The complete paintings of

Bosch

Introduction by **Gregory Martin**

Notes and catalogue by **Mia Cinotti**

Harry N. Abrams, Inc. *Publishers* New York

**Classics of the
World's Great Art**

Editor
Paolo Lecaldano

International Advisory Board
Gian Alberto dell' Acqua
André Chastel
Douglas Cooper
Lorenz Eitner
Enrique Lafuente Ferrari
Bruno Molajoli
Carlo L. Ragghianti
Xavier de Salas
David Talbot Rice
Jacques Thuillier
Rudolf Wittkower

*This series of books is
published in Italy by Rizzoli
Editore, in France by
Flammarion, in the United
Kingdom by Weidenfeld and
Nicolson, in the United States
by Harry N. Abrams, Inc.,
in Spain by Editorial Noguer,
and in Switzerland by
Kunstkreis*

Library of Congress Catalog
Card No. 69-16896
© Copyright in Italy by
Rizzoli Editore, 1966
Printed and bound in Italy

Table of contents

Gregory Martin   Introduction   5

Mia Cinotti   An outline of the artist's critical history   9

Bibliography   11

List of colour plates   16

Outline Biography   83

Catalogue of Works   86

Indexes   Titles   118

Topographical   119

Photographic sources

Colour plates: Dominguez Ramos, Madrid; Emmer, Milan; Francisco Marques (Museu Nacional de Arte Antiga), Lisbon; Foto Ritter, Vienna; Musée des Beaux-Arts, Ghent; Museum Boymans-van Beuningen, Rotterdam; National Gallery, London; Photographie Giraudon, Paris; Réunion des Musées Nationaux, Versailles; Scala, Florence.

Black and white illustrations: Albertina and Akademie der Bildenden Künste, Vienna; Alte Pinakothek, Munich; Amherst College, Amherst, Mass; Archivio Rizzoli, Milan; Art Museum, Princeton University, Princeton; Ashmolean Museum, Oxford; Clowes Fund Collection, Indianapolis; Dominguez Ramos, Madrid; Echte Foto, 'sHertogenbosch; Francisco Marques (Museu Nacional de Art Antiga), Lisbon; Institut Royal du Patrimonie Artistique, Brussels; Karl H. Paulmann, Berlin; Kunsthistorischesmuseum, Vienna; Metropolitan Museum, New York; Musée des Beaux-Arts, Ghent; Museum Boymans-van Beuningen, Rotterdam; Museum of Fine Arts (Edwards, Richardson and Warden collections), Boston; National Gallery, London; Oskar Reinhart, Winterthur; Palazzo Ducale, Venice; Staaliche Museen, Berlin; Städelsches Kunstinstitut, Frankfurt; Statens Museum for Kunst, Copenhagen; Thyssen-Bornemisza, Castagnola-Lugano; Walter Steinkopf, Berlin.

Introduction

The work of Hieronymus Bosch, active probably at 'sHertogenbosch for about thirty-five years from *ca*.1480–1, reveals a culture which today is largely forgotten. And yet his work fascinates because his skill and human perspicacity were such that he can still evoke a response. This is a situation which naturally confronts all the 'old masters'; and it is the duty of art history to link the milieu of the artist with the visual pleasures which we derive from his work, such that the achievement of the man and our response to it is all the richer. However, in the case of Bosch this task is particularly difficult: his culture is a mixture of folklore, adage, astrology and pessimistic, but not greatly influential spiritual beliefs, all popular at the time, but which were so far removed from the mainstream of intellectual thought that they have never attracted much historical study. Thus from the art historical point of view the study of Bosch is often a nightmare of confusing interpretations of abstruse significance, hardly relevant to our way of thinking today; yet despite this, his fascinating vision holds us spellbound.

The study of Bosch is also a nightmare because if we know little about his culture we know just as little about his development as an artist. There are no dated works by him; and although the influence of Netherlandish artists of earlier generations is sometimes apparent and a few parallels can be traced with the work of his contemporaries, we do not know who taught him or whether he ever travelled. Again while the boundaries of his *oeuvre* are fairly well defined, the number of paintings, unanimously accepted as his work, is not large. And even with these masterpieces, scientific analyses concerning condition are scarce. How much repaint there is for instance on *The Garden of Earthly Delights* in the Prado is almost anyone's guess: a glance at detailed reproductions reveals the extent of blistering and loss. A worse case is *The Marriage at Cana* in the Boymans–van Beuningen Museum which is almost certainly largely repaint.

Yet while the meaning of much of his work may have been soon lost to his admirers, it is unlikely that his paintings have been irresponsibly reinterpreted by later restorers to any large extent. For he generally relied on an accumulation of sharply observed detail to express himself, and thus his personality can still speak out loud, clear and unmuffled.

'sHertogenbosch, which lies in southern Holland close to the border with Belgium, was never an artistic centre of any international consequence. Bosch is its only claim to fame in the history of painting – he had no talented predecessors or followers there. Such a situation is unusual, perhaps almost unique, and emphasises the peculiar, isolated status of the man and his works. Yet in spite of this, Bosch is obviously a Netherlandish artist of his time – he could be mistaken for nothing else. This is due both to some of his interests and to his technique. His love of detail, his study of the rougher side of ordinary people, his cool, long landscape views, and distant views of fantastic cities can be found in varying degrees in the art of his predecessors and contemporaries in the Netherlands. His technique of drawing in his design onto the ground, and painting often quite thinly over it is also paralleled by other artists, active mostly in the northern Netherlands at the time.

Our knowledge of Bosch's milieu is such that we are not in a position to define his own standing as a thinker and contributor to his culture. It is hardly conceivable that even his most complex creations were not understood by his circle or patrons (whoever they may have been). And simply because he is the only artist, still admired and remembered, who made visually sophisticated and compelling paintings about subjects often taken from a groundswell of rarely meaningfully uttered attitudes and from ill-charted byways of now abstruse branches of learning, it is obvious that his contribution and status must have been of significance. Thus we can appreciate the wording of the note concerning the obsequies of the artist, dated 9 August 1516, where he is described as *insignis pictor*, in the records of the Brotherhood of Our Lady at 'sHertogenbosch – a body from which Bosch is thought to have received intellectual stimulus.

Much of our awareness of Bosch's genius rests in our admiration for his exotic inventions, sometimes serenely beautiful but more often harrowing; but it is in such a work as *The Seven Deadly Sins* in the Prado that we find the sure basis of his appeal. Here he reveals a Chaucerian quality of telling characterisation and frankness. Each of the scenes, painted round the all-seeing eye of God – whose iris is Christ the Redeemer – depicts one of the seven deadly sins; and there is no need to ponder over the latin nouns for them, written in at the base of each scene, to know what is being described. The look of the bourgeois, leaning over his cottage door watching the progress of a rich man strolling past, has all the sullen ugliness of Jealousy, while the interior showing a fat man gorging himself at table can be nothing other than a description of Gluttony. Bosch here, as often, works to a miniaturist's scale on a large format – and he may have been trained as a miniaturist – but he speaks a simple, universal language. His wit, searching observation and acute understanding of human attitudes and behaviour, prevent him from ever slipping into cliché or failing to make his point.

Bosch's understanding of his fellow men, so clearly expressed in *The Seven Deadly Sins,* did not lead him to admiration for the life enhancing qualities of which at least some can boast. Rather it fed on and stimulated the current of pessimism which runs all through his work. This pessimism is only evident in *The Seven Deadly Sins* in the inscriptions from Deuteronomy added at the top and bottom of the support; but it is the dominant idea behind the triptych also in the Prado known as *The Hay Wain.* Here the same kind of pointed characterisation of human beings is displayed, although the precise symbolic meaning of the cart of hay itself with its cortège being pulled into hell is obscure and disputed. But whether or not by the cart of hay and its cortège, Bosch intended to illustrate the proverb 'the world is a pile of hay, each takes that much which he can grab', to condemn the pursuit of earthly goods, the universal addiction to avarice, or to make clear the inevitability of punishment for sin it is evident that the scene on the central compartment of the triptych in some way draws attention to and satirises the spiritual folly of man's activities, which

stem from the sin of Adam and Eve, depicted on the left-hand wing, and leads to damnation, described on the right-hand wing. Yet despite the fact that only one angel implores the help of Christ in the sky, whose hands are raised as if in despair, the bleak pessimistic message is painted *con amore.* Bosch may stand back and see all too vividly the folly of earthly pursuits, but he convinces both because of his understanding and the sense that he has kept his own despair in control.

Bosch's pessimism runs through much of his work; to a unique degree he saw and expressed what he felt to be the prevalent wickedness of the world. And he devoted all his skill and knowledge towards warning his fellow men away from sin. A recent analysis of the triptych, also in the Prado, of *The Adoration of the Magi* has shown that this heartfelt motive of didacticism lies at the root of all the detail in this apparently traditional picture, in which the pose of the Madonna and Child is inspired by Jan van Eyck. The Madonna and Child are in fact here surrounded by the powers of Evil, and the anti-Christ himself stands at the door of the tumble-down cottage. Thus while his predecessors and contemporaries in their renderings of *The Adoration of the Magi,* sought to inspire the spectator with a sense of love and admiration for God's gift of Christ to the world, Bosch sought to emphasise the odds against which Christ's message had to fight in a world of sin and evil.

This pessimism was probably widely shared at the time, and was no doubt stimulated by the belief that the coming of anti-Christ and the end of the world was imminent. And such fears, based on a searing sense of guilt, led to a great interest in astrology and also in Bosch's case to a fascination for St Anthony – the saint whose successful struggles against the temptations of the devil he so vividly described in the triptych at Lisbon.

The rendering of Hell apart, the Lisbon triptych displays many of the features of Bosch's vision which account for his notoriety today. Hell for Bosch, as is shown on the right-hand wing of *The Hay Wain* is a crazed carnival of cruelty – a fantastic and fascinating nocturnal fairground in which each sin has its separate booth of retribution. His demonic fairground attendants work with a torturer's instinct to convert each sinner's vice from earthly pleasure to everlasting pain. Bosch's idea of Hell was probably inspired by the *Visio Tondali,* an epic of the journey of Tundal through hell, purgatory and heaven, written in the twelfth century. The roots of *The Temptation of St Anthony* at

Lisbon are far more complex, but Bosch's gruesome inventions in it have that quality of repulsive sensual beauty that we find lurking everywhere in the fiery darkness of Bosch's depictions of Hell. Every detail in it has a meaning: temptation and different categories of sin personified, surround the Saint as he is carried to his cell after being beaten by demons on the left-hand wing, or as he sits tempted by the devil on the right-hand wing, or as he turns to bless the spectator in the central compartment. Several of the figures there, near St Anthony, have recently been identified as children of the planets, to whom different sins were attributed at the time; similar and equally obscure identifications have recently been advanced to explain the Prado *Garden of Earthly Delights* and the Boymans–van Beuningen *Prodigal Son*.

The monsters that populate the Lisbon *Temptation of St Anthony* and so much else of Bosch's work were derived from carvings on church pews, bestiaries, and the monsters and grotesques that featured so often in illuminated manuscripts. In Bosch's art each monster is a complex synthesis of literary allusion and association, a sensuous acrostic, which has carefully to be read. Thus the meaning of the whole derives from the sum total of the meaning of each part and the same can be taken for the majority of the paintings themselves.

In this way Bosch's art is an encyclopaedia of medieval thought and beliefs – and thus Bosch becomes one of the greatest medieval painters. His spiritual world was one of visual fantasy, in which attitudes and feelings were expressed by creatures, fearsome for their convincing zoological illogicality.

Yet Bosch flourished in a century when this jungle of complicated beliefs and superstitions, which had grown up over several centuries, nurtured by the subtle minds of medieval sophists, was being razed to the ground by a new reliance on critical, more scientific attitudes. This reliance which lay at the root of the Renaissance – however it is defined – and led to the Reformation, inspired the leading artists of the time to assert the dominating position of man in his world. And while Bosch expressed his pessimism about man's course and showed him overwhelmed by the figments of his fears, guilt and remorse, other Netherlandish artists, following Italian example, showed man flexing his muscles in an ordered world. For them the successful communication of content lay in the manipulation of poses and the moving expression or gesture: for Bosch, at his most ambitious and typical, it required dehumanising the emotions.

It is not so much a tribute to the intricate richness of the culture which Bosch contributed to, that his work should have been admired in the century of his death by such collectors as Philip II, of Spain, the patron of Titian and Veronese. It is rather, of course, a tribute to the man, whose understanding of his fellow men, consistently held convictions and sophisticated handling of the brush were uniquely equipped to give flesh and blood to a vocabulary which to all intents was practically dead. And although Bosch's language is a foreign one to us, it is the genius of the man and our respect for the purpose and motives, which led him to use it with such visual virtuosity that explain our instinctive admiration for his work.

GREGORY MARTIN

7

An outline of the artist's critical history

Bosch's works aroused immediate and lively interest, which rapidly spread from Brabant to Spain, where it remained intense for the best part of the sixteenth century, favoured by the bonds between Spain and the Netherlands. Thus, while Guicciardini, Lampsonius, Lomazzo and Van Mander dwelt on the painter's fantastic aspects, and while De Guevara attempted an assessment of Bosch's naturalism, Brother José de Sigüenza succeeded in appreciating Bosch with an awareness that in some ways anticipated the most acute of modern critics.

A long period of neglect followed, lasting until the end of the nineteenth century; and when Bosch was once more considered, it was mainly in order to redefine his *oeuvre* by denoting unacceptable attributions. Credit for this should go to Justi, Tolnay, Baldass, Friedländer and Combe; their work was more useful than that carried out by those (Lafond, Maeterlinck, etc.) who, having undertaken the interpretation of the artist's work, perceived in the artist only a febrile creator of monsters, an inventor of absurd forms, or an implacable satirist. A substantial contribution has been made by Bax through references to ancient local folklore, theatre, jargon, usage and popular literature, while Tolnay made the first systematic attempt to tackle the problem of the symbolic and allegorical interpretation of the dream world with reference to the ancient 'keys to dreams' and to modern psychoanalysis: in other words, of what has been termed the 'Bosch enigma'. This contribution was followed by others: Fraenger, Wertheim-Aymès, in the field of heretical and esoteric doctrines; Pigler, Cuttler, Brand-Philip, in the field of astrology; again Combe, with his references to alchemy and to the occultism of Tarot cards. Much of the research undertaken has produced convincing clarifications.

Nevertheless, it is also true that the modern increase of interest inspired numberless digressions, of a more or less scholarly nature. The doctrines of Freud and Jung, no less than Breton's rethinking of myths, created the belief that Bosch's fantasies might be the remote ancestor of the inventions of the Surrealists. Thus, a fifteenth-century artist from Brabant suddenly found himself the spiritual father of Tanguy, Dali, Ernst and their followers. It was, and is, a revaluation – if thus it can be termed – based on a skin-deep curiosity: a repertoire of extraordinary wealth is identified with the devices cultivated by the Surrealists. All this presupposes in Bosch a strong desire to impress his contemporaries; as far as we can gather, the latter were not in the least perturbed by his paintings. They continued to commission his works for private houses and for churches and bestowed on Bosch the unreserved esteem due to a devout and industrious man. It would be anachronistic to assume that the concept of the 'cursed artist' might have existed at the time, nor is it convincing to imagine that the painter might have seen himself in this light because of the spiritual unrest that troubled the end of the fifteenth century, or because of the terror with which the dawn of the year 1500 was awaited. A romantic interpretation of the Apocalyptic prophecy presented this date – as it had the year 1000 – as the year that was to bring the end of the world. Bosch was neither more haunted by visions nor more sensitive than many miniaturists, sculptors, xylographers, poets and narrators of his own and of the two or three previous centuries. Others, before and after Bosch, have been impressed by astrology, Tarot cards, magic, alchemy, abnormalities, *ante litteram* Mormonism, folklore, satire, hallucinations, monsters, deviltries, tortures and deformities. More than anyone else, however, Bosch influenced the later expression of these preoccupations. Fraenger's hypothesis that Bosch belonged to an Adamite sect worshipping the divinity of the sexual act is interesting; however, it must be kept in mind that not all of Bosch's work is equally obsessed with evil. Modern criticism has appreciated Bosch's purely painterly qualities: his colours, his forceful line, the subtle light-effects and the beautiful landscapes. Something more than this appreciation is required, however, for a proper understanding of Bosch. The subject-matter of his paintings is almost entirely concerned with moral issues, with the struggle of good against evil: the spectator cannot ignore this essential factor. But for all its research, modern criticism remains baffled by the meaning of most of Bosch's work. As Erwin Panofsky has put it: 'We have bored a few holes through the door of the locked room, but somehow we do not seem to have discovered the key.' *Early Netherlandish Painting* (Cambridge, Mass. 1953) Vol. I, p. 357.

... although he was among the first to paint in oils, he contrived to be somewhat more fluent than the others ... M. A. MICHIEL, *Notizie d'opere di disegno*, 1521–43

Not long ago, I discovered another type of painting, which is called 'gryllos'. It was so named by Antiphylos, after he had portrayed a man whom he called Gryllos in jest; and henceforth, thus was this kind of painting known. Antiphylos, who was born in Egypt, had learned from his teacher Ctesidemos this sort of painting which I find resembles that which our age highly praises in Bosch, or Bosco as we call him, who always showed himself to be so unusual in that he depicted freakish figures and peculiar attitudes ... F. DE GUEVARA, *Comentarios de la pintura*, 1560–2 ca.

Bosch never painted anything other than the natural in all his lifetime unless it were on the subject of Hell or Purgatory; his inventions were based on the search for very strange, albeit natural things: it can thus be taken as a norm that any painting, even though it bear Bosch's signature, that contains anything monstrous or transcending the limits of nature, may be taken as false and counterfeited unless, as I said, it represents hell or subjects relative to it.   F. DE GUEVARA, letter to Philip II of Spain, 1563

. . . a very noble and wonderful inventor of things fantastic and bizarre . . .   L. GUICCIARDINI, *Descrizione di tutti i Paesi Bassi*, 1567

Oh, Hieronymus Bosch, what does it see, that astonished eye of yours? What is that pallor in your face? Do you perchance see before you the monsters and the flying spectres of Erebus? You seem to have forced a passage into the City of Dis and the abodes of Tartarus, so well has your hand painted all that inhabits the recesses of the depths of Avernus.   D. LAMPSONIUS, *Pictorum aliquot celebrium Germaniae inferioris effigies*, 1572

I regret that you [the daughters of Philip II of Spain] and your brother [the future Philip III] were not able to see the procession [of Corpus Christi] as it takes place here [in Lisbon], although it includes several devils resembling those in Bosch's paintings, which I think would have frightened him. PHILIP II OF SPAIN, letter to his daughters, 1581

. . . in the depiction of odd forms and frightening, horrific dreams, he was unique and truly divine.   G. P. LOMAZZO, *Trattato dell'arte della pittura*, 1584

It would be difficult to describe the astonishing, odd, freakish images of spectres and infernal monsters, often as disagreeable as they are horrid, which J. Bos (*sic*) has conceived in his mind and reproduced with his brush. He was born at 'sHertogenbosch; but I have never been able to find out what date, nor where or when he died. It is apparent only that he flourished in early times, nevertheless he rumples, breaks up and folds the draperies much less than did the painters of old. His style was straightforward, ready and fluid; and he managed to produce a number of his paintings simultaneously. Like many of the old masters, he was in the habit of sketching and drawing on a white compound, proceeding with transparent coatings and making the background one of the contributory factors in the final affect.   C. VAN MANDER, *Het Schilderboeck*, 1604

The difference which in my opinion exists between the paintings of this man and those of others consists in that the latter seek to paint men as they outwardly appear, whereas he has the courage to paint them as they are inwardly.   J. DE SIGÜENZA, *Tercera parte de la Historia de la Orden de San Gerónimo*, 1605

Bibliography

Section A is based mostly on the researches of P. Gerlach in 1967. Section B on the same scholar as far as the Dutch sources are concerned and on X. de Salas as far as the Spanish sources are concerned. Sections D and E are based on the complete bibliography compiled by H.M.F.M.C. van Crimpen for the catalogue of the Bosch Exhibition in 1967.

A DOCUMENTARY SOURCES

1841 Hermans, C. R., Geschiedkundig Mengelwerk, II, 'sHertogenbosch, 1841.
1843–67 Hermans, C. R., *Geschiedenis der Rederijkers in Noord Brabant*, 'sHertogenbosch, 1843–67.
1847 *Compte-rendu des séances de la Commission royale d'histoire*, XIII, p. 115–119, Brussels, 1847.
1848 Hermans, C. R., *Verzameling van kronyken, Charters en Oorkonden betreffende de Stad en de Meijerij van 'sHertogenbosch*, 'sHertogenbosch, 1848, I (vol. II never published).
1858 Pinchart, A., *Notes sur Jérôme van Aeken, dit Hieronymus Bosch, peintre et graveur, et sur Alard du Hameel, graveur et architecte, à Bois-le-Duc*, Bulletins de l'Académie Royale de Belgique 2e S. IV (1858), p. 497–505.
1860 Pinchart, A., *Documents inédits* Archives des Arts, Sciences et Lettres 1e S. I, Ghent 1860, p. 267–78 (formerly issued in: Messager des Sciences Historiques, Ghent 1858, p. 157–68).
1861 (Hermans, C. R.), *De kunstschilder Hieronymus van Aeken of Bos, en de bouwmeester en plaatsnijder Alard du Hamel*, Handelingen van het Provinciaal Genootschap van Kunsten en Wetenschappen in Noord-Brabant 1861, p. 60–74.
1862 Passavant, J. D., *Notizen über Hieronymus van Aeken genannt Hieronymus Bosch und Alart du Hameel*, Archiv für die zeichnenden Künste mit bes. Bezeihung auf Kupferstecher- und Holzschneidekunst und ihre Geschichte VII/VIII (1862), p. 88–92.
1865 Zuiklen, R. A. van, *lijst der schepenen van de stad 'sHertogenbosch*, 'sHertogenbosch, 1865.
1874 Hezenmans, J. C. A., *Hieronymus van Aken*, Onze Wachter II (1874), p. 1–35.
1876 Hezenmans, J. C. A., *De Illustre Lieve Trouve Broederschap*, Onze Wachter II (1870), p. 174–195, 253–284, 341–370, 402–438; reissued 1877.
1887 Hezenmans, J. C. A., *Hieronymus van Aken*, De Dietsche Warande N. (3e) R. I (1887), p. 293–302.
1889 Justi, C. See below under section D.
Viñaza, M., *Adiciones al Diccionario de Céan Bermúdez*, Madrid 1889.
1901 Engelenburg, F. v., *De schilderijvernameling van Damiaan de Goes*, Oud Holland, 19 (1901), p. 193 ff.
1907 Smits. F. X., *De Kathedraal van 'sHertogenbosch*, Brussels 1907

1914 Van Sasse van Ysselt A. F. O., *De voorname huizen en gebouwen van 'sHertogenbosch-Aanteekeningen uit de Bossche Schepenprotocollen Loopende van 1500–1800*, 'sHertogenbosch, 1914.'
1930 Zarco Cuevas, G., in 'Boletín de la Real Academia de la Historia', XCVI, 1930.
1931 Mosmans, J., *De St Janskerk te 'sHertogenbosch*, Nieuwe Geschiedenis, 'sHertogenbosch, 1931.
1932 Denuce, G., *De Antwerpsche 'Konstkamers' Inventarissen van kunstverzameling te Antwerpen in de Zestiende en Zeventiende couwen* (Bronnen voor de Geschiedenis van de Vlaamsche Kunst, II), Amsterdam, 1932.
194.. Sanchez Cantón, F G., *Inventarios Reales desde 1555 a 1834*, Madrid, 194..
1947 Mosmans, G., see below under section D.
1948 Ebeling, M. J. M., *Jheronimus van Aken*, Miscellanea Gessleriana, Antwerp 1948, p. 444–57.
1950 Mosmans, J., see below under section D.
1955 Smulders, F. W., *Een zuster van Jeroen Bosch*, De Brabantse Leeuw IV (1955), p. 97–9.
1957 Smulders, F. W., *De ooms van Jeroen Bosch*, De Brabantse Leeuw VI (1957), p. 55–6.
Smulders, F. W., *Nog een zuster van Jeroen*, De Brabantse Leeuw VI (1957), p. 70–2.
1958 Smulders, F. W., *De schildersfamilie Van Aken*, De Brabantse Leeuw VII (1958), p. 43–6.
1961 Vosters, S. A., *De geestelijke achtergronden van Mencia de Mendoza, Vrouwe van Breda*, De Oranjeboom, 14 (1961), p. 63–64.
1965 Mateo Gómez, J., see below under section D.
1967 Gerlach, P., *De Bronnen voor het leven en het werk van Jeroen Bosch*, Brabantia XVI (1967), p. 58–65; p. 95–104.
Transl.: *Les sources pour l'étude de la vie de Jérôme Bosch*, Gazette des Beaux-Arts, LXXI, Febr. 1968, p. 109–116. *De Bronnen etc., II, Bronnen voor zijn werk*, Brabantia XVI (1967) p. 95–104.
Gerlach, P., *Jheronimus Bosch, Bijdragen* (catalogue of J. B. Exhibition, 'sHertogenbosch, 1967) p. 48–97.

B ANCIENT LITERARY SOURCES
Salas, X. de, *El Bosco en la literatura española*, Barcelona 1943.
Salas. X. de, *Más sobre el Bosco en España*, Homenaje a. J. V. Praag, Amsterdam 1930–1955, p. 108–13.
Gerlach, P., *De bronnen voor het leven en het werk van Jeroen Bosch, II Bronnen voor zijn werk*, Brabantia XVI (1967), p. 98–100 (literaire bronnen).
Antonio de Beatis (*Diario di viaggio*, 1517–18), ed. by L. von Pastor, *Die Reise des Kardinals Luigi d'Aragona durch Deutschland, die Niederlände, Frankreich und Oberitalien, 1517–18, beschrieben von Antonio de Beatis*, Freiburg i. Breisgau, 1905 (Erläuterungen und Ergänzungen zu Janssens Geschichte des deutschen Volkes, IV, 4).
Marcantonio Michiel ('Anonimo

Morelliano'), *Notizia d'opere di disegno* (1521–1543). Ed. by J. Morelli, Bassano 1800 (as 'Anonimo'), by G. Frizzoni, Bologna 1884; by Th. von Frimmel, Vienna 1888 (Eitelberger Quellenschriften, N. F. I.). Wilhelm Molius, *Annales civitates Buscoducensis* (first half XVI century). Not edited, see P. Gerlach, Brabantia XVI (1967) p. 60 and note 12 (transl. Gazette des Beaux-Arts, Febr. 1968, p. 111 and note 12).
Manuscript 8472 of the Brussels Royal Library (c. 1540–50). Ed. by Schutjes in *Geschiedenis van het Bisdom 'sHertogenbosch, IV*, St Michiels-Gestel, 1873, p. 775–779.
Guevara, Don Felipe de, *Comentarios de la pintura* (c. 1560–62), ed. by A. Ponz, Madrid 1788.
Van Vaernewijck, Marcus, *Beroerlicke tyden in die Nederlanden en voornamelijk in Ghendt* (1566–68). Ed. by F. Vanderhaegen, Ghent 1872. French ed. *Troulslesen Flandres . . .*, Brussels, 1905.
Guicciardini, Lodovico, *Descrittione di tutti i Paesi Bassi, altrimenti detti Germania inferiore*, Antwerp 1567. (contemp.). French ed. : *Description de tout le Pays Bas, autrement dit la Germanie supérieure ou Basse Allemagne*, ibid., 1567.
Vasari, Giorgio, *Le vite dei piu eccellenti pittori, scultori e architettori*, Florence 1568² (in first edition, Florence 1550, Bosch is not yet mentioned). Critical ed. by G. Milanesi, Florence 1878–81, 9 vol. (*Vite* vol. 1–7), and C. L. Ragghianti, Milan 1942–50, 4 vols.
Lomazzo, Giovan Paolo, *Trattato dell'arte della Pittura*, Milan 1584; repr. Rome 1844, 3 vols.
Molina, Gonzalo Argote de, *Discurso sobre el libro de la Montería*, Seville 1583. Ed. by Gutierrez de Vega, Bibliotheca Venetoria, Madrid 1882, p. IV, p. 102.
Mander, Karel van, *Het Schilderboek*, Alkmaar 1604, Amsterdam 1618. Ed. in modern Dutch, Amsterdam 1936. 1946³; English ed. by C. van de Wall, New York 1936.
Sigüenza, Fray José de, *Tercera parte de la Historia de la Orden de San Jerónimo*. Madrid, 1605.
Van Balen, Everswijn, Loeff, *Origo opidi Buscoduci* (1608). Manuscript n. 63 of the Rijksarchief in Noordbrabant, composed for the official historian of 'sHertogenbosch Gramage (see below).
Gramage, Jan Baptist de, *Taxandria*, Brussels 1610 (based on the manuscript by van Balen, Everswijn and Loeff, see above).
Manuscript by Henricus van de Leemputte (before 1656), ed. by Schutjes in *Geschiedenis van het Bisdom 'sHertogenbosch, IV*, St Michiels-Gestel, 1873.
Oudenhoven, Jacobus van, *Siliz-Ducis ancta et renata*, Amsterdam 1649 (*Beschrijvinge van de stad en de meyereye van 'sHertogenbosche*); n. ed. 'sHertogenbosch, 1670.
Ponz, Antonio, *Viaje de España* Madrid, 1772, 18 vols. Ed. 1774–83, 1787–94; modem ed. by C. M. del Rivero, Madrid, 1947.

Bermúdez, Ceán, *Diccionario histórico de los mas ilustres profesores de las bellas artes en España*, Madrid 1800.

C GENERAL LITERATURE— MUSEUM CATALOGUES
1875 Crowe, J. A., Cavalcaselle, G. B., *Geschichte der Altniederländischen Malerei*, Leipzig 1875; Italian ed. Florence 1899.
1898–99 Frimmel, Th. von, *Geschichte der Wiener Gemäldesammlungen*, I, Leipzig, 1898–99.
Fierens-Gevaert, *La peinture en Belgique. Les primitifs flamands* III, Brussels 1910, p. 169ff.
1910 Friedländer M., *Von Eyck bis Bruegel*, Berlin 1916. Reissued Berlin 1921.
1927 Eigenberger, R., *Die Gemäldegalerie der Akademie der bildenden Künste in Wien*, Textband, Vienna 1927, p. 47ff (Bosch, Flügelaltar).
1951 Janssens de Bisthoven, A., Parmentier, R. A., *Le Musée communal de Bruges* (Les Primitifs Flamands, I Corpus de la peinture des anciens Pays-Bas méridionaux au quinzième siècle, 1–4, Antwerp, 1951 [Bosch p. 3–12]).
1952 Lavalleye, J., *Collections d'Espagne, I.1* (Les Primitifs Flamands, I I, Répertoire des peintures flamandes des quinzième et seizième siècles. Antwerp, 1952 [Bosch p. 13, 55]). Ed., I, 2, Antwerp 1958 [Bosch p. 22].
1953 Michel E., *Catalogue raisonné des peintures flamandes du XV–XVI siècle*, Paris 1953.
Panofsky, E., *Early Netherlandish Painting*, Cambridge, Mass., 1953, 2 vols.
Davies, M., *The National Gallery, London, I.* (Les Primitifs Flamands, I Corpus de la peinture des Anciens Pays-Bas méridionaux au quinzième siècle, 3, 6–13, Antwerp, 1953 [Bosch p. 18–21]).
1954 Genaille, R., *La peinture dans les Anciens Pays-Bas*, Paris 1954.
1956 Friedländer, M., *Early Netherlandish Painting, from van Eyck to Bruegel*, London, 1956 (see 1916).
1953 Salvini, R., *La pittura fiamminga*, Milan 1958.
1960 Wilensky, R. H., *Flemish Painters*, London 1960.
1961 Eisler, C. T., *New England Museums*. (Les primitifs Flamands, I Corpus de la peinture des Anciens Pays-Bas méridionaux au quinzième siècle, 4, Brussels, 1961 [Bosch p. 33–49]).
1962 Puyvelde, L. van, *La peinture flamande au siècle de Bosch et Breughel*, Paris 1962.
Adhémar, H., *Le Musée National du Louvre, Paris. I* (Les Primitifs Flamands, I Corpus de la peinture des Anciens Pays-Bas méridionaux au quinzième siècle, 5, Brussels 1962 [Bosch p. 20–32]).

D MONOGRAPHS AND MONOGRAPHICAL STUDIES, BOSCH EXHIBITIONS
1889 Justi, C., *Die Werke des Hieronymus Bosch in Spanien*, Jahrbuch der preussischen Kunstsammlungen X (1889),

p. 120–44
(reissued in: Miscellaneen aus drei Jahrhunderten spanischen Kunstlebens II, Berlin 1908, p. 61–93).
1890 Geudens, E., *Jeronimus Bosch, allas Van Aken*, De Dietsche Warande N. (=3e) R. III (1890), p. 5–25.
1898 Dollmayr, H., *Hieronymus Bosch und die Darstellung der vier Letzten Dinge in der niederlandischen Malerei des XV und XVI Jahrhunderts*, Jahrbuch der kunsthistorischen Sammlungen des Allerhöchsten Kaiserhauses XIX (1898), p. 284–310.
1907 Gossart, G., *La peinture de diableries à la fin du moyen-age. Jérôme Bosch, le 'faizeur de dyables' de Bois-le-Duc*, Lille 1907.
1910 Cohen, W., *Hieronymus Bosch*, in: Thieme-Becker Künstlerlexikon IV (1910), p. 386ff.
1914 Lafond, P., *Hieronymus Bosch, son art, son influence, ses disciples*, Brussels-Paris 1914. Reviewed in: Monatsheft für Kunstwissenschaft VII (1914), p. 305–6.
1917 Baldass, L. von., *Die Chronologie der Gemälde des Hieronymus Bosch*, Jahrbuch der preussischen Kunstsammlungen XXXVIII (1917), p. 177–85.
1918 Mather, F. J. Jr., *Paintings by Jerome Bosch in America*, Art in America and elsewhere VI (1918), p. 3–20.
1921 Romdahl, A. L., *Hieronymus Bosch*, Kunsthistoriska Sällskapets Publikation 1921, p. 31–49.
1922 Pfister, K., *Hieronymus Bosch*, Potsdam 1922. Reviewed in: The Burlington Magazine XLV (1924), p. 27 (A.E.P. [opham]); Belvedere. Monatschrift für Sammler und Kunstfreunde III (1923), p. 89–90 (J.M. [eder]).
1923 Schürmeyer, W., *Hieronymus Bosch*, Munich 1923. Reviewed in: Der Cicerone XV (1923), p. 628–9 (V. C. Habicht); Zeitschrift für bildende Kunst LVIII (1924–5), p. 5–6 (F. Winkler); Jahrbuch für Kunstwissenschaft 1923, p. 310–11 (G. Ring); Mitteilungen der Gesellschaft für vervielfaltigende Kunst, Beilage der 'Graphischen Künste' 1923, p. 33.
1925 Tolnay, C. de, *Hieronymus Bosch*, Vienna 1925 (University dissertation, Vienna).
. . . *Der neuentdeckte Hieronymus Bosch*, Der Kunstwanderer 1925–6, p. 378–9.
1926 Baldass, L. von, *Betrachtungen zum Werke des Hieronymus Bosch*, Jahrbuch der kunsthistorischen Sammlungen in Wien N.F. I (1926), p. 103–18.
1927 Friedländer, M. J., *Die altniederländische Malerei* v. *Geertgen und Bosch*, Berlin 1927.
1930 Lommers, L., *Iheronymus van Aecken, genoemd Jeroen Bosch* 'le faizeur de Dyables' *Bij de onthulling van zijn standbeeld* ('s-Gravenhage 1930) (=reprint from: De Hollandsche Revue XXXV [1930]), p. 523–36; see also: p. 356–9).
1934 Parrot, L., *Jerónimo Bosco*, Cruz Raya XVI (1934), p. 41–70.
1936 Hammacher, A. M., *Jeroen Bosch ca 1450–1516*, De Vrije Bladen XIII (1936), Schrift 9. Reviewed in: Prisma

der kunsten II (1937), p. 31–3 (L.B. [rom]); Groot-Nederland XXXIV² (1936), p. 621–2 (J.E. [ngelman]).
Jeroen Bosch, Noord-Nederlandsche primitieven. Museum Boymans, Rotterdam 1936 (Catalogue of the Exhibition).
1937 Friedländer, M. J., *Die altniederlandische Malerei* XIV. *Pieter Bruegel und Nachträge zu den früheren Banden*, Leyden 1937, p. 99–101.
Muls, J., *Hieronymus Bosch*, Leven en Werken, Maandbiad der Radio-Volksuniversiteit Holland N.R. I (1937), p. 1–30.
Tolnay, Ch. de, *Hieronymus Bosch*, Basel 1937. Reviewed in: The Art Bulletin XIX (1937), p. 604 (F. E. Hyslop); L. Amour de l'art XVIII (1937), p. 311–12 (M. Florisoone); Die Graphischen Künste N.F. III (1938) p. 77–9 (L. Baldass); Revue d'histoire ecclésiastique XXXIII (1937), p. 935 (J. Lavalleye); The Burlington Magazine LXXI (1937), p. 293–4 (A. E. Popham).
1938 Baldass, L. von, *Zur künstlerischen Entwicklung des Hieronymus Bosch*, Annuaire des Musées Royaux des Beaux-Arts de Belgique (1938), p. 41–71.
Brion, M., *Bosch*, Paris 1938. Reviewed in: Gazette des Beaux-Arts 6e Pér. XXI (1939), p. 57. (J. B. [abelon]); Beaux-Arts, Chronique des Arts et de la Curiosité, Le Journal des Arts 7 April 1939, p. 6 (P. du Colombier).
1939 Huebner, F. M., *Hieronymus Bosch*, Berlin 1939. Reviewed in: Pantheon, Monatsschrift fur Freunde under Sammler der Kunst XXV (1940), p. 152 (M.G.); De Nieuwe Gids LVI (1941), p. 251–9. (A. A. Haighton); Kunst-und Antiquitäten-Rundschau XLVII (1939), p. 199–200 (K. K. Eberlein).
Vermeylen, A., *Hieronymus Bosch*, Amsterdam 1939.
1942 Huebner, F. M., *Jeroen Bosch als mensch en kunstenaar*, The Hague 1942. Reviewed in: Maandblad voor Beeldende Kunsten XXI (1944), p. 63–4 (C.V. [eth]).
1943 Baldass, L. von, *Hieronymus Bosch*, Vienna 1943. Reviewed by J. Borms, *Een boek over Hieronymus Bosch van Ludwig von Baldass*, Die Nieuwe Rotterdamsche Courant, 1 June, 1944.
Huebner, F. M., *Jérôme Bosch*, Brussels 1943.
1944 Bossche, L. van den, *Jérôme Bosch*, Diest 1944. (Dutch edition: *Jeroen Bosch*, Diest 1944).
1946 Combe, J., *Jérôme Bosch*, Paris 1946.
1947 Boschère, J. de, *Jérôme Bosch*, Brussels 1947.
Combe, J., *Ihieronymus Bosch*, London 1947. (English translation of the French edition of 1946). Reviewed in: Art News XLVII (1948), nr. 3, p. 13; The Studio, Magazine of Beauty CXXXVI (1948), p. 128; The Connoisseur CXXI (1948), p. 58 (H. G. [ranville] F. [ell]).
Daniel, H., *Hieronymus Bosch*, New York 1947. (French translation of the American edition: Paris 1947). Reviewed in: Art News XLVIII (1948), nr. 3, p. 13; Magazine of Art XLI (1948),

p. 283–4 (Ch. Kuhn).
Mosmans, J., *Jheronimus Anthoniszoon van Aken, alias Hieronymus Bosch. Zijn leven en zijn werk*, 'sHertogenbosch 1947. Reviewed in: Das Kunstwerk IV (1950), p. 48; Museum LV (1950), p. 50–1. (W. R. Juynboll); Maandblad voor Beeldende Kunsten XXV (1949), p. 79–80 (C. V. [eth]); Revue d'histoire ecclésiastique XLIV (1949), p. 248–50 (R. Maere).
1948 Brans, J. V. L., *Hieronymus Bosch (el Bosco) en el Prado y en el Escorial*. Traducción castellana del original inédito por M. Cardenal Iracheta, Barcelona 1948. Reviewed in: The Burlington Magazine XCII (1950), p. 119.
1949 Bax, D., *Ontcifering van Jeroen Bosch*, 's-Gravenhage 1949 (Dissertation, ibidem 1948). Reviewed in: Phoenix IV (1949), p. 325 (H. v. G. [uldener]); Kroniek van Kunst en Kultuur XI (1950), p. 214 (Agnostes); The Connoisseur CXXVI (1950), p. 218–19 (A. C. S.); Maandblad voor Beeldende Kunsten XXVI (1950), p. 308 (C.V. [eth]); Erasmus III (1950), p. 762–4 (W. Hirsch); The Burlington Magazine XCII (1950), p. 29 (G. Ring); Museum LVI (1951), p. 118–19 (H. v. d. Waal); Bijdragen v.d. geschiedenis der Nederlanden VI (1951), p. 156–9 (D. Th. Enklaar); Leuvense Bijdragen XLI (1951), p. 12–13 (J. Gessler); Nieuwe Taalgids XLIII (1950), p. 58.
Godfrey, F. M., *Jerome Bosch*, London-New York 1959. Reviewed in: Eldos 1950, nr. 2, p. 46 (J. E. E.).
Leymarie, J., *Jérôme Bosch*, Paris 1949. (Dutch translation: Amsterdam 1949; German translation: Stuttgart-Konstanz 1949).
1950 Bertram, A., *Jérôme Bosch*, London 1950.
Mosmans, J., *Jheronimus Bosch, Maria en Sint Jan, onbekend en laat schilderwerk bewaard in zijne vaderstad*, 'sHertogenbosch 1950. Reviewed in: Die Weltkunst XX (1950), nr. 20, p. 8; Oud Nederland IV (1950), p. 133–6 (H. J. M. Ebeling); Kunst en Kunstleven II (1949/1950), p. 313–14 (W. P. Martens); Museum LVI (1951), p. 147–9 (G. Knuttel Wzn.).
1951 Vogeisang, W., *Hieronymus Bosch*, Amsterdam 1951.
1953 Wilenski, R. H., *Hieronymus Bosch*, London 1953. Reviewed in: Kroniek van kunst en kultuur XIV (1954), p. 93.
1955 Philip, L. Brand, *Hieronymus Bosch*, New York, 1955.
1956 Philip, L. Brand, *Hieronymus Bosch*, New York-London 1956. Teixeira Leite, J. R., *Jheronimus Bosch*, Rio de Janeiro 1956.
1957 Combe, J., *Jérôme Bosch*, Paris 1957 (reprint of the 1946 edition; German translation: Munich 1957).
Wertheim-Aymes, Cl. A., *Hieronymus Bosch, Eine Einfuhrung in seine geheime Symbolik, dargestellt am 'Garten der himmlischen Freuden', am Heuwagen-Triptychon, am Lissabonner Altar und an Motiven aus anderen Werken*, Amsterdam 1957. Reviewed in: De Kroniek van de Vriendenkring van het

Rembrandthuis XII (1958), p. 25–30 (M. Muller); Das Munster X (1957), p. 374–7. (G. F. Hartlaub).
1958 Vogelsang, W., *Hieronymus Bosch*, Amsterdam 1958.
1959 Baldass, L. von, *Jheronimus Bosch*, Vienna-Munich 1959 (reprint of the 1943 edition; American edition: New York 1960). Reviewed in: The Burlington Magazine CII (1960), p. 457–8 (K. G. Boon); The Art Journal XX (1960/1961), p. 246–8 (Ch. D. Cuttler).
Linfert, C., *Hieronymus Bosch, the paintings*, London 1959. Reviewed in Apollo LXXI (1960), p. 207 (H. Shipp); The Burlington Magazine CII (1960), p. 458 (K. G. Boon); Sele-Arte n. 44 (1960), (C. L. Ragghianti).
1960 Delevcy, R. L., *Jheronimus Bosch Etude biographique et critique*. Geneva 1960 (Skira). (German edition: Geneva 1960; American edition: Cleveland 1960). Reviewed in: The Art Journal XX (1960/1961), p. 248–50 (Ch. D. Cuttler).
1961 Wertheim Aymès, Cl. A., *Die Bildersprache des Hieronymus Bosch, Dargestellt an 'Der Verlorene Sohn', an 'Die Versuchung des heiligen Antonius' und an Motiven aus anderen Werken*, The Hague 1961. Reviewed in: De Kroniek van de Vriendenkring van het Rembrandthuis XV (1961), p. 142–4 (M. Muller).
1962 Boschère, J. de, *Jérôme Bosch et le fantastique*, Paris 1962. (Reprint of the 1947 edition).
1963 Bosman, A., *Hieronymus Bosch*, London 1963.
1965 Gauffreteau-Sévy, M., *Jérôme Bosch*, Paris 1965. Reviewed in: Beaux-Arts 1965, nr. 1106, p. 2 (A. Miguel).
Genaille, R., *Jérôme Bosch*, Paris 1965. Huebner, F. M., *Le mystère Jérôme Bosch*, Brussels 1965. (French translation of the German edition of 1939).
Tolnay, Ch. de, *Hieronymus Bosch* I-II, Baden-Baden 1965. (Reprint of the 1937 edition; English edition: London 1966). Reviewed by E. H. Gombrich, New York Review of Books, VIII, 3. 23 February 1967; by R. Hughes, The Studio, 173, Suppl. 9, March 1967; by G. Martin, Apollo, n.s.86, July 1967; by M. Brion, La quinzaine littéraire, n.nn, Febr. 1968.
1966 Cinotti, M., *L'opera completa di Bosch*, Milan 1966.
1967 Jheronimus Bosch, Catalogue of Exhibition at Noordbrabants Museum, 'sHertogenbosch, September-November 1967. Introduction by G. Lemmens and E. Taverne reviewed by G. van Lennep (*A propos de Jérôme Bosch: polémique, tarots et sang-dragon*), Gazette des Beaux Arts, LXXI, March 1968, p. 189–190.
Gauffreteau-Sévy, M., *Hieronimus Bosch, 'El Bosco'*. Traducción, prólogo, apéndice de Juan Eduardo Cirlot, Barcelona 1967 (Spanish edition, see 1965).

E STUDIES ON VARIOUS QUESTIONS AND INDIVIDUAL WORKS

1886 Loo, H. van, *Hieronimus van*

Aken, genaamd Hieronimus Bosch, Kunstkronijk N. (=3e) R. VI (1886), p. 120–4.
1896 Glück, G., Das jüngste Gericht der Wiener Akademie, Kunstchronik N.F. VII (1896), p. 196ff.
1900 Maeterlinck, L., Une oeuvre inconnue de Jérôme Bosch, Gazette des Beaux-Arts 3e Pér XXIII (1900), p. 68–74.
1901 Verreyt, Ch. C. V., Schilderijen, teekeningen en beeldwerken van Noord-Brabanters. Hieronymus van Aken of Bosch, Taxandria VIII (1901), p. 78ff.
1903 Fry, R., Christ mocked, by Jerome Bosch, The Burlington Magazine III (1903), p. 86–93.
Marquand, A., A Painting by Hieronymus Bosch in the Princeton Art Museum, Princeton University Bulletin XIV (1903), p. 41–7.
1903 Schubert-Soldern, F. von, Hieronymus Bosch und Pieter Brueghel der Ältere, Beltrage zur Kunstgeschichte. Franz Wickhoff gewidmet von einem Kreise von Freunden und Schülern, Vienna 1903, p. 73–9.
1904 Gluck, G., Zu einem Bilde von Hieronymus Bosch in der Figdorschen Sammlung in Wien, Jahrbuch der preussischen Kunstsammlungen XXV (1904), p. 174–84.
1906 Frizzoni, G., A Propos du tableau 'Le Jongleur' de Jérôme Bosch au Musée municipal de St Germain-en-Laye, La Chronique des Arts et de la Curiosité 1906, p. 240–1.
Maeterlinck, L., A propos d'une oeuvre de Bosch au Musée de Gand, Revue de l'art ancien et moderne XX (1906), p. 299–307.
Reinach, S., A propos du tableau de Jérôme Bosch au Musée municipal de St Germain, La, Chronique des Arts et de la Curiosité 1906, p. 53.
Schmidt-Degener, F., Un tableau de Jérôme Bosch au Musée municipal de St-Germain-en-Laye, Gazette des Beaux-Arts 3e Pér. XXXV (1906), p. 147–54.
1907 Maeterlinck, L., Le genre satirique dans la peinture flamande, Brussels 1907.
1908 Maeterlinck, L., Les imitateurs de Hieronymus Bosch, à propos d'une oeuvre inconnue d'Henri met de Bles, Revue de l'art ancien et moderne XXIII (1908), p. 145–56.
1910 Phillips, C., The Mocking of Christ, by Hieronymus Bosch, The Burlington Magazine XVII (1910), p. 321–7.
1911 Troubnikov, A., (The Demonism of Hieronymus Bosch), Apollon March 1911, p. 7–19 (Russian text).
1912 Fourcaud, L. de, Le réalisme populaire dans l'art des Pays Bas: Hieronymus van Aken, dit Jérôme Bosch, Paris 1912.
Viola, M., De Heilige Geboorte, Van onzen tijd XIII (1912/1913), p. 185–7.
1913 (Burroughs), B., A Picture by Hieronymus Bosch, The Bulletin of the Metropolitan Museum of Art, New York VIII (1913), p. 130–3.
1914 Friedländer, M. J., Hieronymus Bosch, Stizungsberichte der kunstgeschichtlichen Gesellschaft VI, Berlin

1914, p. 25–8.
Justi, C., Jerónimo Bosch, La España moderna, June 1914, p. 5ff.
(F. Winkler), Studien und Skizzen zur Gemaldekunde 1 (1913/1915), p. 128–9 (Fr. [immel]).
1915 Coster, H. P., Een herinnering aan Heironymus Bosch?, Taxandria XXII (1915), p. 22–3.
1915 Moerkerk, H., Over den Bosschen schilder Hieronymus Bosch, Handelingen van het Provinciaal Genootschap van Kunsten en Wetenschappen in Noord-Brabant 1909/1915, p. 114–16.
Tramoyeres Blasco, L., Un Tríptico de Jerónimo Bosco en el Museo de Valencia, Archivo de Arte Valenciano I (1915), p. 87–102.
1917–18 Six, J., Die Landschaft in dem Johannes des Hieronymus Bosch, Amtliche Berichte aus den Kgl. Kunstammlungen XXXIX (1917/18), p. 261–70.
1919 Demonts, L., Deux primitifs néerlandais au Musée du Louvre, Gazette des Beaux-Arts 4e Pér. XV (1919), p. 1–20.
Mayer, Aug. L., Ein unbekanntes Bild der Bosch-Werkstatt, Der Kunstwanderer 1919–20, p. 244.
1922 Trapeznikow, T., (News from the Roemjantsjew Museum: The Adoration of the Kings, after H. Bosch), Sredi Kollektsionerow 1922, nr. 3, p. 5–10 (Russian text).
Vermeylen, A., Van Jan van Eyck tot Heronymus Bosch, De Stem II (1922), nr. 1, p. 499ff.
1923 Pfister, K., Unbekannte Bilder des Hieronymus Bosch, Belvedere. Monatschrift für Sammler und Kunstfreunde IV (1923), p. 73–5.
Schretlen, M. J., De Kruisdraging, Opgang. Geillustreerd weekblad III (1923), p. 794–5.
Winkler, F., Unbeachtet holländische Maler des 15. Jahrhunderts, Jahrbuch der preussischen Kunstsammlungen XLII (1923), p. 136ff.
1924 Dvorak, M., Kunstgeschichte als Geistesgeschichte, Munich 1924.
1925 Esswein, H., Physiognomisches zur Kunst des Hieronymus Bosch, Ganymed V (1925), p. 11ff.
1926 Schürmeyer, W., Hieronymus Bosch, Opgang, Geillustreerd weekblad VI (1926) p. 49–51.
Konrad, M., Das Weltgerichtsbild im Stadhauses zu Diest, Wallraf-Richartz-Jahrbuch III/IV (1926–7), p. 141ff.
1927 Burroughs, B., The Descent of Christ into Hell by Hieronymus Bosch, Bulletin of the Metropolitan Museum of Art, New York XXII (1927), p. 272–4.
Jamot, P., A propos d'un primitif français preté par le musée d'Amsterdam au Louvre, Revue de l'art ancien et moderne LII (1927), p. 155–62.
Jeltes, H. F. W., Een Hieronymus Bosch in het Rijksmuseum, Elseviers Geillustreerd Maandschrift LXXIV (1927), p. 75–7.
Rouchès, G., La tentation du mourant. Dessin attribué à Jérôme Bosch, Beaux-Arts V (1927), p. 6–7.
1928 Cust, L., The Adoration of the Three Kings by Hieronymus Bosch, Apollo. VIII (1928), p. 55–9.
1930 Lammers, L., Iheronimus van Aeken, genaamd Jeroen Boschschilder,

Het R. K. Bouwblad I (1929–30), p. 365–7.
Michel, E., Musée de Valenciennes. Un panneau de Jérôme Bosch. Bulletin des Musées de France II (1930), p. 64–6.
Schmidt-Degener, F., Hieronymus Bosch, Jaarverslag Vereeniging Rembrandt over 1930, p. 16–19.
Stheeman, A., Een Jheronymus Bosch bij R. W. P. de Vries Elseviers Geillustreerd Maandschrift LXXX (1930), p. 284–6.
1931 Benesch, O., Ein Spätwerk von Hieronymus Bosch, Mélanges Hulin de Loo, Brussels-Paris 1931, p. 36–44.
Cohen, W., Der 'Verlorene Sohn' von Hieronymus Bosch im Boymans-Museum zu Rotterdam, Pantheon VIII (1931), p. 440.
Ephron, W., Zwei Kreuztragungen. Eine Entgegnung, Belvedere. II (1931), p. 114ff
Ephron, W., Hieronymous Bosch. Zwei Kreuztragungen, eine 'planmässige Wesensuntersuchung' mit einem Beitrag: Persönliche Meinung und sachliche Verantwortung von Josef Strzygowski, Zurich-Leipzig-Vienna 1931.
Hannema, D., De Verloren Zoon van Jheronymus Bosch, Jaarverslag Museum Boymans Rotterdam 1931. p. 2–5.
Hannema, E., De Verloren Zoon, van Jheronymus Bosch, Jaarverslag Vereeniging Rembrandt over 1931, p. 8–11.
Henkel, M. D., Neuerwerbungen des Rijksmuseums in Amsterdam, Pantheon, VIII (1931), p. 273ff.
Vogelsang, W., Een vroege navolger van Hieronymus Bosch, Mélanges Hulin de Loo, Brussels-Paris 1931, p. 333–7.
..., Un Jérôme Bosch inconnu, Bulletin de l'art ancien et moderne 1931, p. 370
Dodgson, C., School of Hieronymus Bosch: Sheet of grotesque inventions, Old Master Drawings VI (1931–2), p. 52.
1932 Alvarez Cabanas, A. La Adoración de los Santos Reyes, tríptico de Jerónimo Bosch, Religión y Cultura XIX (1932, p. 408–17).
Benesch, O., Meisterzeichnungen. I Hieronymus Bosch. Die Kruppel, Mitteilungen der Gesellschaft für vervielfaltigende Kunst, Beilage der 'Graphischen Kunste' 1932, p. 3.
Cornette, A., Jérôme Bosch. Saint Jacques le Majeur et le magicien, Trésor de l'art flamand du Moyen Age au XVIIIme siècle, Mémorial de l'exposition d'art flamand ancien à Anvers 1930 par un groupe de spécialistes I, Peintures, Paris 1932, p. 46ff.
Destrée, J., Jérôme Bosch, Bulletin de la Classe des Beaux-Arts de l'Académie royale de Belgique XIV (1932), p 118–22.
Glück, G., Die Darstellungen des Karnavals und der Fasten von Bosch und Bruegel, Gedenkboek A. Vermeylen, Bruges 1932, p. 263–8.
Koomen, P., Een Hieronymus Bosch in Boymans, Maandblad voor Beeldende Kunsten IX (1932), p. 45–9.
Meige, H., L'opération des pierres dans le tête, Aesculape XXII (1932), p. 50–62.
Wehite, K., Rontgenologische Gemäldeuntersuchungen im Städel-

schen Kunstinstitut, Städeljahrbuch VII/VIII (1932), p. 224.
Wolters, A., Anmerkungen zu einigen Rontgenautnahmen, Städeljahrbuch VII/VIII (1932), p. 234.
-s., Ein Maler des Chaos: Hieronymus Bosch, Hochland XXX (1932–3), p. 91–4.
1933 Juten, G. C. A., Jeronimus Bosch, Taxandria XL (1933), p. 310.
1934 Granville Fell, H., A Painting by Hieronymus Bosch, The Connoisseur XCIV (1934), p. 398–9.
1935 Baldass, L. von, Ein Kreuzigungsaltar von H. Bosch, Jahrbuch der kunsthistorischen Sammlungen in Wien N.F. IX (1935), p. 87ff.
1936 Baldass, L. von, Die frühholländische Austellung in Rotterdam, Pantheon XVIII (1936), p. 252–7.
Buchner, E., Ein Werk des Hieronymus Bosch in der Älteren Pinakothek, Münchener Jahrbuch der bildende Kunst N.F. XI (1934–6), p. 297–302.
Chastel, A., La Tentation de St Antoine ou le songe du mélancolique, Gazette des Beaux-Arts 6e Pér. XV (1936), p. 218ff.
Devoghelaere, H., Une oeuvre peu connue de Jérôme Bosch: le 'Saint Jean-Baptiste' de la collection J. Lazaro, L'Art et la vie III (1936), p. 312–18; p. 372–4.
Engelman, J., Over het duivelsche bij Jeroen Bosch, De Groene Amsterdammer, 8 August 1936.
Fierens, P., Jérôme Bosch et les 'Préhollandais', Le Journal des Débats (de Paris) 1936, 1 September, 15 September, 29 September, 13 October.
Florisoone, M., J. Bosch et les primitifs néerlandais à Rotterdam, L'Amour de l'art XVII (1936), p. 302–04.
Hammacher, A. M., De tentoonstelling in Museum Boymans, Elseviers Geillustreerd Maandschrift XCII (1936), p. 203–206.
Hannema, D., De Jeroen Bosch-tentoonstelling Museum Boymans, III Jeroen Bosch, Nieuwe Rotterdamsche Courant 1936, nr. 237.
Hildebrandt, H., Ein Tryptichon mit Flügeln von Hieronymus Bosch, Kunst- und-Antiquitaten-Rundschau XLIV (1936), p. 225.
Hoogewerff, G. J., Hieronymus Bosch, Elseviers Geillustreerd Maandschrift XCII (1936), p. 1–11.
K.. n, P., Tentoonstelling Museum Boymans II 'De Verzoeking van den Heiligen Antonius' uit Lissabon, Algemeen Handelsblad 28 July 1936.
Overbeek, J. M. C. van, Jeroen Bosch Schilder van duivelsche verbeeldingen, Wereldkroniek 1 August 1936, p. 1152ff.
Reik, Th. Een psychologische raadsel, Jeroen Bosch 'Fayzeur de diables', De Groene Amsterdammer, 11 July 1936.
Roggen, D., Het verklaren van het werk van Bosch en Bruegel, Nieuw Vlaanderen nr. 10, 7 March 1936.
Rozendaal, W. J., Hieronymus Bosch, Prisma der Kunsten I (1936), p. 250–5.
Scharf, A., A note on the Exhibition of Flemish Primitives at Rotterdam, Apollo XXIV (1936), p. 232–3.
Schöne, W., Die Versuchung des heiligen Antonius. Ein wenig bekanntes Bild im Escorial, Jahrbuch der preussischen Kunstsammlungen 1936,

p. 57–64.

Schreiner, G., *Jheronymus Bosch*, De Gemeenschap XII (1936), p. 372–83.

Stheeman, A., *De tentoonstelling van Bosch en andere Noord-Nederlandsche primitieven in Boymans*, Op de Hoogte XXXIII (1936), p. 262–8.

Veth, C., *Rotterdam, De tentoonstelling, in Boymans: Jeroen Bosch, Van Geertgen tot Scorel, Noord-Nederlandsche primitieven*, Maandblad voor Beeldende Kunsten XIII (1936), p. 286–90.

Veth, C., *Noord-Nederlandsche primitieven te Rotterdam. Nog enkele opmerkingen*, Maandblad voor Beeldende Kunsten XIII (1936), p. 297–304.

Veth, C., *Was Bosch bevangen door de obsessies van zijn tijd?*, Maandblad voor Beeldende Kunsten XIII (1936), p. 347–9.

Veth, C., *De Hieronymus Boschtentoonstelling*, De Telegraaf 9 July 1936.

Veth, C., *Nog een Verzoeking van Hieronymus Bosch in Boymans*, De Telegraaf 23 July 1936.

Vriesland, V. E. van, *Gedrevenheid en distantie: Jeroen Bosch en zijn jongere tijdgenooten*, De Groene Amsterdammer 12 September 1936.

W. (aterkamp), J., *De Jeroen Bosch-tentoonstelling in Museum Boymans Rotterdam*, Het Gildeboek XIX (1936), p. 173–4.

Beerends, J., *Jeroen Bosch en de Noord-Nederlandsche primitieven*, Het R. K. Bouwblad VIII (1936–7), p. 57–62; 68–71.

Zwartendijk, J., *Jeroen Bosch in het Museum Boymans*, Nieuwe Rotterdamsche Courant 29 August 1936.

Fierens, P., *Au Musée Boymans de Rotterdam: Jérôme Bosch, ses contemporains et ses successeurs*, L'art et les artistes N.S. XXXIII (1936–7), p. 37–42.

1937 Baldass, L. von, *Die Zeichnung im Schaffen Hieronymus Bosch und der Frühhollander*, Die Graphischen Kunste N.F. II (1937), p. 21ff.

Benesch, O., *Der Wald der sieht und hört*, Jahrbuch der preussischen Kunstsammlungen LVIII (1937), p. 258–66.

Devoghelaere, H., *Interprétations de la nef des fous de Jérôme Bosch*, L'Art et la vie IV (1937), p. 43–50.

Dupont, J., *Jérôme Bosch. Le retable de Saint-Antoine du Musée National de Lisbonne*, Laboratoire du Musée du Louvre. Institut Mainini, Brussels-Paris 1937

Dupont, J., *Jérôme Bosch*, L'Art sacré II March 1937, p. 67–70.

Knuttel, G. Wzn., *Hieronymus Bosch en de tengennatuurlijke dingen. Nabetrachting naar aanleiding van de tentoonstelling van Noord-Nederlandsche primitieven in het Museum Boymans*, Summer 1936. De Gids II (1937), p. 64–82.

d'Ors, E., *Hieronymus Bosch*, Almanach des Arts, Paris 1937, p. 235–9.

. . . *Ein neuentdeckter Hieronymus Bosch: Das jüngste Gericht*, Die Kunst. LXXV (1937), p. 153.

Bremmer, H. P., *Hieronymus Bosch*, Beeldende Kunst XXIV (1937–8).

1938 Avermaete, R., *Jeroen Bosch en*

de Noord-Nederlandse primitieven, Van Giotto tot de Vlaamse expressionisten, Brussels 1938, p. 31–7.

Destrée, J., *Jérôme Bosch*, Bulletin de l'Académie Royale des Sciences, des Lettres et des Beaux-Arts de Belgique. Brussels 1938, p. 138.

Fierens, P., *Jérôme Bosch et les 'Préhollandais'*, Le Journal des Débats (de Paris), 1 September 1938.

Gaunt, W., *A fifteenth-century surrealist: Jheronimus Bosch*, The Studio. CXVI (1938), p. 189–96.

Grauls, J., *Taalkundige toelichting bij het Hooi en den Hooiwagen*, Gentsche Bijdragen tot de Kunstgeschiedenis V (1938), p. 156–75.

Hals, A., *Die Rätsel der Bilder von Jeroen Bosch*, Munich 1938 rom.

Lebeer, L., *Het Hooi en de Hooiwagen in de beeldende Kunsten*, De Ets 'Al Hoy', Gentsche Bijdragen tot de Kunstgeschiedenis V (1938), p. 152–5.

Romein-(Verschoor), A., *Jeroen Bosch, meester der duisternis*, Erflaters van onze beschaving, Nederlandse Gestalten uit zes eeuwen I, Amsterdam 1938, p. 76–101.

. . . *A Great Jerome Bosch for San Diego: 'Christ taken in Captivity'*, The Art News XXXVII (1938), 31 December, p. 6.

Rosenberg, J., *Hieronymus Bosch: The heads of two pharisees (?) – Adam and Eve; formerly in the possession of L. Rosenthal, now in an American private collection*, Old Master Drawings XIII (1938–9), p. 62–3.

1939 Brion, M., *Le singe de Dieu: H. Bosch*, La Renaissance. Revue d'Art (1938/1939), nr. 6, p. 17–31.

Couturier, M. A., *La critique et le discernement des esprits*, L'Art sacré IV (1939), p. 37–9.

Gerlach, P. (ater) (=S. Schummer), *De minderbroeder bij Jeroen Bosch*, Franciskaansch Leven XXII (1939), p. 7–11.

Luedecke, H., *Luftkampf. Eine Vision des Hieronymus Bosch vom Ende des XV. Jahrhunderts*, Atlantis. Länder-Volker-Reisen XI (1939), p. 357–9.

Grauls, J., *Ter verklaring van Bosch en Bruegel*, Gentsche Bijdragen tot de Kunstgeschiedenis VI (1939/1940), p. 139–60.

Keyser, P. de, *Rhetoricale Toelichting bij het Hooi en den Hooiwagen*, Gentsche Bijdragen tot de Kunstgeschiedenis VI (1939/1940), p. 127–33.

Roggen, D., *J. Bosch: Literatuur en Folklore*, Gentsche Bijdragen tot de Kunstgeschiedenis VI (1939/1940), p. 107–26.

1940 Angulo, D., *Saint Christopher by Hieronymus Bosch*, The Burlington Magazine LXXXII (1940), p. 1ff.

Escherich, M., *Eine politische Satire von Heronymus Bosch*, Zeitschrift für Kunstgeschichte IX (1940), p. 188–90.

Gils, J. B. F. van, *Het snijden van de kei*, Nederlandsch Tijdschrift voor Geneeskunde II (1940), p. 1310ff.

Odenheimer, D., *The Garden of Paradise by Bosch*, Bulletin of the Art Institute of Chicago XXXIV (1940), p. 106–107.

Veth, C., *Jeroen Bosch door psychiaters verklaard*, Elseviers Geillustreerd Maandschrift XCIX (1940), p. 239.

1941 Friedländer, M. J., *Hieronymus*

Bosch. Ein Vortrag von–, The Hague 1941.

Gelder, J. G., van, *Teekeningen van Jeroen Bosch*, Beeldende Kunst XXVII (1941), nr. 8, p. 57–64.

Kerssemakers, J. W., *Een Studieblad van Jeroen Bosch*, Studiën. CXXXV (1941), p. 226–9.

Marlier, G., *Les visions démoniaques de Jérôme Bosch et de ses émules*, Le Soir, Brussels 18 February 1941, p. 10.

1942 Veth, C., *Max J. Friedländer over Jeroen Bosch*, Aan Max J. Friedländer, aangeboden door enkele vrienden en bewonderaars van zijn werk, The Hague 1942, p. 29–30.

. . ., *Hieronymus Bosch*, Das Niederlandbuch. Sammlung deutscher und niederlandischer Arbeiten, Frankfurt a M. 1942, p. 245–53.

1943 Fraenger, W., *Andacht zum Kinde, Auslegung eines Bildes von Hieronymus Bosch*, Die neue Rundschau LVI (1943), nr. 6, p. 221–6.

1944 Bax, D., *Jeroen Bosch keisnijding*, Historia, X (1944), p. 121–4.

Biltz, K. P., *Philipp II von Spanien und der Maler Hieronymus Bosch*, Maandblad der Nederlandsch-Duitsche Kultuurgemeenschap, January 1944, p, 1–11.

Borms, J., *Onbekend werk van Hieronymus Bosch. Een kruisdraging*. De Nieuwe Rotterdamsche Courant, 17 May 1944.

Tolnay, Ch. de, *A temptation of Saint Anthony by Hieronymus Bosch*, Art in America and elsewhere XXXII (1944), p. 60–5.

1945 Read, H., *Bosch and Dali, A coat of many colours*. Occasional essays, London 1945, p. 55–8.

Tervarent, G. de, *The origin of one of Jérôme Bosch's pictures*. Message Belgian Review, January 1945, p. 44–5.

1946 Combe, J., *Sources alchimiques dans l'art de Jérôme Bosch*, L'amour de l'art XXVI (1946), p. 30–5.

Denvir, B., *A sheet of drawings by Jerome Bosch at Oxford*, The Burlington Magazine LXXXVIII (1946), p. 121–2.

Kleef, N. van, *De Verloren Zoon door Hieronymus Bosch*, De Spectator Kern van Kunst- en Geestesleven, 19 May 1946, p. 1.

Schenk, V. W. D., *Tussen dulvelgeloof en beeldenstorm. Een studie over Jeroen Bosch en Erasmus van Rotterdam*, Amsterdam 1946.

1947 Fraenger, W., *Hieronymus Bosch. Das tausendjährige Reich. Grundzüge einer Auslegung*, Coburg 1947.

Sousa, Trigo de, *Relatório de exame radio-gráfico de um quadro de Bosch 'Tentaçoes de Santo Antão'*, Boletim do Museu Nacional de Arte antiga 1, 1947, fasc. 4 (1949), p. 212–13.

1948 Combe, J., *Jérôme Bosch dans l'art de Pierre Bruegel*, Les Arts plastiques II (1948), p. 435–46.

Contreras, J. de, *Algo más sobre la fortuna del Bosco en España*, Boletín de la Real Academia de la Historia CXXIII (1948), p. 285–95.

Dew, E. T., *The recent cleaning of Bosch's 'Christ before Pilate'*, Record of the Art Museum, Princeton University VII (1948), nr. 2, p. 1–5.

Fraenger, W., *Hieronymus Bosch:*

Johannes der Täufer, Eine Meditationstafel des Freien Geistes, Zeitschrift für Kunst I (1948), p. 163–75.

(Rath, K. von), *Hieronymus Bosch. Die Anbetung des Christuskindes*, Berlin 1948.

1949 Bach, O. K., *Bosch's Vision of Tondalys*, Denver Art Museum Quarterly, Spring 1949, p. 5.

Camp, G. van, *Considérations sur le paysage chez Jérôme Bosch*, Miscellanea Leo van Puyvelde, Brussels 1949, p. 65–73.

Tolnay, Ch., de, *An Early Dutch Panel: A Contribution to the Panel Painting before Bosch*, Miscellanea Leo van Puyvelde, Brussels 1949, p. 49–54.

Fraenger, W., *Johannes auf Patmos. Eine Umwendtafel für den Meditationsgebrauch*, Zeitschrift für Religions- und Geistesgeschichte II (1949/1950), p. 327–45.

1950 Fraenger, W., *Die Hochzeit zu Kana, Ein Dokument semitischer Gnosis bei Hieronymus Bosch*, Berlin 1950.

Larsen, E., *Les tentations de Saint Antoine de Jérôme Bosch*, Revue belge d'archéologie et d'histoire de l'art XIX (1950), p. 3–41.

Neugass, F., *Hieronymus Bosch Anbetung der Könige*, Die Weltkunst XX (1950), nr. 24, p. 1–2.

Pigler, A., *Astrology and Jerome Bosch*, The Burlington Magazine XCII (1950), p. 132–6.

Salinger, M., *Notes on the Adoration of the Magi by Hieronymus Bosch*, The Metropolitan Museum of Art Bulletin, New York IX (1950), p. 96.

1951 Caviggiolo, A., *Jheronimus Bosch*, 1460–1516. Adoration of the kings, Alte und neue Kunst 1951, nr. 7, p. 21.

Fraenger, W., *Hieronymus Bosch in seiner Auseinandersetzung mit dem Unbewussten*, Du. Schweizerische Monatschrift XI (1951), p. 6–18.

Fraenger, W., *Hieronymus Bosch 'Der verlorene Sohn'*, Castrum peregrini nr. 1 Amsterdam 1951, p. 27–39.

Fraenger, W., *Hieronymus Bosch. Der Tisch der Weisheit bisher 'Die sieben Todsunden' genannt*. Psyche, ein Zeitschrift für Tiefenpsychologie und Menschenkunde in Forschung und Praxis V (1951), p. 355–84.

Jacobsen, R., *Jeroen Bosch op de tentoonstelling der Nederlandse primitieven*, Prisma 1951, p. 49–60.

1952 Brans, J. V. L., *Un nouveau Bosch au musée du Prado*, Gazette des Beaux-Arts 6e Pér. XL (1952), p. 129–31.

Fraenger, W., *The Millennium of Hieronymus Bosch. Outlines of a new interpretation*, London 1952.

Castelli, E., *Il demoniaco nell'arte*, Milan 1952.

Janson, C., *Le Christ en croix de Jérôme Bosch*. Bulletin des Musées Royaux des Beaux-Arts (1952), p. 83–8.

Popham, A. E., *A drawing by Hieronymus Bosch*, British Museum Quarterly XVII (1952), p. 45.

Baldass, L. von, *La tendenza moralizzante in Bosch e Bruegel*, Atti del II Congresso internazionale di Studi Umanistici (Rome 1952), Rome-Milan 1953.

1953 Bax, D., Bosschiana. *Verloren*

Zoon – Johannes op Pathmos – Wellusturn – Doornenkroning, Oud-Holland LXVIII (1953), p. 200–208.
Chartel, A., *L'Antéchrist à la Renaissance*, Atti del II Congresso Internazionale di Studi Umanistici (Rome 1952), Rome-Milan 1953, p. 177–186.
Dorfles, G., *Bosch*, Milan 1953.
Fraenger W., *Hieronymus Bosch, Der Verlorene Sohn*, Atti del II Congresso internazionale di Studi Umanistici (Rome 1952), Rome-Milan 1953.
Fraenger, W., *Il Figliol prodigo di Hieronymus Bosch*, Arch. di Filosofia I (1953), p. 127–36.
Janssens, E. P., *Jeroen Bosch*, Schets VI (1953), p. 97–100.
Meertens, P. J., *Over volkskundige elementen in het werk van Jeroen Bosch*, Volkskunde LIV (1953), p. 172–180.
Philip, L. Brand, *The Prado Epiphany by Jerome Bosch*, The Art Bulletin XXXV (1953), p. 267–93.
Seligman, K., *Hieronymus Bosch, The Peddler*, Gazette des Beaux-Arts 6e Pér. XLII (1953), p. 97–104.
Santos, A. Vieira, *Hieronymus Bosch. As Tentaçoes de Santo Antão do Museu Nacional de Arte antiga de Lisboa*, Lisbon 1953.
1954 Beselaere, W. van, *Het Kerstthema by Bosch en Bruegel*, Westvlaanderen III (1954), p. 8–15.
Camp, G., van, *Autonomie de Jérôme Bosch et récentes interprétations de ses oeuvres*, Bulletin des Musées Royaux des Beaux-Arts III (1954), p. 131–48.
Dion, J., *Le concert dans l'oeuf de Jérôme Bosch*, Bulletin des Amis du Musée de Lille 1954, nr. 12, p. 11–12.
Dorfles, G., *Bosch*, Milan 1954.
F., *Frühwerke des Hieronymus Bosch*, Die Weltkunst XXIV (1954), nr. 5, p. 3–4.
Hirsch, W., *Hieronymus Bosch, De tuin der lusten*, Amsterdam-Antwerp 1954.
Walicki, M., *Hieronima Boscha dialog ze s'wiatem*, Prz. artyst. 1954 nrs. 5–6, p. 101–16.
1955 Brans, J. V. L., *Los ermitaños de Jerónimo Bosco, San Juan Bautista en el desierto*, Goya 1955, nr. 4, p. 196–201.
Baltrusaitis, J., *Le Moyen-Âge fantastique*, Paris 1955.
Camp, G. van, *Une Tentation de Saint Antoine à rattacher à l'oeuvre de Jérôme Bosch*, Revue belge d'archéologie et d'histoire de l'art XXIV (1955), p. 29–38.
Fierens, P., *Le réalisme fantastique de Jérôme Bosch*, Bulletin des Amis du Musée de Lille 1955, nr. 14, p. 9–12.
Hirsch, W., *Hieronymus Bosch, The Garden of Delights*, London 1955.
Popham, A. E., *An unknown drawing by Hieronymus Bosch*, Actes du XVIIème Congrès international d'histoire de l'art, Amsterdam 1952 (The Hague 1955), p. 247–51.
R(egteren) A(Itena), J. O. van, *Een schetsblad door Hieronymus Bosch*, Vereeniging Rembrandt, verslag over de jaren 1954 en 1955, p. 24.
Rothe, H., *Hieronymus Bosch, Garten der Lüste*, Munich 1955.
Salazar, A. M., *El Bosco y Ambrosio de Morales*, Archivo español de Arte XXVIII (1955), p. 117–38.

Swarzenski, H., *An unknown Bosch*, Bulletin of the Boston Museum of Fine Arts LIII (1955), p. 1–10.
1956 Bax, D., *Beschrijving en poging tot verklaring van het Tuin der onkuisheld-drieluik van Jeroen Bosch, Gevolgd door kritiek op Fraenger*, Amsterdam 1956.
Calandre de Pita, E., *El drago en un cuadro de El Bosco y en un grabado de Schongauer*, Clavileño 1956, nr. 39, p. 61–5.
Charmet, R., *L'oeuf dans la peinture, symbole et réalité*, Arts, 4 April 1956, p. 14.
1957 Benesch, O., *Hieronymus Bosch and the thinking of the late middle ages*, Konsthistorisk Tidskrift XXVI (1957), p. 21–42; p. 103–27.
Cuttler, Ch. D., *Witchcraft in a Work by Bosch*, The Art Quarterly XX (1957), p. 128–40.
Cuttler, Ch. D., *The Lisbon Temptation of St Anthony by Jerome Bosch*, The Art Bulletin XXXIX (1957), p. 109–26.
Fraenger, W., *Die Natursymbolik des Hieronymus Bosch*, Bildende Kunst V (1957), p. 306–08.
Fraenger, W., *Die Versuchung des hl. Antonius von Hieronymus Bosch*, Archivo di Filosofia III (1957), p. 155–63.
Fraenger, W., *Hieronymus Bosch, Der Busser St Hieronymus*. Castrum peregrini XXXII (1957/1958), p. 5–13.
Fraenger, W., *Der vierte König des Madrider Epiphanias-Altars von Hieronymus Bosch*, Deutsches Jahrbuch für Volkskunde III (1957). p. 169–98.
Hartlaub, G. F., *Hieronymus Bosch, Wege und Abwege der Deutung*, Das Münster X (1957), p. 374–7.
Macgreevy, Th., *Deux tableaux Boschesques à Dublin*, Miscellanea Prof. Dr. D. Roggen, Antwerp 1957, p. 105–11.
... *Une restauration extraordinaire: Le Portement de Croix de Jérôme Bosch*, Connaissance des Arts LXIII (1957), p. 50–3.
1958 Fraenger, W., *Hieronymus Bosch. Die Versuchung des hl. Antonius*, Hessische Blätter für Volkskunde XLIX–L (1958), p. 20–7.
H., *Der Geburtstag des Hieronymus Bosch*, Die Weltkunst XXVIII (1958). nr. 20, p. 31.
Lebeer, L., *Frans Hogenberg, Al Hoy (Tout es foin)*, Trésors de la Bibliothèque Royale de Belgique 1958, p. 134–7.
Philip, L. Brand. *The Peddler by Hieronymus Bosch. A Study in detection*, Nederlands Kunsthistorisch Jaarboek IX (1958), p. 1–81.
Santos, A. V., *Subsidios para um estudo sobre o triptico 'Tentaçoes de Santo Antão' do Museu de Lisboa*, Boletim do Museu Nacional de arte antiga III (1958), nr. 4, p. 19–24.
... *Révélation au Musée des Beaux-Arts de Gand, un chef-d'oeuvre retrouve son vrai visage*, Connaissance des Arts LXXI (1958), p. 37–7.
1959 Brans, J. V. L., *Filips II en Hieronymus Bosch*, Dietsche Warande en Belfort 1959, p. 139–46.
Erdgren, L., *'Lustarnas trädgard'*, Paletten 1959, nr. 2, p. 46–53.

Holten, R. von, *Hieronymus Bosch und die Vision des Tondalus*, Konsthistorisk Tidskrift XXVIII (1959), p. 99–109.
Masson, A., *Le Jardin des Délices*, Critique 1959, nr. 144, p. 427–32.
Mateo Gómez, I., *El grupo de los jugadores en el 'Jardin de las Delicias' del Bosco*, Archivo español de arte XXXII (1959), p. 253–6; XXXIII (1960), p. 427–30.
Schoute, R. van, *Le portement de Croix de Jérôme Bosch au Musée de Gand. Considérations sur l'exécution picturale.* Bulletin de l'institut royal du patrimoine artistique II (1959), p. 47–58.
... *Vonst van een grisaille-schildering van Hieronymus Bosch in het Stedelijk Museum te Brugge*, Handelingen van het Genootschap voor Geschiedenis 'Société d'Emulation' te Brugge XCVI (1959), p. 253–4.
... *Jerome Bosch 'The Adoration of the Magi'*, Philadelphia Museum of Art Bulletin LV (1959/1960), p. 1–2.
1960 Baltrusaitis, J., *Réveils et prodiges*. Paris 1960.
Lurker, M., *Der Baum in Glauben und Kunst unter besonderer Berücksichtigung der Werke des Hieronymus Bosch*, Baden-Baden/Strasbourg 1960.
Tolnay, Ch. de, *Remarques sur quelques dessins de Bruegel l'Ancien et sur un dessin de Bosch récemment réapparus*, Bulletin des Musées Royaux des Beaux-Arts IX (1960), p. 3–28.
1961 Bax, D., *Jeroen Bosch' Drieluik met de gekruisigde martelares*, Amsterdam 1961.
Pemán, C., *Sobre la interpretación del viadante al reverso del 'Carro de neno' del Bosco*; Archivo español de arte XXXIV (1961), p. 125–39.
Rosenberg, J., *On the meaning of a Bosch drawing*, De artibus opuscula XL. Essays in honour of Erwin Panofsky, New York 1961, p. 422–6.
Tolnay, Ch. de, *Two drawings after a lost triptych by Hieronymus Bosch*, Record of the Art Museum, Princeton University XX (1961), p. 43–8.
1962 Meertens, P. J., *Volkskundige elementen in het werk van Jeroen Bosch* II Volkskunde LXIII (1962), p. 1–16.
Pondelíček, I., *Some reflections on fantastical painting*, Výtvarne umeni 1962, p. 106–11.
Steppe, J., *Problemen betreffende het werk van Hieronymus Bosch*, Jaarboek Koninklijke Academie voor Wetenschappen, Letteren en Schone Kunsten van Belgie XXIV (1962), p. 156–67.
Sulzberger, S., *Jérôme Bosch et les maitres de l'enluminure*, Scriptorium XVI (1962), p. 46–9.
1963 Chartel, A., *L'Europe de la Renaissance. L'âge de l'Humanisme*. Paris, 1963; Engl. ed. London 1963.
Fraenger, W., *'Das Lied des Moses' als Zentralmotiv der Lissaboner 'Versuchungen des St Antonius' von Hieronymus Bosch*, Castrum peregrini LVIII (1963), p. 5–79.
Fraenger, W., *Ein Leitwort Jacob Grimms zur Ausiegung der Lissaboner 'Versuchung des heiligen Antonius' von Hieronymus Bosch*, Jacob Grimm zur 100. Wiederkehr seines Todestages, Berlin 1963, p. 240–90.
Mateo Gómez, I., *El grupo de la cueva en el panel central del 'Jardin de las*

delicias' del Bosco, Archivo español de arte XXXVI (1963), p. 253–7.
Tolnay, Ch. de, *The Paintings of H. Bosch in the Philadelphia Museum of Art*, Art International VII (1963), nr. 4, p. 20–8.
Vinken, P. J., *Controverse over Marskramer van Jeroen Bosch*, Vrij Nederland 20 July 1963.
1964 Blote-Obbes, M., *De symboliek van de uil bij Jeroen Bosch*, Volkskunde LXV (1964), p. 24–6.
Meertens, P. J., *Volkskundige elementen in het werk van Jeroen Bosch* III, Volkskunde LXV (1964), p. 49–60.
M. (eertens), P. J., *Prof. Dr W. Fraenger*, Volkskunde LXV (1964), p. 30–2.
1965 Hemphill, R. E., *The personality and problem of Hieronymus Bosch*, Proceedings of the Royal Society of Medicine LVIII (1965), nr. 2, p. 137–44.
Mateo Gómez, I., *El Bosco en España*, Madrid 1965.
1966 Biedrzynski, R., *Der Garten der Lüste. Die Bildwelt des Hieronymus Bosch*, Feldafing 1966.
Debevere, R., *Is de 'Keisnijding' van Jeroen Bosch ?*, Ons Erfdeel X (1966–7), nr. 2, p. 113–22.
Gerlach, P., *Jeroen Bosch. Ter gelegenheid van de 450ste gedenkdag van zijn sterven*, Brabantia XV (1966), p. 208–209.
Kröber, H. J., *Unbekannter Bosch in Kairo*, Kristall XXI (1966), nr. 27, p. 27–35.
Praz, M., *The canticles of Hieronymus Bosch*, Art News Annual XXXII (1966), p. 55–69.
Spychalska-Boczkowska, A., *Material for the Iconography of Hieronymus Bosch's Triptych the Garden of Delights*, Studia Muzealne V (1966), p. 49–95.
1967 Gerlach, P., *De interpretatie van Jeroen Bosch*, Brabantia, XVI (1967), p. 184–92.
Gerlach, P., *Jeroen Bosch een ketter... een volgeling van Jacob van Almaengien ?*, Brabants Heermn XIX (1967), p. 34–9.
Gombrich, E. H., *The Earliest Description of Bosch's Garden of Delight*, Journal of Warburg & Courtauld Institutes XXX, 1967, p. 403–06.
Kurz, O.: *Four tapestries after Hieronymus Bosch*, Journal of Warburg & Courtauld Institutes XXX, 1967. p. 150–63.
Mateo Gómez, J., *El Jardin de las delicias, a propósito de una copia temprana y un tapiz*, Archivo Español de Arte, p. 40, n. 157, Jan.-Mar. 1967, p. 47–53.
Poch-Kalous, M., *Hieronymus Bosch in der Gemäldegalerie der Akademie der bildenben Künste in Wien*, Vienna 1967.
Scher, S. K., *Hieronymus Bosch: an exercise in attribution*, Bulletin Rhode Island School Design (Providence), LIII, 1966–7, nr. 2.
1968 McGrath, R. L., *Satan and Bosch. The visio Tundali and the monastic vices*. Gazette des Beaux-Arts, LXXI, Jan. 1968, p. 45–50.

The paintings in colour

List of plates

THE CURE OF FOLLY
Plate I
Whole
The Seven Deadly Sins

Plate II
Whole

Plate III
Detail: tondo of *Hell*

Plate IV
A Detail: panel of *Envy*
B Detail: panel of *Gluttony*

Plate V
Detail: panel of *Pride*

THE MARRIAGE AT CANA
Plate VI
Detail of upper central part

Plate VII
Detail: figures at left

THE CONJURER
Plate VIII
Detail: the onlookers

THE SHIP OF FOOLS
Plate IX
Detail: the boat

TRIPTYCH OF THE FLOOD
Plate X
Central part of *The World after the Flood*

Plate XI
A Tondo of *The Devil in the Country*
B Lower part of *The Evil World*

VISIONS OF THE HEREAFTER
Plate XII
Central part of *The Ascent into the Empyrean*

Plate XIII
Lower part of *Hell*

TRIPTYCH OF THE HAY WAIN
Plate XIV
Shutters of *The Path of Life*(?)

Plate XV
Bust of the central figure of *The Path of Life* (?)

Plates XVI–XVII
Comprehensive view of the open triptych (*Original Sin – The Hay Wain – Hell*)

Plate XVIII
Upper part of *Original Sin*

Plate XIX
Upper part of *Hell*

Plate XX
Detail of the group on the wain

Plate XXI
Details of *The Hay Wain*:
A Landscape at upper left –
B Landscape at upper right –
C Figures at left centre – *D* Figures at right centre – *E* Figures at lower left – *F* Brawlers at the centre towards the bottom –
G Figures at lower centre –
H Figures at lower right

Plates XXII and XXIII
Central detail of *The Hay Wain*: the brawlers around the wain

TRIPTYCH OF THE GARDEN OF DELIGHTS
Plates XXIV–XXV
Comprehensive view of the open triptych (*The Garden of Eden – The Garden of Delights – Musical Hell*)

Plate XXVI
Details of *The Garden of Eden*: *A* and *B* Hilly structures at upper left and right – *C* Animals around upper left – *D* Animals and monsters around centre right – *E* Animals around centre left – *F* Animals and monsters at centre right – *G* Vegetation around centre left – *H* Animals and monsters at lower right

Plate XXVII
Central detail of *The Garden of Eden*: Christ and Eve

Plate XXVIII
Details of *Musical Hell*: *A*, *B* and *C* Landscape at the top – *D*, *E*, *F*, *G*, *H* and *I* Damned, demons, and diabolic contrivances and instruments in the central part toward the top

Plate XXIX
Lower part of *Musical Hell*

Plate XXX
Fountain at upper centre of *The Garden of Delights*

Plate XXXI
Trophy at upper right in *The Garden of Delights*

Plates XXXII–XXXIII
Central detail of *The Garden of Delights*: the pond of voluptuousness, the cavalcade of lust and the fountain of youth

Plate XXXIV
Details of *The Garden of Delights*: *A*, *B* and *C* Vegetable and stony structures at top, left and around the centre – *D*, *E*, *F* and *G* Figures, animals, monsters and vegetation in the central part toward the top – *H* and *I* Figures, animals and vegetable monstrosities at centre left

Plate XXXV
Details of figures, animals and monstrous vegetables of *The Garden of Delights*: *A*, *B* and *C* Around centre right – *D*, *E*, *F* and *G* In the lower middle part, at the centre and at right – *H* and *I* At the bottom, at left and at the centre

Plate XXXVI
Detail around lower left of *The Garden of Delights*: the lovers

Plate XXXVII
Nudes at lower right in *The Garden of Delights*

ST CHRISTOPHER
Plate XXXVIII
Detail: Landscape to the left

Plate XXXIX
Central detail: the saint and the Infant Jesus

Plate XL
Rural detail around lower right

ST JOHN THE BAPTIST IN THE WILDERNESS
Plate XLI
Whole

TRIPTYCH OF THE TEMPTATION OF ST ANTHONY
Plates XLII–XLIII
Detail of the landscape at upper left in *The Temptation of St Anthony*

Plate XLIV
Detail of lower part of *St Anthony's Aerial Torment and His Return to His Retreat*

Plate XLV
A Upper detail of the *St Anthony's Aerial Torment and His Return to His Retreat*
B Central detail of *The Temptation of St Anthony*

Plate XLVI
A Upper detail of *The Meditation of St Anthony*
B Detail of lower left of *The Temptation of St Anthony*

Plate XLVII
Detail of lower left of *The Meditation of St Anthony*

TRIPTYCH OF THE JUDGEMENT (VIENNA)
Plate XLVIII
A Upper detail of *The Last Judgement*
B Detail of centre left of *The Last Judgement*

Plate XLIX
Details of figures, animals, monsters and instruments of torture in *The Last Judgement*: *A* and *B* Centre – *C* Centre right – *D*, *E* and *F* Lower centre – *G* and *H* At bottom, left and right

THE CROWNING WITH THORNS
Plate L
Whole

Plate LI
Head of the figure at upper right

Plate LII
Figure at lower left

THE TEMPTATION OF ST ANTHONY
Plate LIII
Detail of landscape at centre left

'THE PRODIGAL SON'
Plate LIV
Detail of the house

Plate LV
Detail of the protagonist

TRIPTYCH OF THE EPIPHANY (MADRID)
Plates LVI–LVII
A Comprehensive view of the closed triptych (*The Mass of St Gregory*): *B–C–D* Comprehensive view of the open triptych (*St Peter and the Donor – The Adoration of the Magi – St Agnes and the Donor*)

Plate LVIII
Detail of St Joseph in *St Peter and the Donor*

Plate LIX
Upper detail of *The Adoration of the Magi*: Jerusalem

Plates LX and LXI
Central detail of *The Adoration of the Magi*: the roof of the hut

CHRIST BEARING THE CROSS
Plate LXII
Whole

Plate LXIII
Detail of figures at lower left

Plate LXIV
Detail of figures at lower right

COVER ILLUSTRATION
Central detail, toward lower left, of *The Garden of Delights*

In the captions at the foot of the colour plates the indication is given (in centimetres) of the actual dimension (width) of the painting, or of the part of the painting reproduced in it

PLATE I   THE CURE FOR MADNESS Madrid, Prado [No. 1]
Whole (35 cm.)

PLATE II   THE SEVEN DEADLY SINS Madrid, Prado [No. 2]
Whole (150 cm.)

PLATE III   THE SEVEN DEADLY SINS Madrid, Prado [No. 2]
Tondo of *Hell* (diameter 36.3 cm.)

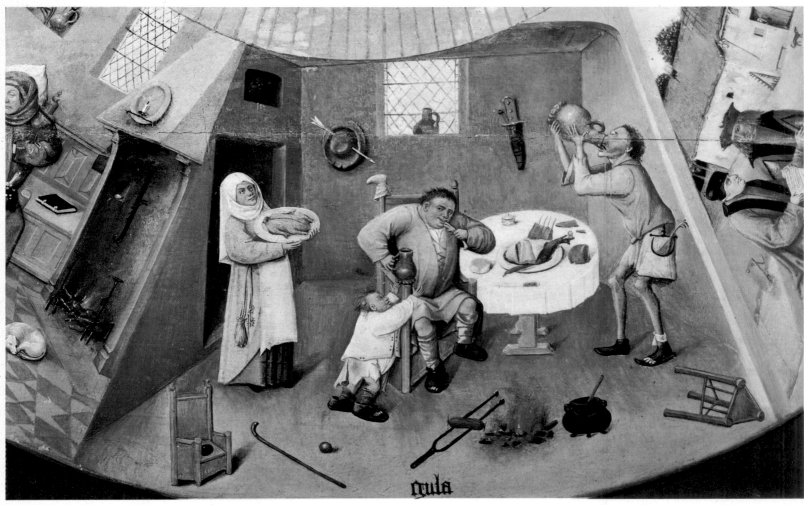

PLATE IV THE SEVEN DEADLY SINS Madrid, Prado [No. 2]
Panels of *Envy* (49 cm.) and *Gluttony* (43.5 cm.)

PLATE V THE SEVEN DEADLY SINS Madrid, Prado [No. 2]
Panel of *Pride* (actual size)

PLATE VI   THE MARRIAGE OF CANA   Rotterdam, Boymans-van Beuningen Museum   [No. 3]
Detail (30.9 cm.)

PLATE VII THE MARRIAGE OF CANA Rotterdam, Boymans-van Beuningen Museum [No. 3]
Detail (39.5 cm.)

PLATE VIII   THE CONJURER   Saint-Germain-en-Laye, Musée Municipal   [No. 6]
Detail (34.1 cm.)

PLATE IX   THE SHIP OF FOOLS Paris, Louvre [No. 16]
Detail (32 cm.)

PLATE X TRIPTYCH OF THE FLOOD Rotterdam, Boymans-van Beuningen Museum [No. 25]
Detail of *The World after the Flood* [No. 25 D] (36 cm.)

PLATE XI   TRIPTYCH OF THE FLOOD   Rotterdam, Boymans-van Beuningen Museum [No. 25]
Tondo of the *Devil in the country* [No. 25 C] (diameter 30 cm.) and detail of the *Evil world* [No. 25 D] (36 cm.)

PLATE XII   VISIONS OF THE HEREAFTER Venice, Palazzo Ducale [No. 26]
Detail of the *Ascent into the Empyrean* [No. 26 D] (38 cm.)

PLATE XIII   VISIONS OF THE HEREAFTER   Venice, Palazzo Ducale   [No. 26]
Detail of the *Hell*   [No. 26 B]   (39 cm.)

PLATE XIV   TRIPTYCH OF THE HAY WAIN Madrid, Prado [No. 21]
Panels of the *Path of life* [No. 21 A] (90 cm.)

PLATE XV   TRIPTYCH OF THE HAY WAIN Madrid, Prado [No. 21]
Detail of the *Path of life* [No. 21 A] (actual size).

PLATES XVI-XVII TRIPTYCH OF THE HAY WAIN Madrid, Prado [No. 21]
Comprehensive view of the open triptych [Nos. 21 B, 21 C and 21 D] (190 cm.)

PLATE XVIII   TRIPTYCH OF THE HAY WAIN Madrid, Prado [No. 21]
Detail of the *Original Sin* [No. 21 B] (36 cm.)

PLATE XIX   TRIPTYCH OF THE HAY WAIN Madrid, Prado [No. 21]
Detail of the *Infernal Constructions* [No. 21 D] (45 cm.)

PLATE XX   TRIPTYCH OF THE HAY WAIN Madrid, Prado [No. 21]
Detail of the *Hay Wain* [No. 21 C] (31.4 cm.)

PLATE XXII   TRIPTYCH OF THE HAY WAIN   Madrid, Prado   [No. 21]
Detail of the *Hay Wain*   [No. 21 C]   (31.2 cm.)

PLATE XXIII   TRIPTYCH OF THE HAY WAIN Madrid, Prado [No. 21]
Detail of the *Hay Wain* [No. 21 C] (31.2 cm.)

PLATE XXVI   TRIPTYCH OF THE GARDEN OF DELIGHTS Madrid, Prado [No. 30]
Details of the *Garden of Eden* [No. 30 B] (small ones: 36.7 cm.; large one: 75.3 cm.)

PLATE XXVII   TRIPTYCH OF THE GARDEN OF DELIGHTS Madrid, Prado [No. 30]
Detail of the *Garden of Eden* [No. 30 B] (39.7 cm.)

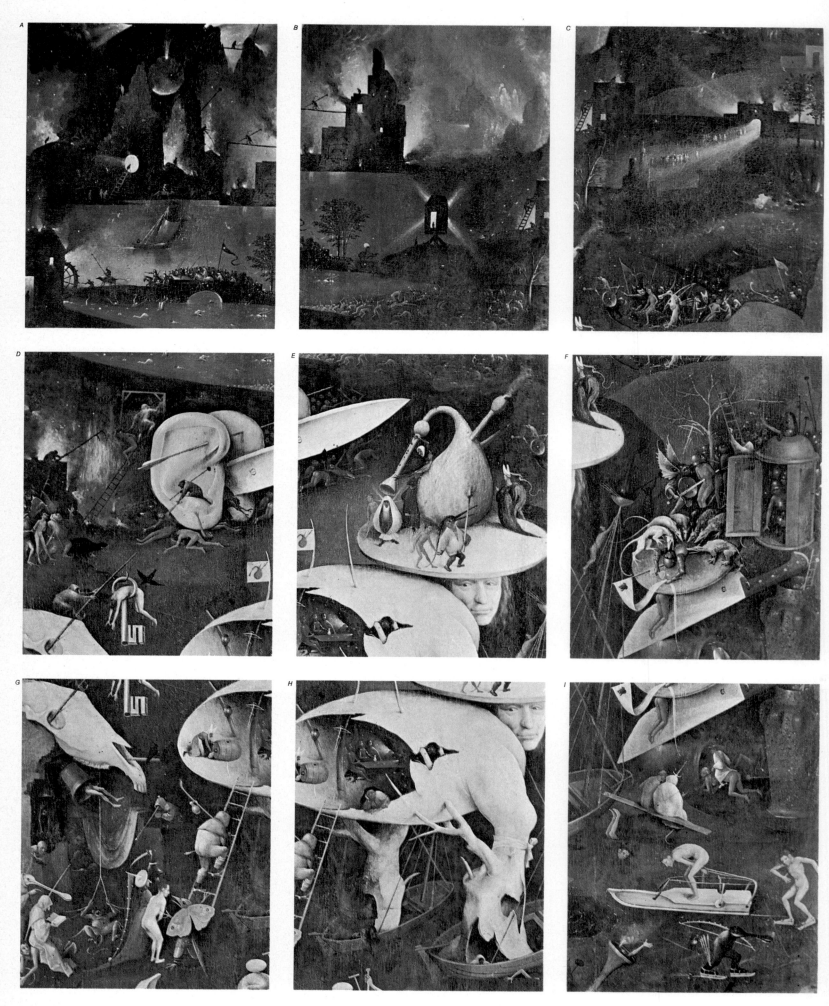

PLATE XXVIII   TRIPTYCH OF THE GARDEN OF DELIGHTS Madrid, Prado [No. 30]
Details of the *Musical Hell* [No. 30 D] (each, 33.8 cm.)

PLATE XXIX   TRIPTYCH OF THE GARDEN OF DELIGHTS   Madrid, Prado   [No. 30]
Detail of the *Musical Hell*   [No. 30 D]   (97 cm.)

PLATE XXX   TRIPTYCH OF THE GARDEN OF DELIGHTS Madrid, Prado [No. 30]
Detail of the *Garden of Delights* [No. 30 C] (28.4 cm.)

PLATE XXXI   TRIPTYCH OF THE GARDEN OF DELIGHTS Madrid, Prado [No. 30]
Detail of the *Garden of Delights* [No. 30 C] (29.6 cm.)

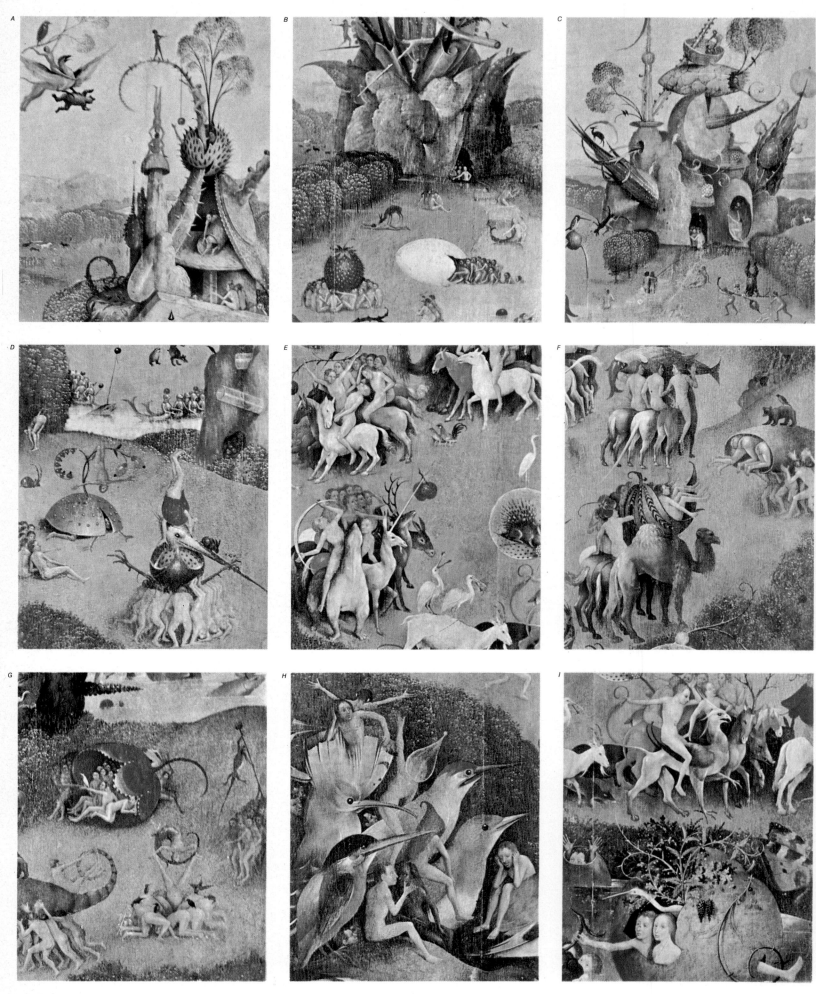

PLATE XXXIV TRIPTYCH OF THE GARDEN OF DELIGHTS Madrid, Prado [No. 30]
Details of the *Garden of Delights* [No. 30 C] (each, 16.2 cm.)

PLATE XXXV   TRIPTYCH OF THE GARDEN OF DELIGHTS Madrid, Prado [No. 30]
Details of the *Garden of Delights* [No. 30 C] (each, 16.2 cm.)

PLATE XXXVI   TRIPTYCH OF THE GARDEN OF DELIGHTS   Madrid, Prado   [No. 30]
Detail of the *Garden of Delights*   [No. 30 C]   (actual size)

PLATE XXXVII   TRIPTYCH OF THE GARDEN OF DELIGHTS Madrid, Prado [No. 30]
Detail of the *Garden of Delights* [No. 30 C] (actual size)

PLATE XXXVIII   SAINT CHRISTOPHER   Rotterdam, Boymans-van Beuningen Museum   [No. 36]
Detail (38.7 cm.)

PLATE XXXIX   SAINT CHRISTOPHER   Rotterdam, Boymans-van Beuningen Museum   [No. 36]
Detail (28 cm.)

PLATE XL   SAINT CHRISTOPHER   Rotterdam, Boymans-van Beuningen Museum   [No. 36]
Detail (24.7 cm.)

PLATE XLI　SAINT JOHN THE BAPTIST IN THE WILDERNESS　Madrid, Lázaro Galdiano Museum　[No. 34]
Whole (40 cm.)

PLATE XLIV   TRIPTYCH OF THE TEMPTATION OF SAINT ANTHONY   Lisbon, Museu Nacional de Arte Antiga   [No. 43]
Detail of the *Flight and Fall of Saint Anthony*   [No. 43 C]   (48.2 cm.)

PLATE XLVI   TRIPTYCH OF THE TEMPTATION OF SAINT ANTHONY Lisbon, Museu Nacional de Arte Antiga [No. 43]
Details of the *Meditation* [No. 43 E] (27.4 cm.) and of the *Temptation of Saint Anthony* [No. 43 D] (58.8 cm.)

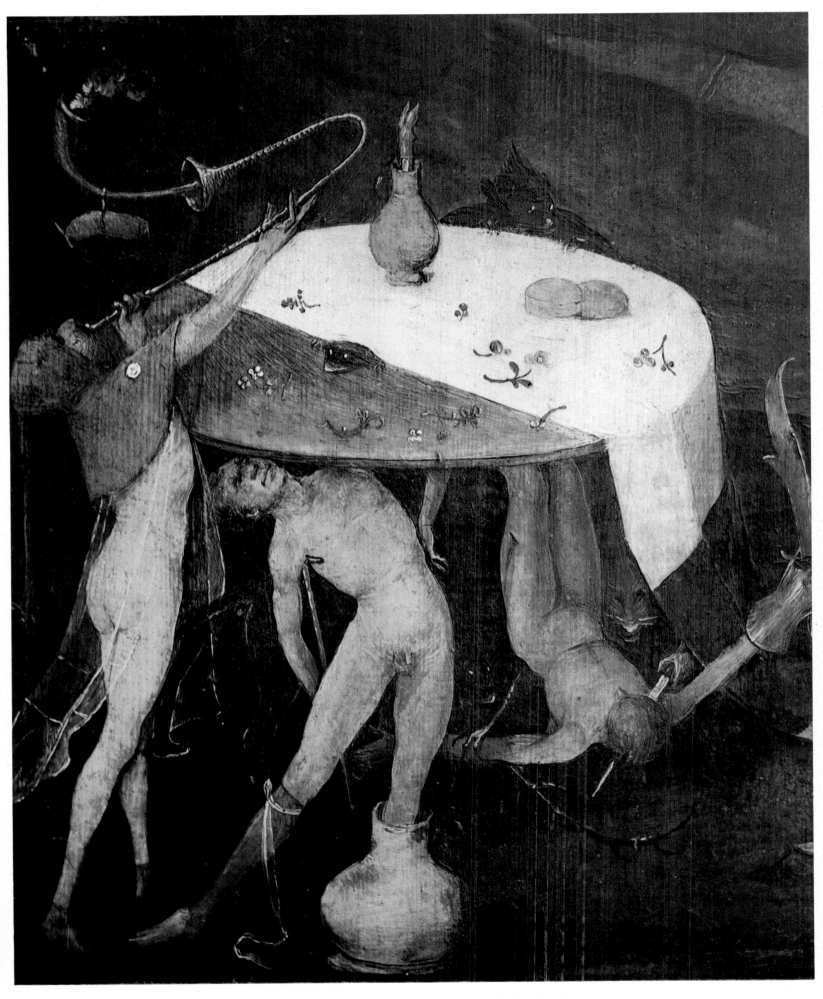

PLATE XLVII   TRIPTYCH OF THE TEMPTATION OF SAINT ANTHONY Lisbon, Museu Nacional de Arte Antiga [No. 43]
Detail of the *Meditation of Saint Anthony* [No. 43 E] (26.2 cm.)

PLATE XLVIII   TRIPTYCH OF THE JUDGEMENT IN VIENNA   Vienna, Akademie der bildenden Künste   [No. 50]
Upper (127 cm.) and central (45.1 cm.) details of the *Last Judgement*   [No. 50 D]

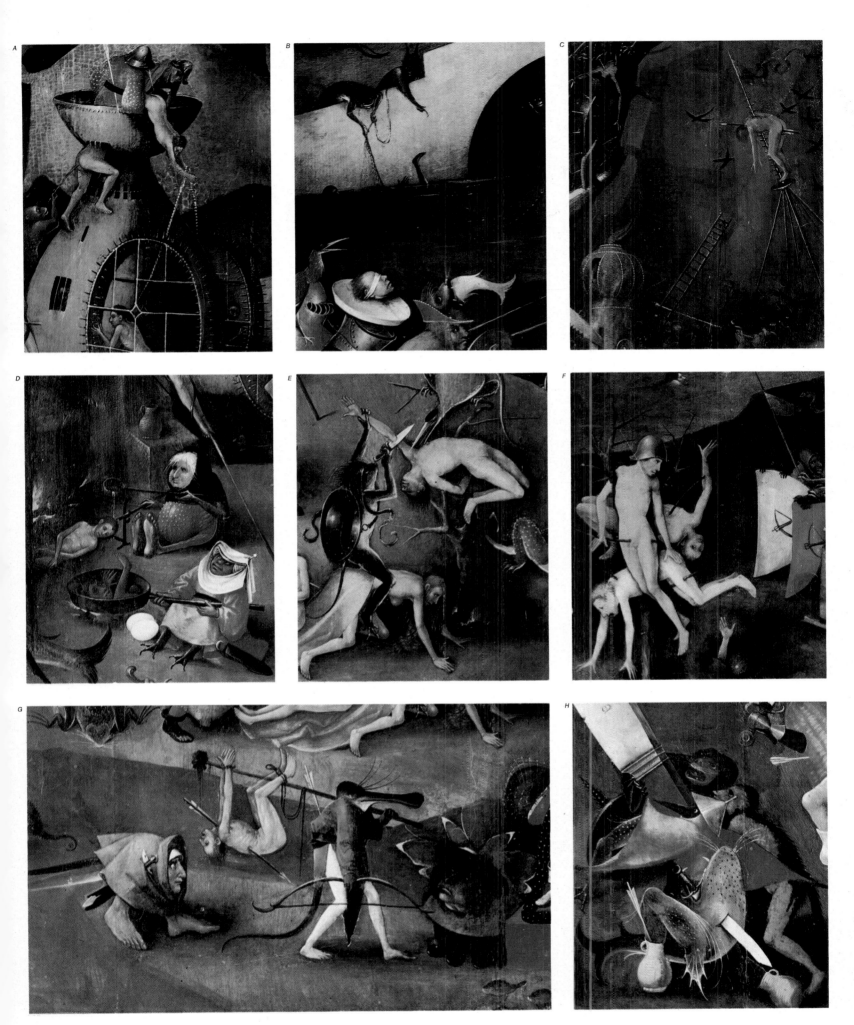

PLATE XLIX TRIPTYCH OF THE VIENNA LAST JUDGEMENT Vienna, Akademie der bildenden Künste [No. 50]
Details of the *Last Judgement* [No. 50 D] (small ones, 17.6 cm.; the large one, 38.4 cm.)

PLATE L   THE CROWNING WITH THORNS London, National Gallery [No. 57]
Whole (58.5 cm.)

PLATE LI   THE CROWNING WITH THORNS London, National Gallery [No. 57]
Detail (actual size)

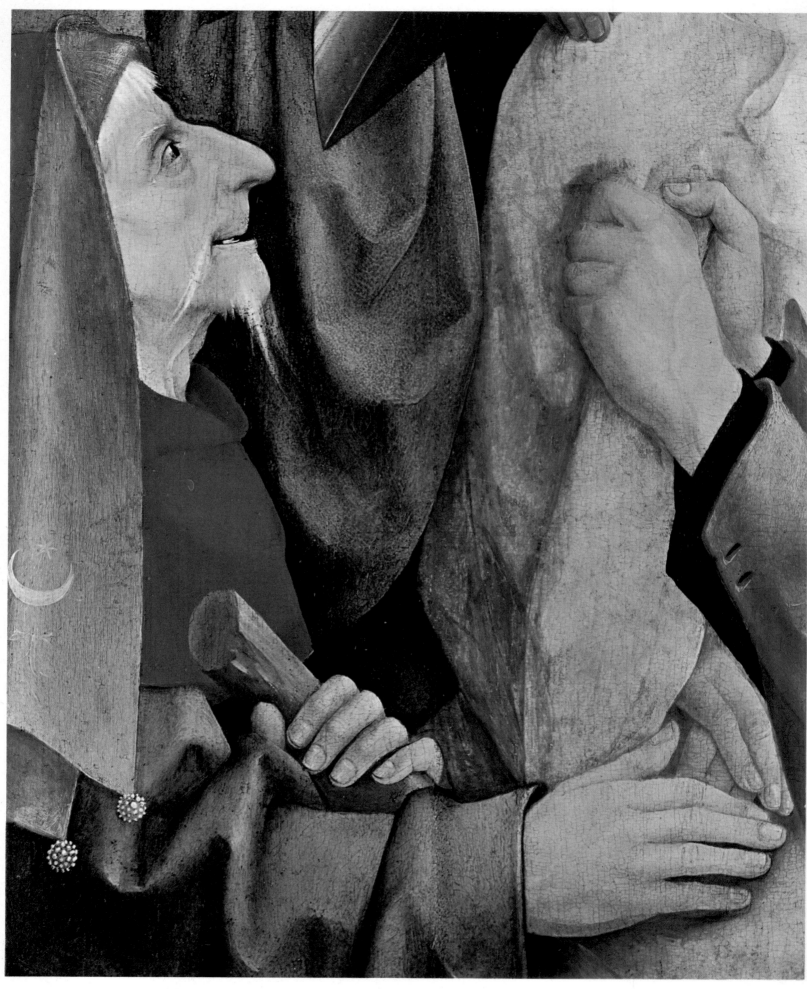

PLATE LII   THE CROWNING WITH THORNS London, National Gallery [No. 57]
Detail (33.6 cm.)

PLATE LIII   THE TEMPTATION OF SAINT ANTHONY Madrid, Prado [No. 59]
Detail (30 cm.)

PLATE LIV   THE PRODIGAL SON   Rotterdam, Boymans-van Beuningen Museum   [No. 61]
Detail (actual size)

PLATE LV THE PRODIGAL SON Rotterdam, Boymans-van Beuningen Museum [No. 61]
Detail (30.4 cm.)

PLATES LVI-LVII   TRIPTYCH OF THE MADRID EPIPHANY [No. 62]
Comprehensive view of the closed triptych [No. 62 A]   (66 cm.)   and of the open triptych [Nos. 62 B, 62 C and 62 D]   (138 cm.)

PLATE LVIII   TRIPTYCH OF THE MADRID EPIPHANY [No. 62]
Detail of *Saint Peter and the donor* [No. 62 B] (actual size)

PLATE LIX   TRIPTYCH OF THE MADRID EPIPHANY [No. 62]
Detail of the *Adoration of the Magi* [No. 62 C] (33.6 cm.)

PLATE LX   TRIPTYCH OF THE MADRID EPIPHANY [No. 62]
Detail of the *Adoration of the Magi* [No. 62 C] (28.6 cm.)

PLATE LXI   TRIPTYCH OF THE MADRID EPIPHANY [No. 62]
Detail of the *Adoration of the Magi* [No. 62 C] (28.6 cm.)

PLATE LXII   CHRIST BEARING THE CROSS   Ghent, Musée des Beaux-Arts   [No. 70]
Whole (83.5 cm.)

PLATE LXIII   CHRIST BEARING THE CROSS   Ghent, Musée des Beaux-Arts   [No. 70]
Detail (actual size)

PLATE LXIV   CHRIST BEARING THE CROSS   Ghent, Musée des Beaux-Arts   [No. 70]
Detail (actual size)

The works

Key to symbols used

In order to throw into immediate relief the essential elements of each work, the heading of every entry bears, after the number of the painting (which follows the most reliable chronological sequence, and to which reference is made whenever the work is cited throughout the volume), a series of symbols relating to: 1 the execution of the painting, that is to say its degree of authenticity; 2 the technique employed; 3 the type of base; 4 the location; 5 the following other data: whether the work is signed, dated, whether it is at present complete in all its parts, whether it was finished. As for the other numbers inserted under the same heading, the upper ones indicate the dimensions of the painting in centimetres (height and width), and the lower ones the dating of the painting; when such data cannot be stated with certainty, but only approximately, they are preceded or followed by an asterisk *. All the elements provided record the opinion prevailing in modern art historiography: important dissensions and further details are elucidated in the text.

Execution

⊞ Autograph

⊞ With assistance

⊞ With collaboration

⊞ With extensive collaboration

⊞ From the workshop

⊞ Generally attributed

⊞ Generally not attributed

▩ Traditionally attributed

▩ Recently attributed

Technique

◉ Oils

◉ Fresco

◉ Tempera

Base

◉ Panel

◉ Wall

◉ Canvas

Location

⦂ Accessible to the public

⦂ Private collection

○○ Whereabouts unknown

○○ Lost work

Additional data

⊟ Signed work

⊟ Dated work

⊟ Part or fragment

⊟ Unfinished work

Key to these symbols provided in text

Information supplied in the text:
We gratefully acknowledge the generous contribution of documents and unpublished data made by: the city of 'sHertogenbosch in the persons of H. J. H. Bossink, archivist of the Town Hall, H. Hens, archivist of the Diocese and of the Cathedral, and Father Gerlach of the Archives of the Capuchin Minorities; Prof. Xavier de Salas, Deputy Director of the Prado Museum in Madrid, and Mr Alfonso E. Pérez; the Director of the Lisbon Museum, Prof. Abel Le Moura; the Director of the Art Library of the Sforza Castle in Milan, Dr Alberto Lorenzi.

List of abbreviations

AASL: Archives des arts, sciences et lettres (Ghent)
AB: The Art Bulletin
ACSU: Atti del II Congresso internazionale di studi umanistici (Rome 1952)
AEA: Archivo español de arte y arqueologia
AF: Arte figurativa
AI: Art International
AMBA: Annuaire des Musées royaux des Beaux-Arts de Belgique
AQ: Art Quarterly
ARF: Archivio di filsofia
AV: L'art et la vie
BAS: Bulletin of the Art Institute of Chicago
BL: The Brabantse Leeuw
BM: The Burlington Magazine
BMB: Bulletin of the Museum of Fine Arts in Boston
BMNA: Boletim do Museu nacional de Arte antiga
BPM: Bulletin of the Princeton Museum of Art
BR: Belgian Review
BRAH: Boletin de la Real Academia de la Historia
BRB: Bulletin des Musées Royaux de Bruxelles
CAJ: College Art Journal
CRS: Cristianesimo e ragion di Stato (Rome 1952)
DJV: Deutsches Jahrbuch für Volkskunde
EH: L'Europe humaniste (Bussels 1954)
GB: Gentsche Bijdragen
GBA: Gazette des Beaux-Arts
H: Oud Holland
HBV: Hessische Blätter für Volkskunde
HVP: Homenaje a J. A. van Praag (Amsterdam 1957)
JKS: Jahrbuch der kunsthistorischen Sammlungen
JKW: Jahrbuch für Kunstwissenschaft
JPK: Jahrbuch der preussischen Kunstsammlungen
KC: Kunstchronik
KT: Konsthistorisk Tidskrift
MG: Miscellanea Gessleriana (Antwerp 1948)
MJ: Münchner Jahrbuch der bildenden Kunst
ML: Mélanges Hulin de Loo (Brussels 1931)
MR: Miscellanea Roggen (Antwerp 1957)
NKJ: Netherlandsch Kunsthistorisch Jaarboek
NV: Nieuw Vlaanderen
PNBC: Provinciale Noord-Brabantse Courant
RAAM: Revue de l'art ancien et moderne
RBAH: Revue belge d'archéologie et d'histoire de l'art
RL: Revue du Louvre
RUB: Revue de l'Université de Bruxelles
SA: SeleArte
SJ: Städel Jahrbuch
TB: Thieme Becker Künstler Lexicon
ZBK: Zeitschrift für bildende Kunst
ZK: Zeitschrift für Kunstgeschichte
ZRG: Zeitschrift für Religion und Geistesgeschichte,

Outline Biography

Hieronymus Bosch's first biographers, who were full of respect for their subject, – Lampsonius (1572), De Guevara (1560–62), Van Mander (1604) – created the impression of a personality lost in legend less than a century after his death, even though his contemporaries had held him in high esteem. He was called *insignis pictor*, when he died, and this high esteem also applied to the social behaviour of one of the wealthiest inhabitants, so it seems, of his native 'sHertogenbosch. In Bosch's day, such esteem was generally considered of greater value than an outstanding reputation in the field of art; the painter seems to have been exclusively devoted to workshop and church, absorbed in his work, the administration of his property, and the association with the pious and distinguished brotherhood of which he was a leading member: in other words, he was a very worthy citizen. We are not told that he even left his native town, but the possibility of some travel, if only to Antwerp, cannot be excluded.

It was not until Justi (1889) that a thorough biography appeared; since this initial re-assessment, Tolnay's book (1937) has been regarded as the most important pioneering work, from which subsequent serious criticism has sprung. What scarce material has been scraped together concerning Bosch, rests for the most part on two archival sources of far from rigorously verifiable reliability. These are documents relating to the Brotherhood to which the painter belonged, that of Our Lady in 'sHertogenbosch: the first (*Rekeningen Van St Jan*) includes the Brotherhood's accounts and was drawn up in its surviving form immediately after the artist's death, about 1519, albeit as a copy of the original, now lost. The second (*Lyst van levende en overleden bruders van 1330 tot 1640*), recording the brethren's date of registration and of death, appears written by various hands, but the same handwriting is found for the period from 1330 to 1567, from which it can be inferred that the part concerning Bosch was

written only around the latter year. Little reliance can be placed upon a third source (*Namen ende Wapenen der Heeren Beeidigde Broeders soo gestelijke als wereltlijke van de seer oude ende seer doorlugtige Broederschap van Onse Lieve Vrouw birme de Stad 'sHertogenbosch*), a catalogue of the brethren's names and coats-of-arms, which dates back only to 1750 approximately (report by P. Gerlach, 1966) despite the note that states it to have been written in 1606.

The documentary facts available on the painter's family are somewhat more definite: their surname was 'Van Aken' (see also below, **1453**), referable to a possible provenance from the city of Aachen. As for the rest, the infrequent, though occasionally reliable allusions to Bosch's artistic activity remain almost sterile because the corresponding works have been lost. There are no letters from the artist himself, writings addressed to him by others, etc. to provide any more direct evidence for the historian.

1418 A Jan van Aken dies at 'sHertogenbosch; he was the owner of a house facing the bell-tower of St John's Cathedral, and can perhaps be identified as a furrier of the same name who had acquired civic rights in 1399 and might have been a relative.

1423–4 The archives of the cathedral at 'sHertogenbosch carry repeated mention of a painter by the name of Jan van Aken, who was almost certainly Bosch's paternal grandfather and who might be assumed to have been the son or grandson of the furrier mentioned above. In his turn, this Jan had five sons: (in their probable order of seniority) Jan, Hubert, Goossen (mentioned in documents of 1488–9), Anthonis and Thomas (mentioned in archival papers dated 1447 and 1451); the last three were also painters.

1424 A letter (in the archives of the Godshuizen – the Hospice – of 'sHertogenbosch) mentions a certain 'Peter, called Peter of Aachen, son of the late Gerard,

known as 'Gerard of Aachen', who may have been related to the artist.

1431–2 Jan van Aken is reported to have painted 'properties for the miracle-plays of Our Lady': and this is, in fact, the only documentary note that connects a Van Aken painter (not, however, Bosch) with sacred drama.

1444 In this year (though some maintain 1434), or a little earlier, a 'Van Aken' appears to have painted one or more frescoes (unquestionably one representing the Crucifixion) in the cathedral of 'sHertogenbosch, displaying characteristics that were later to be developed in Bosch's works. Historians are for the most part inclined to consider Jan van Aken as their author, but there is no reason why they should not be ascribed to one or other of his three painter sons.

c. 1450 Birth of Bosch. According to a suggestion advanced by J. Mosmans (Het Huisgezin, 30-9-1958; GBA, 1959), the date of Bosch's birth would be 2 October 1453 (his future wife was born the same year see **1480–1**). However, no convincing documentation has yet been published to confirm this date, which some old historiographers put back to about 1435, deducing it from the artist's 'decrepit' appearance in the portrait contained in the Recueil d'Arras (reproduced here); others hold it to be quite compatible with a possible birth date fifteen years later. At any rate, the majority of the scholars tends to accept the years between 1450 and 1460, since the former date was asserted in the 17th century by J. B. Descamps (though the grounds for this are unknown), and the latter by Justi (1889) on the basis of the painter's appearance in his engraved portrait, published in 1572 by Cock's widow. Ebeling believed – though his views met with little or no support – that Bosch might have been born between 1460 and 1462 as, according to him, he became a master painter in 1487–8, a title which was generally acquired between the age of twenty-five and twenty-seven (but, see below, **1487–8**).

He was the son of Anthonis, son of Jan van Aken (see **1423–4**), cited in documents from 'sHertogenbosch referring to the years 1472, 1474, 1476 and 1481, and the father of another Anthonis and of Jan. Katherine, Heberta, Goossen as well as Hieronymus (the order of seniority is doubtful). Pinchart (1860) indicated the last-named as the son of a

Laurent van Aken, mentioned in 1464 as a citizen of 'sHertogenbosch; but the descent stated above is confirmed by the patronymic 'Anthoniszoon' (or 'Anthonissen' and 'Anthonissoene') under which Bosch was later registered in the Brotherhood of Our Lady. Bosch's mother was the daughter of a tailor; as for his brother Goossen, it is known that he inherited their father's workshop (which might prove that he was Hieronymus' elder), and in all likelihood continued to manage it, given that he supplied two shutters for an altar in the Cathedral of St John at 'sHertogenbosch, mentioned in 1481.

'Jeroen (or Joen) van Aken (or Aeken and Acken)' was the painter's real name and as such (with one or the other patronymic, or with the

Drawing (Vienna, Albertina) by P. Bruegel the Elder variously dated between 1560 and 1565 (the signature is apocryphal). The painting is generally viewed as a satirical self-portrait; nonetheless, some scholars regard it as the idealised portrait of Bosch, in view of the fact that a copy (1556–8 ca.) of the present drawing, also considered authentic (London, V. Korda Collection), bears the inscription: Effigies Heronimi Bos ad vivum delineata a Pietro Breugelio, discipulo suo, a(nn)o 1537 (Portrait of Hieronymus Bosch drawn from life by Peter Breugel, his disciple, in the year 1537). The inscription appears to have been added in the seventeenth century; at any rate its content ('drawn from life') is in contrast with the fact that the man allegedly portrayed died in 1516.

Latinised appellation of 'Jheronymus' and 'Jeronimus' – or with the impeccably Latin one of 'Hieronymus') he was registered both in the registers of his Brotherhood and in official papers. It is to be noted that such a variety of readings contributed to Ebeling's belief that in Bosch's day another

painter, or two other painters, bearing the same Christian name were active in 'sHertogenbosch (but see **1511–12**). However, in his own works he signed himself 'Jheronymus Bosch'; the following quotation appears (1509–10) in the registers of the Brotherhood of Our Lady: *Jheroninus van Aken, scilder, dis hem scrift Bosch*, that is to say 'Jheronimus van Aken, painter, who signs himself Bosch'. This represents the only valid ground for confirming his probable birth in 'sHertogenbosch, even though in the painter's time no Van Aken appears in the registers listing the people newly entitled to rights of citizenship (but such registers are no longer complete). It may be needless to recall that 'sHertogenbosch is the same as Bois-le-Duc; it is less well

known that 'Den Bosch' is still in current use as the abbreviation of the city's name. It can be assumed that the adoption of this name (just as 'Bruegel', [probably] the name of his own native village, was used by the famous Flemish master; and so many other artists, before and after, from Bassano to Cortona and to Empoli, identified themselves with their place of origin), and the surrendering of the family surname might have been the result of Hieronymus' wish to differentiate himself from his brother Goossen, who may have acquired such a surname before him. Be that as it may, the designation of Bosch which was later to prevail in Spain was 'Geronimo Bosco' or 'el

Signature in the central panel of The Triptych of the Hay Wain *in Madrid (21 C)*

Signature in the central panel of The Triptych of the Epiphany, *also in Madrid (62 C)*

Bosco'; in Italy, 'Gerolamo Boschi Fiamengo' (half a century after the painter's death, Guicciardini called him 'Bosco di Balduc'); in Flanders, 'Bos', a version also sometimes found in other countries.

1454 14 MARCH–8 AUGUST Death of Jan van Aken, Bosch's grandfather. Whether or not he was the author of the frescoes mentioned in 1444, he could not have been Bosch's direct teacher, unless the improbable date of 1435 is accepted for the latter's birth. Nevertheless, this does not invalidate the theory (Tolnay, Puyvelde etc.) that Bosch was introduced to art in his own family, where – even excluding his brother – the people still in a position to instruct him included his father, Anthonis (who did not die before 1481), and at least one of his two painter uncles, Goossen, certainly still active in 1488.

1461 The town of Arras is seized by mass hysteria, and hundreds of people are publicly tortured and executed on charges of witchcraft. The second half of the fifteenth century was to witness many similar incidents; another major example (within the region that is interesting for the purposes of this study) took place in 1468 with the sack of Ghent, in the course of which major public tortures were staged. These tragic episodes were no doubt connected with an increasing mystico-sadistic preoccupation in people's minds, aimed at combating the action of the Devil, who was obsessively described everywhere, at every moment. This preoccupation was to be very much a part of Bosch's pictorial world.

1475 Death at Zwolle of the Dominican friar Alain de la Roche, whose image-creating sermons belong in the tradition of the great Netherlandish mystics. In such sermons he described 'animals symbolising the sins, with horrific genital organs that produce torrents of fire, clouding the earth with their smoke, the vagrant whore who gives birth to apostates, alternately devouring them and spewing them, embracing them and fondling them'. These – and other – visions are clearly not unrelated to those illustrated by Bosch.

1478 G. Leeu printed at Gouda a Netherlandish version of Jacobus de Voragine's *Golden Legend*: the work is among the principal sources for the life of St Anthony, to whom Bosch devoted many works, including the Lisbon Triptych (*Catalogue*, 43).

1478–94 Allaert de Hameel, architect and engraver (some of his prints after Bosch's works are extant) (*Catalogue*, 53 and 130) supervised the builder's works in St John's Cathedral at 'sHertogenbosch, completing the south wing of the transept and beginning the central wing. The grotesque and demoniacal figures on the rampant arches of the choir – which had been usual in church decoration at least since the pre-Romanesque period – have been cited as among the many probable sources of Bosch's inspiration.

1480–1 Bosch bought two compartments belonging to the old altar-piece of the Brotherhood of Our Lady in 'sHertogenbosch, which his father had left unpainted (Mosmans, 1931). In the corresponding document he is referred to as *Jeroen de maelre* (Jerome the painter), which seems to confirm that he was already a master painter.

1480 or **1481** 15 JUNE For the first time Bosch is mentioned as being married. The wedding probably took place about 1478; his wife was Aleyt, born in 1453 of Postellina (daughter of a pharmacist; Postellina died in November 1472) and Goyart van de Meervenne known as Brant, the son of Goyart (Smulders), a well-to-do nobleman. Aleyt's dowry consisted of some land inherited at Oirchot (Oorschot), a village thirty kilometres from 'sHertogenbosch. After April 1482, in his quality of 'husband and representative' of Aleyt, Bosch is often reported to be engaged in financial transactions on behalf of his wife (3 January and 21 March 1483, 29 December 1487, 26 February and 1 October

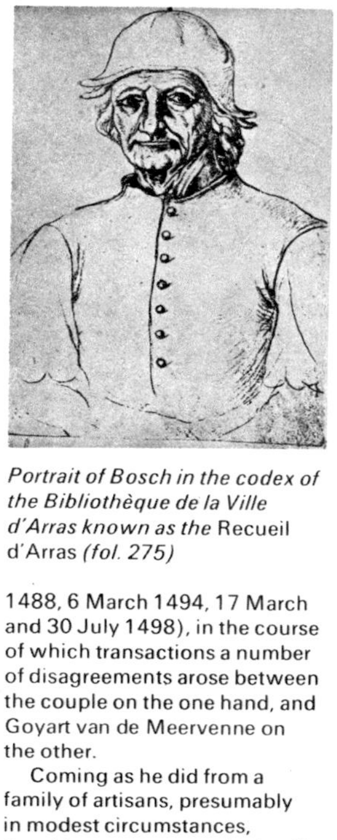

Portrait of Bosch in the codex of the Bibliothèque de la Ville d'Arras known as the Recueil d'Arras *(fol. 275)*

1488, 6 March 1494, 17 March and 30 July 1498), in the course of which transactions a number of disagreements arose between the couple on the one hand, and Goyart van de Meervenne on the other.

Coming as he did from a family of artisans, presumably in modest circumstances, Bosch's status was undoubtedly much improved by his marriage to a rich patrician woman; it is certain, at any rate, that after his wedding he must have been very well-off, given that he paid considerable taxes, among the highest in 'sHertogenbosch (Hebeling). Such a position of prosperity was held to explain (Tolnay) the artist's possibility of expressing his own views – not always very orthodox, it seems, with regard to the Church – and his own criticism of the world – the powerful and the clergy included – which otherwise would have been precluded from him, or at any rate limited. It should be noted, nevertheless, that some liberties were quite usual in those days, and not only within the sphere of popular iconography – presumably protected, at least to some extent, by anonymity – but even in the representations intended for religious buildings.

1482 The *editio princeps* of the Dutch version (*Het Boek van Tondalus vysioen*) of the *Visio Tungdali* by an anonymous Irish author, was published in Antwerp (though possibly published ten years earlier); two years later it was reprinted in 'sHertogenbosch, edited by Leempt. The well-known poem tells of a knight – Tondalus (Tantalus, Tantale, Tantaly, Tantall) of Ireland, living in the twelfth century – who, after an impious and corrupt life, was granted by divine mercy the possibility of having his soul visit the hereafter and, after three days, to return repentant inside his own body: it is the most dismal of the medieval visions, peopled with monsters, serpents, souls doomed to very subtle punishments (an example of the most refined of them: before they reach Hell, the reprobates must make their way through Paradise, resplendent with gold, jewels and purple). The work is considered as one of the principal sources of demoniac iconography, and its relevance to Bosch's pictorial world can not be ignored.

1484 The artist inherited from his brother-in-law a small property at Roedeken, near Oirchot. This year is also that of the Papal Bull *Summis desiderantes affectibus*, which was the starting point for the great persecutions against sorcerers and magic.

1486–7 'Jeronimus Anthonissoen van Aken' entered the Brotherhood of Our Lady (*Lieve Vrouwe Broederschap*) annexed to the Cathedral of St John at 'sHertogenbosch, and was a member until his death. As early as 1488 he appears as a 'notabel' among the brethren, and he is then registered in 1489, 1493, 1498, 1503, 1508 and 1512 (see also **1516**). Most scholars attribute considerable importance to the artist's membership in such a brotherhood, by means of which, among other things, he was able to establish friendly relations with the architect-engraver Allaert de Hameel (see **1478–94**), also registered in the charitable institution during his long stay in 'sHertogenbosch. In the first century after it was founded (1318), the adherents were almost wholly taken up with religious veneration, particularly of the Virgin; but in the fifteenth century they also began to devote themselves to charity work, perhaps inspired by the Brethren of the Common Life.

The Brethren of the Common Life were a manifestation of the religious impetus which sprang up in the Netherlands during the fourteenth century: in 1343 Jan van Ruysbroeck withdrew, at the age of fifty, to a hermitage in the Soignes forest near Brussels, where, until his death (1381), he dictated edifying compositions and attracted many disciples. One of these, Geert Groote, later founded at Deventer the association of the Brethren of the Common Life which in 1387 became the Congregation of Windesheim, destined to multiply until it numbered, toward the end of the fifteenth century, as many as one hundred and fifteen communities. Among other activities, the Brethren opened two schools in 'sHertogenbosch (1424 and 1480), taking up the name of 'Hieronymites'. The young Erasmus of Rotterdam spent about three years in one of these communities. The schools provided the brethren with the means of subsistence, as did the transcription of manuscripts and, later, the publication of books. The Brethren spread a new spirit of religious life, engaged on the one hand in the fight against the heretical sects, on the other in polemics against the corruption of the clergy. It was inevitable that a stand of this kind, clearly anticipating the Reformation, should arouse mistrust and worse: from a *Chronicon Windeshemse* it appears that during 1384 Geert Groote had publicly to defend a brother-member from the slanders of the Minorites; and other defensive interventions occurred later; finally, brought before the Council of Constance in 1418, the association was acquitted of any suspicion, thus ensuring for itself a period of free activity, which lasted until after Bosch's time. The anti-clericalism revealed in Bosch's work is related to the similar reforming tendencies of the Brethren.

A connection was conjectured (Fraenger, 1947) between the artist and the sect of the *Homines Intelligentiae*, revolving round the clandestine heresy of the Brethren and Sisters of the Free Spirit, widespread in Germany and in the Netherlands since the beginning of the fifteenth century but dating back at least two centuries earlier. From the records of a trial held about 1411 before the tribunal of the Archbishop of Cambrai (published by Balusius in 1679, then by Frederick in 1889) it appears that charges were brought against the movement – or at least against one of its lay exponents, the illiterate Aegidius Cantor – for believing, among other things, that: the whole of mankind is destined to salvation; hell does not exist; evil, like good, depends on the divine will; man cannot deserve eternal life; the repression of sinners is worse than sin itself; there will be no resurrection of the flesh; preaching is useless and priests should be humbled; a deflowered woman, with neither husband nor resources, has the same merits as a virgin. From the answers supplied by Cantor, the defendant, it might be deduced that the adepts of the Free Spirit understood sexual intercourse as a heavenly delight; in particular (this was their 'cult of Adam', whence their designation of 'Adamites') they were said to strive for the union of spiritual and sensual love to re-establish themselves within the innocence of the Progenitors or, better still, within the original hermaphrodite identity of Adam when he still contained Eve, from whom was to spring redemption, the new Eden. But all this appears rather vaguely from the testimonies, while nothing documents the existence, among the members of the sect, of novices and initiates or the fact that only the latter were in possession of a particular esoteric language (Puyvelde, 1962). An explanation for the divergence between Bosch's religious paintings and his great polyptychs has been attempted (by Fraenger): the first were said to stem from commissions by churches or individuals of strict Catholic observance; while in the others the exceptionally fantastic contents included heretical elements, by order of the sect of the Free Spirit (see **1496**). Although devoid of any documentary basis (almost nothing is known about the original purchasers of Bosch's extant works), this thesis met with some agreement, but was then firmly rejected by Bax (1949 and 1956), Mosmans (1950), and much discouraged by others. Moreover, ever since 1330, the harshest attacks made against the sect of the Free Spirit were due to Ruysbroeck; so that to assume Bosch's simultaneous adhesion to the principles of the Common Life – created by Ruysbroeck – and to those of the Free Spirit suggests a strange inconsistency.

The Brotherhood of Our Lady had a white swan as its coat-of-arms (the members were also known as the 'Brethren of the Swan'), and a 'banquet of the swan' was held yearly (in 1498–9 Bosch offered a swan for one of these feasts). A flag or sign bearing the snow-white bird appears in some of Bosch's paintings, such as *The Prodigal Son* (*Catalogue*, 61). The members of the association, in addition to belonging to the musical group of St John's Cathedral, were in charge of the staging of religious performances.

1487 On the initiative of the German inquisitor Henricus Kramer and of Jacobus Sprenger – a disciple of Alain de la Roche (see **1475**) – the *Malleus maleficorum* was published in Strasbourg; it declared that God, in order to punish mankind, has allowed the Evil One to establish himself on earth and to found the breed of sorcerers, whose practices were described, as well as the means of fighting them.

1487–8 The archives of the Brotherhood of Our Lady record that the painter 'Jerome' donated the congregation a sum of money. According to Ebeling (doubtfully followed by Van Puyvelde), the presumable motive was the achievement by the donor of the title of master painter; but this is in open contrast with the designation applied to Bosch in the document dated 1480–1 (Tolnay). In 1488 the artist presided at the banquet of the Brethren of Our Lady.

1488–90–1491–2 Within this period Bosch painted the shutters of the altarpiece on the high altar of the Brotherhood of Our Lady (see *Catalogue*, 14). The céntral section of this altarpiece had been carved in 1476–7 by Adriaen van Wesel from Utrecht; the wings were added in 1488–9 by Goyart Cuper, when Bosch gave his services in this connection.

1490 P. van Os published at Zwolle a translation of the *Lives of the Saints*, drawn from the writings of St Athanasius, which included the life of St Anthony (see **1478**).

1492 7 FEBRUARY Master 'Joen' prepared, on two old bedsheets, the drawing for a stained-glass window to be placed in the chapel of his Brotherhood in the cathedral at 'sHertogenbosch and which in 1493–4 was to have been executed by Willem Lombard. Because of this, it was

assumed that Bosch also designed the polychromatic windows for the choir of the same cathedral, unquestionably carried out by Henricken Bueken; but no proof exists.

1494 Appearance in Basel of the first edition of Sebastian Brant's vernacular poem *The Ship of Fools* (*Narrenschiff*), which immediately enjoyed great popularity.

In 1498 J. Bade (Judocus Badius Ascenius) – completing the Latin version by J. Locher (*Navis stultifera*, Basel 1497) – was to publish the *Ship of the She-Fools* (*Stultiferae naves*). There is an evident connection between the themes of these poems and that of the well-known painting by Bosch, now in Paris (*Catalogue*, 16).

1496 Baptism in 'sHertogen-bosch, in the presence of Philip the Fair, of the Jew Jacob de Almaengien, whom Fraenger (1949–50; 'Du', 1951) believed to have been the Grand Master of the Free Spirit (see **1486–7**) and to have commissioned Bosch's 'emblematic' paintings. There is no historial documentation to support this theory: we only know that Almaengien entered the Brotherhood of Our Lady, to which Bosch also belonged, but that he reverted to Hebraism.

1503–4 The account book of the Brotherhood of Our Lady records a payment made by Henrich Massereels and by

Lucas van Erpe on the delivery to Bosch (presumably so that he could paint them) of three shields commissioned by the knight Jannen van Baex.

1504 From a document in the archives of the Département du Nord at Lille it appears that the sum of thirty-six pounds was paid to Bosch, on account for a painting nine feet high and eleven wide representing the Last Judgement, with Heaven and Hell, commissioned by Philip the Fair (*Septembre l'an* xvc quatre. *A Jeronnimus Van aeken dit bosch peintre dem (eurant) au bois le duc la somme de trente six livres dudict pris En prest et paiement a bon compte Sur ce qu'il lui povoit et pourroit estre deu sur ung grant tableau de paincture de neuf pietz de hault et unze pietz de long Ou doit estre le Jugement de dieu assavoir paradis et Infer que icellui S(eigneu)r lui avoit ordonné faire pour son très noble plaisir Pour ce icy par sa quintancy Rend(ue) ladicte somme de* xxxvi *L (ivres).* (Trans. P. Gerlach, Brabantia 1967, p. 64, note 2). (1504 September. To Jeronimus van Aeken, known as Bosch, residing in 'sHertogenbosch, the sum of thirty-six pounds, on account for what might be due (for) a large painting, of nine feet in height and eleven in width, in which must be (represented) the Judgement of God, to wit paradise and hell, which Monseigneur commanded him to make for his very noble pleasure). The work cannot be pinpointed with any certainty, although attempts have been made to identify it with the Vienna *Judgement* (*Catalogue*, 50) or, better still the fragmentary one in Munich (48).

1508–9 The priors of the Brotherhood of Our Lady requested the advice of Bosch and Jan Heynste (or Heyns), the architect of their chapel in the cathedral of 'sHertogenbosch concerning the polychromatic painting and gilding of the carved altarpiece (see **1488–90**), inviting them to examine the work on completion. In the same year the Brotherhood awarded the painter a modest payment for the model of a copper candelabrum (or similar object) (see also **1511–12**).

1511–12 Hieronymus designed a cross, or a Crucifix, perhaps for a surplice commissioned by his Brotherhood. Ebeling's hypothesis that a master of Bosch's reputation and, what is more, related through his wife to one of the most outstanding families in the town, cannot have been the author of this, and of the other small work mentioned above (**1508–9**), was criticised by Tolnay, who brought forward the examples of Dürer, Michelangelo, Titian, etc. often engaged in tasks of secondary importance, and argued that the scant remuneration might be justified precisely by Bosch's prosperity, which may have led him to accept the mere covering of expenses.

Alleged portrait of Bosch, dated 1585, by an unknown Flemish painter (Amherst College, Mass)

Moreover, it does not appear from the surviving (though incomplete) rosters of the brethren of Our Lady, that other painters were registered in the Brotherhood at that time; therefore, it was perhaps natural that he should have been asked. Consequently, Ebeling's thesis, according to which two or three painters by the name of 'Jeron' were then active in 'sHertogenbosch, cannot rest on these assumptions.

1516 The inventory of property owned at Malines by Margaret of Austria, sister of Philip the Fair (see **1504**) and Regent of the Netherlands since 1507, lists a *St Anthony* painted by Bosch, apparently unrelated to commissions by Philip the Fair (*Ung moyen tableau de Sainct-Antoine, qui n'a couverture ne feullet, qui est fait de Jheronymus Bosch, et a esté donné à Madame par Jñoane, femme de chambre de madame Lyonor)* (Pinchart; De Boom. RUB, 1930–1).

1516 9 AUGUST In the chapel of the Brotherhood of Our Lady, in St John's Cathedral at 'sHertogenbosch, a solemn funeral service was held for the 'late brother Jerome of Aschen known as Bosch, illustrious painter', who had probably died a few days earlier.

1517 Antonio de Beatis, accompanying Cardinal Luigi d'Aragona, saw in the palace in Brussels of Henry III of Nassau, Regent of the Netherlands, a painting (or paintings) which, in his description, sounds very like the so-called *Garden of Delights* now in Madrid. (cf. E. H. Gombrich, Journal of the Warburg & Courtauld Institutes, xxx, 1967, pp. 403–6).

1520 Don Felipe de Guevara inherited from his father, Diego, the art collection – including works by Bosch – which was at Brussels (see **1570**). It is impossible to ascertain when Guevara's artistic patrimony was formed. Presumably, as far as Bosch's works are concerned, Don Diego – the promoter of the ties between the Houses of Austria and of Spain, notably the marriage of the future regent Margaret (see **1516**) to Juan of Castille and Aragon – acquired them while he was at Malines (1507–15) when staying with Margaret, who had conferred upon him the honorary

appointment of Keeper of the Tapestries. He may also have bought from Prince Henry, in Brussels. It is known that a love of art and interest in antiquities was very strong in the De Guevara family (cfr. A. De Morales, *Discurso general de las anti güedades*, 1565).

1521 M. A. Michiel saw three paintings by Bosch in the residence of Cardinal Grimani at Venice (*Catalogue*, 26 and 98).

1523–4 Damião de Gois, the agent of Juan III bought a painting by Bosch on the theme of the Patience of Job (see 109).

1531 Settlement of the inheritance of Aleyt van de Mervenne, Bosch's widow.

1560–2 Shortly before his death (1563) de Guevara wrote the *Comentarios de la pintura*, where various pages are devoted to Bosch (see page 10).

1568 In the second edition of Le Vite, Vasari mentions the works of Bosch.

1570 16 JANUARY Philip II of Spain bought various paintings, among which a panel (*The Hay Wain* (*Catalogue*, 21)) and five canvases by Bosch (*Three Blind Figures* (*Catalogue*, 120), *Flemish Dance* (121), *Blind Men Boar-hunting* (122), *A Witch* (123), *The Cure of Folly* (124)) from the widow and the son of Felipe de Guevara (the respective document, drawn up by Simancas, was published by Justi (1889) *Notas de las pinturas compradas a D. a. Beatriz de Haro y de Ladrón de Guevara mujer e hijo de D. Felipe de Guevara*).

1574 15 APRIL Philip II of Spain, who in the meanwhile had acquired other works by Bosch, had nine of these paintings transferred to the Escorial (*Catalogue*, 2, 21, 44, 62, 111, 112, 113, 114, 115), and decided to display the panel of *The Seven Deadly Sins* in his own room (*Catalogue*, 2). A dozen other works by Bosch are said to have remained in the Royal Palace at Madrid, where most of them were lost (perhaps as a result of fires which, as is known, destroyed canvases by Titian, etc.).

1586 Ambrosio de Morales described the triptych of *The Hay Wain* (*Catalogue*, 21) in the commentary to the *Tabla de Cebes*, published in *Las obras del Maestro Fernán Pérez de Oliva*. He mentioned that the painting belonged to King Philip II (therefore, the remark dates back to at least 1570); but, on the whole, the commentary could be considerably earlier, since the artist attributes it to his 'years of youth', when he was studying in Salamanca (1530–2 ca.); at any rate, Morales had been familiar with the collection of Diego de Guevara since at least 1544–5, as he was at the time tutoring a son of the collector's, the younger Diego (see A. M. Salazar [AEA, 1955]).

HIERONYMO BOSCHIO PICTORI.

Quid fibi vult, Hieronyme Bofchi,
Ille oculus tuus attonitus? quid
Pallor in ore? velut lemures fi
Spectra Erebi volitantia coràm

Afpiceres? Tibi Diús auari
Crediderim patuiffe receffus,
Tartareasque domos · tua quando
Quicquid habet finus imus Auerni

Tam potuit bene pingere dextra.

Portrait of Bosch reproduced in Lampsonius' Collection, published at Antwerp in 1572

Catalogue of Works

The origins and the evolution of Bosch's art still present one of the most fascinating problems of Flemish painting. The very term 'Flemish' can give rise to controversy, as 'sHertogenbosch is on the borders of Brabant, already within the Dutch sphere of influence: so that the critics who have attempted to trace the painter's formative process could turn either to the tradition of the great Flemish 'Primitives' of the South, from Van Eyck to Van der Weyden, or to the rather more distant northern centres of Haarlem and of Delft. The total lack of documentary information on Bosch's apprenticeship and on his possible movements outside his native town, has encouraged research in both directions. Thus, we find the oft-repeated name of Bouts (Baldass, 1943) from Haarlem, who died in 1475, at the beginning of Bosch's career, and from whose solemn lyricism the latter may well have borrowed; of Geertgen tot Sint Jans (Dollmayr, 1898), also from Haarlem, with his weightless, slightly spare figures, but this could have been merely a case of artistic exchanges, Geertgen being some ten years younger than Bosch; of the 'Master of the Virgo inter Virgines' (Cohen, 1910; Winkler, JPK, 1923), active in Delft in 1470–1500, one of the 'most prolific, forceful and accomplished' painters of so-called Dutch Provincialism (Panofsky, 1953), with the expressionism of his firmly delineated figures. At the same time, in the south credit was given to the centres of Brussels with Van der Weyden (Justi, 1889; Baldass), or of Antwerp (Justi), and to the two founders of Flemish painting: the Master of Flémalle — or Robert Campin, as the case may be – especially for the schemes of the *Epiphanies* (Hymans, GBA, 1893; followed by others), and Van Eyck (Baldass) for a certain physiognomical solemnity and the broad feeling for landscape.

Baldass placed particular emphasis on the Dutch models, insisting on the keen characterisation of types, peculiar also to Bosch; he also referred to Schongauer's engravings (already mentioned by Dvořák (1924), especially as concerns the diabolical inventions), and above all to the 'Master E.S.', a High-Rhenish artist active about 1440–67, still within the sphere of International Gothic, who might have provided Bosch with models, both iconographic and compositional.

It is impossible, however, to establish a certain knowledge by Bosch of his great predecessors, and it is as well to keep in mind the works he would definitely have seen in his native town. These are the 1444 *Crucifixion* ascribed to the grandfather or uncle of Bosch (q.v.); the frescoes which survive in the Cathedral, a *Tree of Jesse*, a *St Nicholas* and a *St Peter with St James*, all from the beginning of the fifteenth century.

As important as paintings are ms. illustrations, woodcuts and prints, and illustrations to books. The Convent of the Order of St Bridget (founded 1434) at Condewater, just outside 'sHertogenbosch, produced illustrated ms. books of devotion, and of course the Netherlands, especially Utrecht, were famous for the production of these books until the invention of printing. Brant's *Narrenschiff*, illustrated by the young Dürer has already been mentioned; other popular works were the *Sterfboeck* (Ars Moriendi) and the *Grand Calendrier des Bergers*, where Hell is treated in detail; Sir John Mandeville's *Peregrinationes*, with its pre-occupation with astrology, was, according to A. Spychalska – Boczkowska (1966) an important source for *The Garden of Delights*.

1 Pl. I

A much more difficult problem than that of the artistic origins is presented by the evolution of Bosch's career, with the corresponding chronology of the works, given the fact that no dated painting has come down to us. The critics distinguish three periods: youth, maturity and final period; according to Tolnay: 1475–80, 1480–1510, 1510–16; according to Combe, 1475–85, 1485–1505, 1505–16. It is to Tolnay (1937) that credit is due for overcoming the system (Baldass, 1917) whereby the most 'medieval' works (such as *The Delights*) were dated to the first period, and the more 'realistic' ones (like *The Hay Wain*) to the final period; the sequence followed here is therefore the one now most generally accepted.

1 48×35
1475-80

The Cure of Folly
Madrid, Prado
The inscription traced in Gothic letters at the top and at the bottom, *Meester snyt die Keye ras // Myne name is lubbert das*, means: 'Master, dig out the stones (of folly), my name is *lubbert das*' (literally 'castrated dachshund', which stands for a deceived, simple-minded person). A painting of

this theme was displayed in the dining room of the Bishop of Utrecht, Philippe de Bourgogne; in 1524 it was listed in the inventory of the Castle of Duurstede; it is probably the same that appeared in 1570 among the six works by Bosch which Philip II of Spain bought from the De Guevara heirs (Justi, 1889 (*Catalogue*, 124)): in the list drawn up by Simancas it is described as a square canvas, not as a panel; it is therefore difficult to admit that it may be the painting of the Prado, as has been maintained (Tolnay, 1965). In the inventory of the paintings present in the Royal Palace of Madrid at the death of Philip II (1598) it is said to be 'ruined'; its dimensions are also indicated 1½ *braccia* (yards) on all sides, and they do not match those of the panel in question. It is probable instead, that it may be the painting which in 1794 was in the Quinta of the Duque del Arco (Justi). The fact that at the king's death the painting was in poor condition leads to the conjecture that a copy of it was made: this, however, does not appear to be the painting of the Prado, which is of fine quality (but some critics, e.g. Philip, do not agree), datable to the late fifteenth century on the basis of its execution (Tolnay). Critics are divided in their opinion as to its authenticity: those who accept it (e.g. Tolnay), consider it to be one of Bosch's earliest works. Tolnay held it to be the earliest known painting by Bosch, while Friedländer (1927) dated it to about 1490. Gossart (1907) and Demonts (1919), on the other hand, rather implausibly stated it to be his last work, because of its genre-painting realism. Doubts as to its authenticity have been advanced by Baldass (1959); Dollmayr (1898 ['Master M']); Cohen (1910) Brand-Philip (1958), and Boon (B M, 1960) rejected it altogether. Baldass, who at one point thought it authentic (1917),

Copy of 1, with variants (Amsterdam, Rijksmuseum)

later preferred to consider it as the copy of a lost work, where Bosch's followers might have combined stylistic elements of his youthful and mature periods (note the contrast between the simplified figures and the landscape), also adding some elements foreign to the artist (such as the meadow whose close blades of grass are all

equal). Mrs Philip (1958) includes it in her proposed series of four roundels, depicting four low professions, with their astrological and elemental connotations. She considers this Prado picture to be a later version (one of several) of an original by Bosch.

Bax (1962) rejects her interesting theory of the four dishonest professions, because, he says, the 'stone-cutter', never existed in fact. He was only a figure of speech, used to indicate the lengths to which people's folly and gullibility could go.

There are four surviving copies of this work with variants and with a greater number of figures, listed by L. Brand-Philip; in the best of these (Rijksmuseum of Amsterdam), dated to about 1550 (Friedländer), the tondo is surrounded by demoniac figures painted in grisaille.

2  120×150 1475-80

The Seven Deadly Sins
Madrid, Prado

The work appears among those which Philip II had moved to the Escorial in 1574 (no. 8 of the inventory drawn up on that occasion [Justi, 1889]). It is signed 'jheronimus bosch' in black on a dark background, below the lower scroll; Tolnay (1965) does not mention this signature, possibly considering it apocryphal. Almost certainly it was originally a table top. The main point of view, clearly indicated by the vertical compositions of the four tondi and by the inscriptions, distinguishes it from the painted tables of South Germany during the first part of the 1500s (Baldass, 1959), which display four points of view and continuous scenes. Having lost its original utilisation (surely within the devotional sphere), it aided the devout meditations of the King of Spain, who had it hung up in his bedroom as reported by Brother de Sigüenza (1605), who also saw another panel by Bosch with tondi illustrating The Seven Sacraments. De Guevara, in 1560-2, was the first to mention it as a work by Bosch. Almost all modern critics are in agreement as to the attribution (including Baldass, albeit with some doubt that it might be the copy of a lost work). Its authenticity was refuted only by Dollmayr (1898) who ascribed the painting, as well as many others by Bosch, to a certain 'Master M', and by Gossart (1907), who maintained it to be by a contemporary of Bruegel the Elder. Believed at one point to be a late work (Baldass, 1917), in view of the stylistic accomplishment of the landscapes and of the interiors, it was rightly claimed for the initial period by Tolnay (1937), later followed by the rest of the critics, reference being made to the costumes datable to the 1470-80 decade (Baldass). The theme is bound to a unitary conception, on the motif of life and death. The

main tondo, identifiable with the eye of God, bears in the 'pupil' the figure of Christ standing up in the sepulchre; in its turn, the 'iris' might be assimilated to the sun's rays, giving us the biblical equation of Christ with the sun (Tolnay). In the 'cornea', symbolising the world (Tolnay, Combe), are distributed the seven deadly sins, indicated by the respective inscriptions, within trapezoidal compartments arranged like a wheel. At the corners, inside four smaller tondi, the Four Last Things, the inevitable outcome of human vicissitudes: Death and Judgement at the top, Hell and Heaven at the bottom. The various inscriptions in Gothic letters display a still archaic taste for 'spoken' comment. At the centre, under the 'pupil': *Cave cave d(omi)n(u)s videt* (Beware, the Lord sees). On

2 Pls. II–V

the scrolls, the following passage, at the top: *Deutero-(nom)iu(m) 32 / / Gens absque consilio e(st) et sine prudentia / / utina(m) sapere-(n)t et i(n)telligere(n)t ac novissi(m)a providere(n)t* (Deuteronomy XXXII). (For they are a nation void of counsel, neither is there any understanding in them. O that they were wise, that they understood this, that they would consider their latter end); and at the bottom: *Absconda(m) facie(m) mea(m) ab eis: et considerabo novissi(m) a eorum* (I will hide my face from them, and I will see what their end shall be). The moral content is at any rate evident, with a clear link between the theme of the sins and the eschatological theme, gathered into a single cycle: only Fraenger (1951) advanced his usual interpretation of heresy, naming the painting *The Table of Wisdom* (see Outline Biography **1496**) and claiming it to have been commissioned by the Grand

Master Jacob Almaengien to lead the adepts to the stage of pure contemplation during the assemblies of the Free Spirit. The wheel-like arrangement was new in painting, although already present in medieval miniatures and woodcuts representing the Liberal Arts, the Vices and the Virtues, and in fifteenth-century woodcuts illustrating the Sins, the Months, the seven days of Creation. These are iconographic references, but not models for Bosch's painting. Bosch quite altered the traditional concept, replacing the scenes in the style of medieval 'mysteries', or the allegorical figures of the sins, usual until then, with excerpts from everyday life, where sin takes concrete form. Thus, with an entirely personal poetic vigour, the artist expressed his

moralising vision by using a popular form and so opened new paths for Netherlandish painting.

'Ira', Wrath (lower central panel) – is illustrated by two drunken peasants set against an open country landscape with a farm. Baldass (1959) noted that the same sort of farm also appeared in a work by Bosch known through a copy: *Abigail before King David* (14). The central position of Wrath, is a move away from the traditional medieval view that Pride was the principal sin (Baldass). Following the circle from left to right, next comes Pride ('Superbia'): an elegant middle-class woman, standing with her back to the viewer before a wardrobe, tries on a head-dress while the Devil holds the looking-glass for her. The figure is given that enigmatic intensity which is the true essence of Bosch's vision. In Lust ('Luxuria'), two couples inside a half-open tent enjoy a country banquet, cheered by

two jesters: the masked one anticipates the evil coarseness of the series of beggars, buffoons and cripples which parade through Bosch's paintings; musical instruments indicate, as so often in Bosch's work, worldly frivolity. Sloth ('Accidia'), is represented by a man dozing before the fireplace, indifferent, while Faith, clasping her Bible, holds out her rosary to him as a reminder of prayer. Gluttony ('Gula') is a prominent theme in scenes of debauchery in Netherlandish art: the vulgarity of the details is governed by sharp observation, at its sharpest here in the figure of the child, fat and greedy like the adults, echoing Bosch's oft-repeated motif of the bad example set for children, (Combe, 1946 and 1957). Emblematic touches such as the little owl above the door, or the

hat pierced by an arrow, prefigure the symbolism of the later paintings. In Avarice ('Auaricia'), set in the country, a dishonest judge takes money simultaneously from both applicants. Envy ('Inuidia') finds concrete form in the representation of a city street with a burgher attempting the seduction of another's wife, speaking to her through the grating; the merchant who looks crossly at the nobleman with a falcon on his fist, while holding in his hand a bone coveted by the dog that has before it yet other bones, in their turn longed for by another dog (Combe). Four of the scenes are set in the open air, three of them indoors; but the same sky forms the uninterrupted ring-shaped background for all the compositions, lightening the horizon in the landscapes, shining through the windows in the interiors. The central radiated tondo with the eye of God is harshly imprinted against this sky, crossed by wisps of diaphanous clouds: thus, the symbolic intention is imposed on the naturalistic rendering which is always in Bosch's work subordinated to the moral theme.

An engraving of the *Ars moriendi* by the 'Master E.S.' was suggested as the model for the Death in the upper left-hand tondo (Tolnay; Baldass); but Bosch's scene is also a comment on life as the dying man's wife in another room, in the background, is counting the inheritance money. The Last Judgement and Heaven – on the right, top and bottom – are hieratic compositions: thus, in the first, Christ on the globe stands out among saints, apostles and four trumpet-blowing angels; the scene of the Judgement is reduced to the first phase of the resurrection of the dead, without any distinction between the damned and the elect. In Heaven, St Peter admits a soul to the celestial crowd while a devil tries to claim the next applicant; in the centre is a raised platform at the back of which Christ enthroned appears among angels. In the Hell – the tondo in the lower left-hand corner, which begins the long series of Bosch's hells, – the composition becomes livelier. For each capital sin, indicated with its Latin name (from upper left: 'Luxuria', 'Gula', 'Inuidia', 'Accidia', 'Ira'; at the bottom: 'Superbia', 'Auaricia') the appropriate punishment is meted out in accordance with an apocalyptic conception that is found in Dante. But Dante, although influential in Italy, was hardly read North; the representations of Hell in northern miniatures and engravings were probably based in large part on Tondalus' Vision. As we have seen, this appeared in print in Antwerp in 1475, in 'sHertogenbosch in 1484. The misers boil in a cauldron; the wrathful man is pierced by a sword on a rack, the proud look at themselves in the devil's mirror (the evil symbol of the toad climbs on the woman's abdomen); the gluttonous man is fed toads and snakes; the bed of the lustful is attacked by monsters; the envious man is torn to pieces by dogs; the slothful man is pounded at on the anvil: in connection with this detail, Tolnay (1965) referred to a drawing of deviltries in the Kupferstichkabinett of Berlin, which may be by Bosch and which he believes to be a youthful work. The state of preservation is not very good: there are cracks and poor restorations, especially along the joint of the strips that make up the wooden panel.

The Marriage at Cana
Rotterdam, Boymans-van Beuningen Museum
The painting was made known by Pfister ('Belvedere', 1923) and thoroughly analysed for the first time by Baldass (1926). It belonged to the Koenigs

Collection in Haarlem, whence it reached the museum in 1940 as part of the Beuningen donation. Tolnay (1965) wondered whether it might not be identifiable as the 'Wedding banquet in the style of Bosch' mentioned in the inventory of Rubens' collections. The work was cut down in the two upper corners, and widely restored, especially in the heads of the figures: G. Ring (JKW, 1923) provided a good reproduction executed prior to the restorations. The two dogs are an eighteenth-century addition, as documented by the old copy (Collection of Dr J. H. van Heek, 'sHeerenberg), which also shows a second musician to the left of the one shown in our picture. In another copy with variants – an early 1500s drawing in the Rothschild Collection at the Louvre (Boon, BM, 1960), the figure of the donor, introduced by a holy bishop, is shown. This may reflect the original composition. There is general agreement as to the attribution, except for Boon. The L-shape of the table, with the bride facing the viewer and Christ on the short side, might have been borrowed from Giotto's scheme for the Scrovegni (Tolnay), which spread in the North during the 15th-16th century. According to Tolnay, Bosch might have drawn his inspiration from a lost work by the Master of Flémalle who also failed to represent the lateral walls of the interiors. A more evident reference is to *The Last Supper* by Dirk Bouts in the church of St Peter at Louvain (Baldass), in view of the strict parallelism in the disposition of the figures, but Combe rejected this idea, noting the oblique, unstable movement of Bosch's composition; at any rate, the archaic appearance of the figures and the compression of the space, resulting from the raised perspective, put this work among those of the youthful period (according to Baldass, the costume of the donor sitting next to Christ reflects the fashion of about 1480).

Here also, as in other youthful works by Bosch, there are bizarre but inconspicuous details: the smoking victuals brought in by the servants, the head of a boar and a swan, exhale rays of fire which cause one of the servants to draw back; on the capitals of the Gothic chapel, a winged urchin, cupid or devil shoots an arrow at his companion, who cowers in a hole in the wall; on the raised platform on the left, a musician cheers the banquet by playing on the bagpipe, usually considered a sexual and evil symbol; in the background, the master of ceremonies of the banquet, with a wand in his hand (Bax, 1949, called attention to miniatures of the 1400s representing wedding feasts and including a similar character) is very like a sorcerer intent on casting mysterious spells on the victuals and on the objects of the sideboard. The canopy usually placed over the bridal couple is placed over

Copy of 3, prior to the insertion of the dogs (Location unknown)

Copy of 3, with figures of donors (Paris, Louvre, Rothschild Collection)

Christ instead. A child richly dressed and garlanded, has risen from an elaborately inlaid chair opposite Christ, and stands facing the bride and groom holding a cup or chalice in his right hand and raising his left in a solemn gesture.

The prevalence of the allusions has encouraged the most complicated interpretations. Tolnay, believing Christ's gesture of benediction to be directed not at the pitchers but at

3 Pls. VI–VII

the child's chalice, viewed the scene as a representation of the miracle of the Eucharist which was foreshadowed by the transformation of water into wine at Cana – Christ's look and gesture are towards the mysterious child and his chalice; Tolnay would like to interpret the Child as the Early Church. In contrast to this scene of holy mystery, is the evil of this world, embodied in the sorcerer (which is what he holds the master of ceremonies to be) who stands next to the altar of magic (the sideboard). The objects on the sideboard are thought to refer to Christian liturgy (the bread, the wine pitchers and the little flask of oil, the small statue of the pelican, a symbol of Christ, that of St Christopher with the globe on his shoulders) and to the contrasting evils of lust (the two dancing nudes) and of heresy (the sea-urchin [Combe, 1946 and 1957]). The swan too, with the crescent of heresy on his breast, is said to be a cursed food (Tolnay; Combe): Combe pointed to the fourteenth century mystics' interpretation which held the swan to be a symbol of debauchery, a long way from the divine word, and also recalled the Flemish saying about the swan being 'white on the outside, black on the inside', allusive to hypocrisy. However, Tolnay did not fail to note that the swan, with its dark meat, was considered a choice food in the banquets of the period, including those of the Brotherhood of Our Lady, to which Bosch belonged (see Outline Biography **1486–7**). In his turn, Baldass pointed out the sinister appearance of the guests and the presence of the evil little owl; while Fraenger (1950) suggested a general astrological meaning related to the Sons of the Moon, and thought the painting to portray the heretical marriage of

Almaengien to a Jewess (see Outline Biography, **1496**). The explanation provided by Bax (1949) rests instead on the life of the period; he recalls that the Marriage at Cana is celebrated by the Church on the same day as the Epiphany, 6 January, which is also Twelfth Night. He sees the feast as a depiction of a Twelfth Night revel (when swans and boars' heads were eaten), which is in pointed contrast to Christ's holy miracle. Puyvelde (1962), faithful to his systematic explaining away of Bosch's enigmas, referred only to the miraculous feast of the Gospels, animated by the imaginative touches that sprang from the painter's own fancy.

5

4 ⊞ ⊗ 82×54,8 1475-80 ▤ ⋮

Christ and the Adulteress
Philadelphia, Museum of Art (Johnson Collection)
At one time this was thought to be the copy of a work by Bouts (Puyvelde); latterly, Lucie Ninane and J. van Gelder identified it as the possible copy of a lost work by Bosch, and it was published by Tolnay (AI, 1963). The theme, borrowed from the Gospel according to St John VIII: 1–11 (Tolnay, 1965) recalls the moment when Christ, after tracing an inscription on the ground, pronounces the words: 'He that is without sin among you, let him cast the first stone at her'. As far as can be judged from a copy, the style of the figures, the treatment of space and the architectural setting justify its placing in the period of *The Marriage of Cana* (3).

5  14,5×12 1475-80

Two Priestly Heads
Rotterdam, Boymans-van Beuningen Museum
This small panel, the authenticity of which is difficult to prove in view of its very poor state of preservation (Tolnay, 1965), was ascribed to Bosch by P. Haverkorn van Rijsewijk (*Jaarverslag*, 1903) and published again by Baldass (1943 and 1959) as being very close to *The Marriage of Cana* (3) on the basis of the human types, who are thought to portray two bad Jewish priests.

6   53×65 1475-80

The Conjurer
Saint-Germain-en-Laye, Musée Municipal
Nothing is known about the origin of the painting, which entered the museum with the Ducastel bequest in 1872. After the first attribution by Hymans (GBA, 1893), most critics acknowledged its authenticity. It was thought to be the copy of a lost work by Friedländer (1927 [dubitatively]), Brand-Philip (1958), and Baldass (1959) who in 1917 held it to be an original of the final period. We incline to consider

6 Pl. VIII

public, with all the figures in three-quarters view; while in the painting the two protagonists assume a profile position, preferred in the late-Gothic period (Baldass, 1959).

The subject constitutes another chapter in the history of human stupidity. The conjurer causes frogs to come out of a simpleton's mouth (Combe drew attention to the popular expression 'to swallow a frog', standing for credulity) while an accomplice profits by the opportunity to steal her

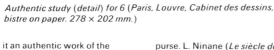

Authentic study (detail) for 6 (Paris, Louvre, Cabinet des dessins, bistre on paper. 278 × 202 mm.)

it an authentic work of the initial stage, connecting it, however, not to the time of the *Ecce Homo* in Frankfurt (10) (Tolnay; Puyvelde (listing it as the last painting of the first period)), but to that, earlier by a few years, of *The Cure of Folly* (1) and of *The Seven Deadly Sins* (2) (Baldass; Linfert), of which *The Conjurer* constitutes a more mature stage. In the autograph sketch preserved in the Louvre (Tolnay, 1965) the scene is limited to the two essential poles: the illusionist and the

purse. L. Ninane (*Le siècle de Bruegel*, 1963) noted that the accessories pertaining to sleight-of-hand have remained unchanged: the tall hat, the funnels, the hollow balls to be fitted one inside the other. The little owl peeping from the basket is part of the charlatan's equipment, but Combe thought it a symbol of heresy, which fascinates the souls of unsteady Christian faith; while, as concerns the conjurer, he referred to the esoteric world of Tarot cards, and particularly to the Fool, the first of the Major

Arcana. An involved interpretation was advanced by Fraenger (1950), according to whom the scene represents a ritual castration of heretics in a satirical key; Pigler (1950) and L. Brand-Philip, linked the painting to popular prints showing the 'Children of the Planets'. Mrs Brand-Philip would like to include the picture — on the basis of the details added in the Philadelphia copy — in her conjectured series by Bosch of the planets, the four elements and the four temperaments. *The Conjurer* would represent the Element of Water, the phlegmatic temperament and the planet Moon (see also 1, 61).

L. Brand-Philip made known several copies of the painting, which appears repainted in various areas: one in a private collection in California, with the scene painted in the form of a tondo, set inside a frame painted in grisaille with 'watery' scenes (as the Amsterdam version of *The Stone-Cutter* is a tondo in a frame painted with 'airy' motifs in grisaille). Another copy is in the Wilstach Collection in Philadelphia (formerly in the Crespi Gallery in Milan (Schmidt-Degener, 1906)), with a background (as in the engraving by Balthasar van de Bos in the Graphische Sammlung in Munich), which the copyist has crammed with genre elements; others in the Ostier Collection in New York (Bosch Catalogue n. 35, formerly in the Heinemann Gallery, Munich. See Friedländer 1927) and the Nicholson Collection, New York.

7  1475-80

Concert in the Egg
A copy of this work (oils on canvas, 107 × 125 cm.; Lille Musée Wicar) came in 1890 from the Morhange Collection. Another copy (73 × 107 cm.), perhaps closer to the date of the original, much more abbreviated in both form and details, is in the Roland Barny d'Avricourt Collection in Paris; formerly Pontalba de Senlis Collection, published as authentic by S. Reinach (*Tableaux inédits ou peu connus*, 1906).

The datings suggested for the lost original vary between the time of *The Conjurer* (6) and that of *The Triptych of the Hay Wain* (21) (Baldass, 1917 [who published the Lille copy]) or of *The Ship of Fools* (16) (Combe, 1946 and 1957 [who, through the presence of the egg, an alchemic symbol, suggested a dating prior to the Lisbon Triptych, 43]). The preliminary drawing by Bosch, in the

(Left) Copy of 6, with variants (Philadelphia, Museum of Art, Wilstach Collection) (Right) Engraved copy of 6 (Munich, Graphische Sammlung)

Kupferstichkabinett in Berlin (on the reverse side of a *Temptation of St Anthony*) is stylistically close to that of *The Conjurer* (6). It is likely that the symbolic elements dead fish, pitcher, little owl, overturned funnel, demoniac fire, erotic allusions such as the dove-cote, the stork, the lute were multiplied by the copyist on the basis of more mature compositions by Bosch. The Lille copy, judged to be subsequent to Bosch's death through some details in the costumes (Ninane, *Le siècle de Bruegel*, 1963) is in fact much later, as indicated by the words on the score (Mirimonde, GBA 1964) *Toutes les nuictz (nuits) que sans vous 'e me couche, pensant à vous...* (All the nights that without you I lie, thinking of you...): they are the beginning of a love song set to music by Thomas Crecquillon and published in 1561.

8   74×54 1480-85

The Epiphany (The Adoration of the Magi)
Philadelphia, Museum of Art (Johnson Collection)
The painting came from the collection of the Earl of Ellenborough, and it is unanimously attributed to Bosch as a youthful work. Because of the peculiar detail of the broken wooden pillar in the fore corner of the hut, Tolnay pointed to a miniature of the Utrecht missal of 1425-30, in the Walters Art Gallery in Baltimore. The event is limited to essentials: the star is shown (it is usually lacking in the Dutch Epiphanies of the latter half of the fifteenth century [Tolnay]), but not the retinue of the Magi (see the above-mentioned miniatures of the early fifteenth century). An interesting detail is introduced in the biblical episode of the falling manna, represented on the sleeve of the negro king Caspar. Tolnay notes that this

biblical prodigy was usually considered in the Middle Ages as a prefiguration of the Last Supper (*Biblia pauperum*, *Speculum humanae salvationis*), and placed in relation with the Eucharist; a passage from the Gospel according to St John (iv:33), where Christ and manna are identified ('the bread of God is he which cometh down from heaven and giveth life unto the world'). Mosmans (1947) thought the youngest king to be a self-portrait, wearing a medallion of the patron saint, St Jerome.

9 70.5×59 1480-85

The Crucifixion
Brussels, Musées Royaux des Beaux-Arts
The panel, representing Christ on the cross between the Virgin, St John, St Peter and a kneeling donor, was formerly in the Franchomme Collection (and, previously, in the Fétis

Copies of 7: (left) Lille, Musée Wicar; (right) Paris, R. Barry d'Avricourt Collection

9

Collection) of Brussels. Tolnay (1937 and 1965) denied that it might be the work mentioned in 1511–12 (see Outline Biography). The dating is debatable: Friedländer (1927) set it at the mature period and perceived in it (1921) reminiscences of Rogier van der Weyden; Tolnay argued, however, that the broken lines of the bodies already appear in the frescoed *Crucifixion* — dated 1444 — in the Cathedral of 'sHertogenbosch (tentatively ascribed to Bosch's grandfather, Jan van Aken), with which he found other links in Christ's position with legs together and feet nailed one on top of the other, rather than crossed as in Rogier's work; he set the work in the middle period, noting the contrast between the colours, based on vermilion, pink, grey, black, which occur in early works and the advanced style of the draperies and of the landscape, which recall mature and late works. Baldass first (1926) dated it to the intermediate period of the *St John on Patmos* (33), but later moved the dating to a time between the end of the youthful stage (AMBA, 1938, and 1943) and early maturity (1959), referring to an altar-painting in the Utrecht Museum (about 1480), and to the costume of the donor, which belongs to the ninth decade of the century. According to Combe (1946, 1957), Delevoy (1960), Puyvelde (1962), it is a youthful work.

10

Preliminary drawing for 7 (Berlin, Kupferstichkabinett)

10 ⊞ ✪ 75×61 1480-85 ▤ ⋮

Ecce Homo Frankfurt, Staedelsches Kunstinstitut Originally part of the Maeterlinck Collection in Ghent (L. Maeterlinck, in GBA, 1900) and subsequently in the R. von Kaufmann Collection in Berlin, the work was bought by Staedel in 1917. It is the first of

Bosch's sacred compositions with crowds of figures, and one of the last of his youthful period. The arrangement of the two groups recurs in engravings of the same theme, such as a woodcut of the middle of the fifteenth century in the Bibliothèque Nationale in Paris (Combe, 1946 and 1957) or the engraving by Schongauer in Brussels (Tolnay); the type of the Christ covered with blood can also be found in graphic arts, rarely in painting (Combe). Baldass (1959) noted the thick-set proportions of the figures, typical of the youthful works and, concerning the group on the right, pointed to a drawing of *The Disputation with the Doctors* in the Pierpont Morgan Library in New York, also catalogued by Tolnay

(1965); while, with reference to the costumes and the human types, he mentioned the group of the Jews in Van Ouwater's *Resurrection of Lazarus*. The sinister types of the evil crowd, present in the work of the Master of Flémalle (Tolnay, 1965 pointed to *The Marriage of the Virgin* in the Prado), and in Schongauer's *Passion* (Dvořàk, 1924) are already sharply characterised here, and were to find ever more intense and ruthless pictorial expression in Bosch's constant contraposition of evil and good in the works of his mature period. Tolnay rejected the reference made by Roggen (NV, 1936) to the leather masks worn at 'sHertogenbosch during processions, as possible models for Bosch, noting that they were not masks of a caricature type

Copies of 12: (left) Paris, Louvre; (right) Settignano (Florence), Weinzheimer Collection

but rather intended to represent the faces of holy persons, such as the Holy Women and the Apostles. An archaic taste typifies the three inscriptions: *Crucifige eu(m), Ecce Homo* and *Salva nos Chr(ist)e r(e)de(m)ptor,* which express, at the centre, at the top and at the bottom, the three attitudes of the actors of the tragedy: the bestial members of the crowd, Pilate's cowardly detachment, the cry of sorrow rising from mankind yearning for salvation (the lower left-hand corner, next to the inscription, originally bore the figures of the donor, still visible under Roentgen rays [Wolters, S J, 1932]). Various evil symbols accentuate the sinister atmosphere, such as the owl looking out of the window of Pilate's house, the toad represented in relief on the shield to the right, the crescent which appears on one of the halberds and on the red flag hanging from the balcony of the Town Hall, in the background with the view of a city. A copy of this work is in the Rijksmuseum of Amsterdam (Friedländer) and another was in the Brockmann sale at Christie's, London, in 1931 (Tolnay).

11 ⊞ ⊕ 73×58 ⊟ ⦂

Ecce Homo Boston.
Museum of Fine Arts
This version of the subject is similar in many parts to the Frankfurt *Ecce Homo* (10), but is a workshop product, created by utilising various Bosch-like elements (Tolnay). Baldass (1959) called attention to the Ascent of Calvary in the background, unusually set in the town square, and resembling that painted by Bosch at the height of his mature period on the reverse of *St John on Patmos* (33). An opinion favourable to its authenticity was expressed by Swarzenski, who was the first to publish it (BMB, 1955) and Panofsky (AMBA, 1956), who extolled the iconographic innovation – later taken up, to illustrate the same theme, by Lucas van Leyden, and by Rembrandt in his 1655 engraving – of the *ostentatio Christi,* with the Redeemer in the foreground, at the centre of the composition. According to Eisler (*Corpus,* 1961) the panel, which appears heavily scraped and repainted in some parts, is a workshop copy, carried out with some assistance from the master, of a now lost original. At present, the composition has been put together at the Boston Museum with two wings bearing figures of saints and donors: but Tolnay questioned this reconstruction, believing that the exterior of the wings (not shown), especially in the case of the draperies, points to Bosch's mature style, and is of high quality, still within the sphere of the workshop. The coat-of-arms on the inside of the left wing is probably that of the eminent Van Oss family of 'sHertogenbosch, and the kneeling donor bears on his cloak the fleur-de-lis, emblem of the Brotherhood of Our Lady, to which Bosch also belonged.

12 ⊞ ⊕ 1480-85 ⊟ ⦂

Jesus among the Doctors
This work is known through several copies, of which the best are preserved in the Louvre (oil on panel, 74.2 × 58 cm.; originally from the Musée de Cluny), at the Museum of Art in Philadelphia and in the Weinzheimer Collection at Settignano (Tolnay, 1965).

H. Met de Bles (attributed), copies of 13 A and B in their presumable entirety (formerly in Ghent, Maeterlinck Collection)

The original was placed by Tolnay in the period of *The Conjurer* (6), but it might best be placed, in view of the similarity of figures and environment, closer to the Frankfurt *Ecce Homo* (10) (Combe, 1946 and 1957). Contrary to the traditional iconography, the infant Jesus is not sitting on a pulpit but among the doctors. With regard to the theme, see also 131.

11

The Triptych of the Judgement
(Fragmentary)

13  34,5×21

A. The Death of the Just Man
New York, Private collection (formerly Wildenstein Gallery)
Together with the following panel (13 B), this was part of a triptych with the Last Judgement (now lost) at the centre (Tolnay, 1965): an old copy of the whole, signed 'Jeronimus bosch' on the right wing but ascribed to Herri Met De Bles, was at one time in the Maeterlinck Collection in Ghent (L. Maeterlinck, RAAM, 1908; Lafond, 1914). These two wings, which were cut down at the top and bottom, came from the Bromberg Collection in Bremen, and were made known by Tolnay (BPM, 1961), who dated them to the end of the youthful period.

This wing, formerly on the left, represents a heavenly scene: the death of the just man, with the procession of the saved souls and their arrival in Heaven. Some eccentric and allusive touches, anticipating the more disquieting combinations of the

Last Judgement, in the Ghent copy, noting a series of motifs entirely new in the Flemish iconography of hells, such as the valley, the river, the bridge, the infernal machines, in the creation of which Bosch was inspired by *The Vision of Tondalus* (see Outline Biography, **1482**), and which he variously elaborated in his Judgements and Hells.

13 33,4×19,6

B. Death of the Reprobate
New York, Private collection (formerly Wildenstein Gallery)
Right wing (see 13 A). The death of the reprobate is an anticipation of infernal punishments: devils and monsters assail his bed, take possession of his soul and torment it, while in the background the damned are led towards the gates of hell. In the foreground appear two *grylli*, small monsters consisting only of a head and legs, typical of Bosch's world, but here, in fact, lacking that convincing quality that is the constant feature of Bosch's abnormal representations. Even the gesticulations of the figures, with their disproportionately long limbs, although characteristic of the artist, are rendered with an excess of zeal.

Probable copies (perhaps partial) of 14 (Switzerland, private collection)

Brotherhood of Our Lady, representing the episode of Abigail and David. Baldass (1959) thought that the two paintings reproduced here (51 × 37 cm.), part of a private Swiss collection, might be copies of it. The inner sides, portraying Solomon and Bathsheba, were painted only in 1521–2 and 1522–3 by Gielis van Hedel of Brussels, known as Van de Bosche, whom Ebeling believed to be a follower or relative of Bosch. In the 1545 accounts mention is again made of the wings painted on the outside by 'meester Jeronimus'

making: installed only in 1492 and seldom opened because of the work being carried out in the chapel, it was still awaiting the finishing touches in 1508–9 (see Outline Biography).

15 92,6×30,8 1490-1500

The Death of the Miser
Washington, National Gallery of Art (Kress Collection)
Originally in the Van der Helst Collection in Vienna, then in that of Samuel H. Kress (1951). After the first mention of Glück (*Bruegels Gemälde*, 1932), by Baldass (1935) and by Tolnay (1937), the critics appear to be in agreement as to the attribution. The subdued range of the colours, which induced Friedländer (1937) to describe it as a grisaille, led to the belief that it is the outside wing of a lost triptych, perhaps representing a Last Judgement. The upper left-hand corner appears to have been added, and was repainted, like the one on the right; other repaintings have covered a rosary on the fore wall, and a jug below the man standing at the foot of the bed. The rough sketch, done in black, shows through distinctly. The composition is linked to the lively drawing with white touches, now in the Louvre (a copy, according to Tolnay; an original, according to Boon [BM, 1960]). The style of the painting falls within the series of works grouped around *The Triptych of the Hay Wain* (21). Iconographic references have been made to engravings, such as *The Annunciation* by the Master of the Amsterdam Cabinet (Combe) and others; as for the perspective of the bed, Tolnay pointed to the Master of Flémalle (Werle altarpiece in the Prado) and to Van der Weyden. At the supreme moment, the miser – a noble knight, judging by the armour at lower right – is unable to make the choice between the Crucifix, pointed out to him by the angel, and the money purse brought by a devil. The scene of the inner struggle between good and evil is repeated at the foot of the bed, where the miser (according to Tolnay, the figure embodies indecision) tells his beads with one hand while with the other he throws

coins into a bag held by a devil inside the coffer.

16 57,8×32,5 1490-1500

The Ship of Fools
Paris, Louvre
The history of the painting is unknown: it was donated to the Louvre in 1918 by Camille Benoît. The lower part is missing and Tolnay (1965) did not feel it could be identified with the fragment of *The Allegory of Pleasures* (17) as Mrs Brand-Philip suggested. Critics are in agreement as to the attribution, though not to the dating: Puyvelde set the painting in the first period, Baldass (1959) about 1500, Demonts (1919) considered it subsequent to 1500, Michel and Adhémar (*Corpus*, 1962) attributed it to the last period (1510–16); Tolnay rightly believed it to be contemporary with, or slightly earlier than, *The Triptych of the Hay Wain* (21) which he dated to 1485–90, while in our opinion the latter picture belongs to the years 1500–2. The subject is a satire on the corruption of society and the clergy, not without references to the folklore and the literature of the period. The motif of the ship of the pleasure-seekers was a very familiar one in the Flanders of

Preliminary drawing for 15 (Paris, Louvre). On the back of the sheet: a helmet and the late-Gothic inscription 'Jeronimus Bos van Antwerpen'

Preliminary drawing for, or copy of, 16 (Paris, Louvre). The tree is represented as it was originally in the painting, before the later additions

13 A

mature works, can be perceived here and there, as for instance in the naked soul riding the large fish, and in the figure crawling into the tent, with a bird poised on its behind. The quality of the drawing, the flatness of the figures and the unconvincing quality of the grotesque details could justify some doubt as to its authenticity. However, without any knowledge of the original, it is impossible to make a firm judgement. Tolnay made an interesting analysis of the central part representing the

13 B

14 1488-92

Abigail and David, Solomon and Bathsheba
Formerly in the Cathedral of 'sHertogenbosch
A lost work, known through documents (Mosmans, 1931, 1947 and 1950; Ebeling, 1948) from which it appears that between 1488–90 and 1491–2 (see Outline Biography) Bosch painted the outside of the shutters for the altarpiece of the

and, on the inside, by Gielis. But in the history of 'sHertogenbosch up to 1565 and in the *Taxandria* (1610), the only name mentioned is the most famous one, that of Bosch. Such evidence, and the difficulty of admitting that the interior of the wings might have remained bare for over thirty years, induced Tolnay (1965) to conjecture that Van Hedel's contribution might have been limited to a repainting. It must be noted, however, that this altarpiece was a long time in the

the fifteenth century (Enklaar, *Tijdskrift voor Geschiedenis,* 1933; Bax, 1949): the blue boat, laden with a libertine party, was celebrated as early as 1413 in Jacob van Oestvoren's poem *De Blauwe Scuut;* it used to appear in the carnival parades of Brabant, and gave its name to a brotherhood found in several Dutch towns, devoted to feasting and merrymaking (D. M. Enklaar, 'De Blauwe Schuit' *Tijdschrift voor Geschiedenis* XLVIII 1933). But Bosch's boat is not painted blue. Moreover, Sebastian Brant's satirical poem *Narrenschiff* was published in German (see Outline Biography) and in Latin in 1494; the 1498 edition contains many engravings, in no way related, however, to Bosch's painting, as claimed by Demonts and Combe; the highest expression of the theme is found in Erasmus' *Praise of Folly* (1509). The connection with Brant's work (Demonts), accepted at one point also by Tolnay (1937), would provide a date *post quem,* but the types of the friar, of the nun and of other characters appear to have been inspired by Oestvoren's poem (Enklaar).

The panel may have been part of a diptych or triptych dedicated to the theme of folly (Demonts; Tolnay): represented

P. van der Heyden (Bosch inv., Cock publ.), prints after 16 or after similar lost compositions: above, The Valve-boat, *1562; below,* die blau Schuyte, *1559*

here is the rudderless boat drifting perhaps towards fools' paradise, Brant's *Narragonia;* Hélène Adhémar thinks it is the Ship of the Church, and on the point of being wrecked. Bosch's drawing in the Vienna Academy, with the ship in flames run though by an evil genius who drags it along while walking on the bottom of the sea, is said by Tolnay to have been the model for a lost hell of the fools, being the right-hand wing of the putative triptych. However the drawing has no connection with our painting other than in the motif of the boat, which, as Boon observes (Catalogue of Bosch exhibition, 1967, 53) is a recurrent theme with Bosch. Attempts have been made to interpret the painting in a psychoanalytic key by identifying the erotic symbols (Solier, *Art fantastique,* 1961);

15

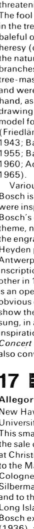

16 Pl. IX

but the various elements are better explained in the climate of the period, as a satire on one of the seven sins or of the five senses. Represented here are 'Gula' and 'Luxuria'; most of the characters are intent on food and drink — one has had too much and is vomiting over the

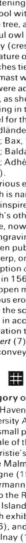

17

boat's side. The monk and the nun, as well as being obviously foolish characters, evidently have a sinful relationship (cherries, according to Bax, have erotic connotations); they are indulging in profane music-making too. 'Ira' is also shown, in the detail of the woman threatening the man on the left. The fool with cap and bells sits in the tree, and above the baleful owl and the flag of heresy (crescent moon) explain the nature of the boat. The branches tied to the top of the tree-mast were originally fewer and were added to by a later hand, as shown by a grisaille drawing in the Louvre, either a model for the painting, or a copy (Friedländer, 1927; Baldass, 1943; Bax, 1949; Popham, 1955; Baldass, 1960; Boon, 1960; Adhémar, 1962; Tolnay, 1965).

Various engravings, in which Bosch is named as 'inventor', were inspired by this and by Bosch's other versions of the theme, now lost: among them the engravings by P. van der Heyden published by Cock at Antwerp, one in 1559, with the inscription *die blau schuyte,* the other in 1562, wherein the boat is an open mollusc valve, an obvious erotic reference; both show the score of a song being sung, in accordance with an inspiration traceable to *The Concert* (7), where the egg also conveys an erotic meaning.

17 ⊞ ⊗ 51×35 1490-1500 ▤ ⦂

Allegory of Pleasures

New Haven (Conn.), Yale University Art Gallery
This small panel, which was in the sale of the Clark Collection at Christie's in London (1928), to the Malmedé Gallery in Cologne (1936), to the Silbermann Gallery in New York, and to the Rabinowitz Gallery in Long Island, appeared in the Bosch exhibition in Rotterdam (1936), and was first published by Tolnay (1937), who suggested it might depict an

episode concerning the Prodigal Son. Cut down at the top and on the right, it probably formed the lower left-hand part of a larger composition; Tolnay (1965) noted that, in view of its size and colours, it cannot be the lower part of *The Ship of Fools,* as claimed by L. Brand-Philip (also quoted by Adhémar (*Corpus,* 1962) who, in her turn, believed it to have been a whole symbolising May or Spring) and by Ch. Seymour jr. (*The Rabinowitz Collection,* 1961), according to whom it might have constituted, with *The Death of the Miser* (15), the wings of a lost triptych. Baldass (1959) believed it, instead, to be part of a panel illustrating the Deadly Sins; Bax (1949) viewed it as the summer feast of a merry party, and interpreted the various objects as symbols of forbidden love. The fragment depicts, in a lively style akin to that of *The Ship of Fools,* and with a delightful lightness of touch, Lust (a couple of lovers under a tent) and Gluttony, in the shape of a sort of Flemish Silenus (Seymour) bestriding a floating cask from which wine spills: this figure inspired the 'Carnival' of Bruegel's *Carnival and Lent* in Vienna. The coat-of-arms on the tent is that of the Bergh family, eminent in 'sHertogenbosch and in The Hague.

18

18 ⊞ ⊗ 13×5 *1490-1500* ▤ ⦂

Head of a Woman

Rotterdam, Boymans-van Beuningen Museum
This small fragment came to the museum (1958) with the Van Beuningen donation and was made known by Tolnay (1965). It has some similarity to the heads in *The Ship of Fools* in the sharp, profile rendering. The head is not, however, a caricature but a deeply-felt life-study in quite another mood. Formerly ascribed to Bruegel the Elder, although in the manner of Bosch, it cannot be definitely ascribed to our painter.

19 🔳 ⊕ 57,2×32 ▤ ⦂
1490-1500

A. The Ascent of Calvary
Vienna, Kunsthistorisches Museum
This small panel, originally arched, appears to have been cut down by some twenty centimetres at the top, and by two or three at the bottom (Baldass, 1959). It is the surviving left wing of a lost altarpiece, probably representing Golgotha at the centre and the Entombment (or Descent from the Cross or Lamentation [Baldass]) in the right wing, in accordance with the scheme adopted on the reverse of *St John on Patmos* in Berlin (33) (Tolnay, 1965). It was bought from Goudstikker of Amsterdam (1923); the cleaning carried out in the subsequent decade eliminated the repaintings which concealed the landscape in the upper part and the top of the tree-trunk cross of the good thief. The attribution is unanimous, except for a groundless attempt made by W. Ephron (1931) to exchange its authenticity with that of the copy formerly in the Weinberger Collection in Vienna. In the light of other works of the early maturity comprising small figures (Tolnay) the work was dated about 1480 (Baldass), but more generally to the beginning of the mature stage, about 1485–90 (Tolnay; Combe). The two thieves with their escort, among them the anachronistic figure of the friar confessing the good thief (the motif was to be taken up by Bruegel), are placed in a kind of proscenium behind which looms the principal scene formed by the group of the victim, the executioners and Simon of Cyrene. In a new iconographic interpretation, the latter does not help in bearing the cross, but merely touches it lightly (Tolnay), so that the whole material and moral weight of the progress toward death centres on the small figure of Christ. As concerns the iconography of the cross, with the transverse arm passing behind the head instead of projecting, Tolnay recalled a Van Eyckian tradition – different from the French-Flemish and traceable to the school of Giotto and that of Siena. With regard to the cruel speed of the march and the evil types, he noted analogies with the fifteenth-century tradition of Master Francke and Multscher; the detail of the clogs spiked with nails, was often included by Dutch and Flemish artists in the fifteenth and sixteenth centuries. According to some (Baldass, 1926), the painter himself 'eyewitnesses' this tragedy in the face looking out at the viewer, behind the soldier in armour at lower left.

19 🔳 ⊕ diam. 29,5 ▤ ⦂
1490-1500

B. Child at Play
On the reverse of the preceding panel, the naked child with the walker and the toy windmill painted in grisaille within a black tondo on a red ground, has been interpreted as an allegory of human foolishness (Bax, 1949; Baldass, 1959; Linfert, 1959) or as the child Jesus, the unsuspecting first stage in a life that is to be concluded by the final sacrifice; Tolnay referred to examples in Italian painting; Combe believed the tondo to symbolise the universe and recalled a similar juxtaposition of child Redeemer and sorrowing Christ in two engravings by the 'Master of the Amsterdam Cabinet'. However Boon (Bosch Catalogue) points out that the reverse sides of triptych volets were often unconnected with the principal subject; the figure of the child would have probably corresponded to a figure or scene painted on the back of the opposite shutter.

20 🔳 ⊕ 46,5×36,5 ▤ ⦂
1500*

The Ascent of Calvary
Formerly in London, Arnot Gallery
A badly damaged copy of a lost work (Tolnay, 1937 and 1965; Combe, 1947 and 1957), belonging to the period of the Vienna *Calvary* (19A). Only Baldass believed it to be an original (1935, 1943 and 1959); but this is disproved by the unusual technique of tempera on canvas as well as by the considerable spaciousness and the Italianate monument (Tolnay suggesting 1530–40). Among the most noticeable variants, compared with the Vienna painting, are the horsemen riding behind Christ, the progress of the thieves in two distinct groups in the background, the landscape representing Golgotha and Jerusalem. Simon of Cyrene's pose seems to pre-figure that in the later *Ascent of Calvary* in Madrid (44).

The Triptych of the Hay Wain

The first of Bosch's great satirical-moral allegories that has come down to us in its entirety (Madrid, Prado). It is already described in *Tabla de Cebes* by Morales (see Outline Biography, **1586**), and then in the work by Brother J. de Sigüenza (1605). It was one of the six paintings bought in 1570 by Philip II from the De Guevara heirs (Justi, 1889): listed as no. 1 in the document drawn up by Simancas; in 1574 it was sent to the Escorial with other works. The complete work now in the Prado is that from the Casa de Campo, signed in the central panel; it entered the collection of the Marquis of

The dating, formerly put to the last period, about 1510 (Baldass, 1917), was later rightly moved back to early maturity: according to Tolnay (1937 and 1965), 1485–90; Baldass, about 1500; in our opinion perhaps slightly later (1500–02), bearing in mind the sequence of works of the 1490–1500 decade (*Cataloque*, 15, 16, 17, 19) and the style of the clothes and head-dresses which begins about 1500 (Mateo Gómez): the pointed neckline, the head-dress and the sleeves of one of the female figures in the foreground of the central panel, made their appearance soon after this date.

Bosch's thought follows that of the fourteenth- and fifteenth-century mystics (Combe, 1958): a meditation on the follies of the world, observed in the antecedent fact (left wing, representing Original Sin), in the realisation (central panel, with the throng of sinners around the large hay wain) and in the final consequence (right wing,

20

Salamanca and was later split up: the central part went to Aranjuez after its purchase by Isabella II (1848); the right wing ended up in the Escorial, the other in the Prado, where the triptych was reassembled after 1914. There exists a second version of fine quality, now in the Escorial; it is signed in the left wing (22). This version is held to be an authentic work by all the early critics (Justi, 1889; Cohen, 1910; Maeterlinck, 1914; Lafond, 1914) as well by L. Brand-Philip (1953) and by Baldass (1959 [although he was of the opposite opinion in 1943]), the last-named scholar relying on points of pictorial technique (see 21 B). The authenticity of the Prado version was maintained by the directors of the museum, Sotomayor and Sánchez Cantón, and it was upheld by Tolnay (1965) especially as regards the exterior and interior of the wings; by Linfert (1959), Delevoy (1960) and Puyvelde (1962). Combe (1946 and 1957), on the other hand, apparently mixed up the two versions (the centre he reproduced as the one in the Prado, is in fact that of the Escorial).

illustrating the punishments of hell). When closed, the polyptych portrays a pilgrim, wandering without rest through the evil world.

In addition to the Escorial version (22), the theme was also treated in an engraving by Remigius Hogenberg of the end of the sixteenth century, inspired by the triptych, but in which the hay wain is replaced with an apple cart. For the engraving and the tapestry bearing the theme of the central panel, see 21 C.

21 🔳 ⊕ 135×90 ▤ ⦂
1500-02

A. The Path of Life (?)
The exterior of the wings forms a single composition: a shabbily dressed vagrant, snarled at by a dog which he wards off with his staff, walks wearily along a road leading to a small shaky bridge (for which Tolnay, 1965, referred to Psalm 24:4). The figure, which is extremely close to the so-called *Prodigal Son* in Rotterdam (61), has been related to an engraving by 'Master E.S.', *The Great Garden of Love* (Baldass, 1926), and to the Fool, the twenty-second Major Arcanum in Tarot cards

19 A

19 B

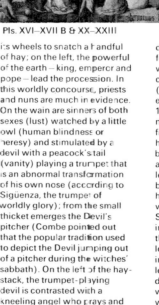
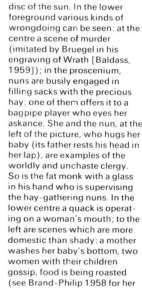

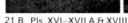

21 A Pls. XIV–XV 21 B Pls. XVI–XVII A & XVIII 21 C Pls. XVI–XVII B & XX–XXIII 21 D Pls. XVI–XVII C & XIX

(Combe, 1946 and 1957), an occult symbol of mindlessness, or of expiation, or of the last stage of the initiation. In the landscape background are represented: on the left a robbery, on the right a couple dancing to the sound of a bagpipe (a sexual symbol); at the back of the airy landscape, sloping down in hills and valleys can be seen the sinister outline of the gallows. The meaning is not perfectly clear, but the painting must be to some extent an allegory of Man's journey on Earth, beset on every side by danger, sin and death.

21 ⊞ ⊗ 135 × 45 1500 - 02

B. Original Sin
Interior of the left wing. In a setting subdivided into three fields by the skilful arrangement of the groves we see the Fall of

the Rebel Angels, the Creation of Eve, the Temptation, the Expulsion from Eden. The slightly 'primitive' mannerism of the figures, typical of northern painting of the nude, also marks the angel, garbed in Gothic raiment, and God the Father, clothed like a bishop. As concerns the nudes, Tolnay (1965) felt they recalled less the bold images of Van Eyck than the figures of proto fifteenth-century miniatures, such as the *Très riches heures* in Chantilly. The Fall of the Angels, who are changed into large insects, is a totally novel iconographic invention: one example of the many startling metamorphoses that Bosch's fertile imagination wrought with created things.

21 ⊞ ⊗ 135 × 100 1500 - 02

C. The Hay Wain
Central panel, signed

'Jheronimus bosch' at lower right, in Gothic letters. A great hay wain, against a fine airy landscape, is being dragged towards the right-hand wing (Hell) by a number of monstrous beings with animal heads. These are perhaps masks (Tolnay, 1965) like those used in the processions which included diabolical scenes, or Bosch may have intended to show a transformation that is already taking place. Combe (1946 and 1957) referred to fifteenth-century woodcuts illustrating the metamorphoses of Ulysses' companions; according to Brother Sigüenza (1605) the monsters are symbols of the various sins (in such a case, the scaly fish, a symbol of purity, might appear derisively). A frenzied throng of people of all classes follows the progress of the wain, ready to tear each other to pieces or end up under

its wheels to snatch a handful of hay; on the left, the powerful of the earth – king, emperor and pope – lead the procession. In this worldly concourse, priests and nuns are much in evidence. On the wain are sinners of both sexes (lust) watched by a little owl (human blindness or heresy) and stimulated by a devil with a peacock's tail (vanity) playing a trumpet that is an abnormal transformation of his own nose (according to Sigüenza, the trumpet of worldly glory); from the small thicket emerges the Devil's pitcher (Combe pointed out that the popular tradition used to depict the Devil jumping out of a pitcher during the witches' sabbath). On the left of the hay-stack, the trumpet-playing devil is contrasted with a kneeling angel who prays and looks up at Christ, revealed among the clouds within the

disc of the sun. In the lower foreground various kinds of wrongdoing can be seen: at the centre a scene of murder (imitated by Bruegel in his engraving of Wrath [Baldass, 1959]); in the proscenium, nuns are busily engaged in filling sacks with the precious hay; one of them offers it to a bagpipe player who eyes her askance. She and the nun, at the left of the picture, who hugs her baby (its father rests his head in her lap), are examples of the worldly and unchaste clergy. So is the fat monk with a glass in his hand who is supervising the hay-gathering nuns. In the lower centre a quack is operating on a woman's mouth; to the left are scenes which are more domestic than shady: a mother washes her baby's bottom, two women with their children gossip, food is being roasted (see Brand-Philip 1958 for her

interpretation of the hog's head and the washing of the baby as an allegory of the five senses) and finally a man (another charlatan, perhaps, owing to his tall hat) showing a little girl the fun of the fair – the hay-gathering.

The meaning of Bosch's allegory has been uncovered during the last few decades. Brother de Sigüenza, writing in the early seventeenth century, remarked that the painting seemed to go back to the passage in Isaiah: 'All flesh is grass'; Charles de Tolnay (1937) was reminded of the Flemish proverb 'The world is a haystack and each man grabs from it what he can'. In the following year Jan Grauls (in *Gentsche Bijdragen tot de Kunstjeschie-denis*) pointed out that this proverb, although clearly interesting, could not be traced further back than 1823; he discussed however a mid-sixteenth-century print depicting a hay wain surrounded by a number of people, with explanatory verses. Grauls explained through reference to contemporary literature and art that hay was equated with vanity, and to chase after hay was to chase after worldliness and emptiness . . . . He showed (GBK, 1939) that in 1563 in Antwerp a hay wain had actually been dragged through the streets in a procession, to the accompaniment of a song whose words were about the futility of worldly ambitions. In 1955 A. M. Salazar published the description by Ambrosio de Morales (published 1586, written about 1544) of Bosch's picture, in which he said that the picture was an allegory of man's pursuit of vanities, and that hay meant 'nothing' in Flemish.

In the Royal Palace in Madrid there is a sixteenth-century tapestry based on Bosch's picture which confirms this interpretation: the wain is enclosed within a crystal globe, indicating the world (Baldass, 1959, and see O. Kury, 1967). Dorfles (1953, before the publication of Salazar's paper) wanted to equate the wain with the Tarot symbol of the chariot drawn by two sphinxes.

21 ⊞ ⊗ 135×45 1500-02

D. Hell
Interior of the right wing, depicting infernal architecture and punishments of the reprobates. In the lower part, in a 'proscenium' recalling that of *The Ascent of Calvary* (20), the glutton is devoured by a monster with human legs, the envious man is torn apart by dogs (but Bax, 1949, interpreted the scene as the punishment of a wanton couple). The actual foreground is formed by the bridge crossed by the souls which the devils drive toward the infernal tower, still under construction. The woman on the ground with the toad in her lap symbolises pride. The man transfixed by a spear, who is riding an ox and holding a liturgical chalice, was interpreted by Tolnay as a plunderer

of churches, and by Combe (1946 and 1957) as a knight of death – typical of late fifteenth-century miniatures; the latter critic also referred to the knight of *coppe* (a suit in Italian playing-cards, corresponding to hearts) in Tarot cards. The fire in the background develops the theme already hinted at in *The Deadly Sins* (2): among other things, the detail of the hanged man reappears (Combe). Bosch undoubtedly had in mind as a literary source *The Vision of Tondalus* (see Outline Biography, **1482**), where both the knight with the chalice and the infernal bridge are described. The representations of creatures half-way between the animal and vegetable worlds (note the dog with a tree-branch tail) were to be developed in subsequent compositions with ever more disquieting exchanges between the vegetable, mineral and animal kingdoms.

22 ⊞ ⊗ 140×232

Triptych of the Hay Wain
Escorial, Monastery of San Lorenzo
Identical with the Prado version (21), except for very small variants, such as the jug on the table next to the monk (central panel); and the different pictorial rendering of Adam's legs (21 B). Signed 'Jheronimus bosch' in the lower part of the left wing. The painting shows restorations in various places, notably in the landscape of the central panel

23

and in the group to the left of the wain. L. Brand-Philip (1958) and Baldass (1959) considered this to be Bosch's original version (see 21); Dollmayr (1898) attributed it to his 'Master M.'. The exterior of the wings, representing the wanderer, was always considered a workshop product (Friedländer, 1927). The triptych may not be a copy made in Spain, but a version elaborated in Bosch's own workshop. In 1939 the two triptychs were brought together in the Prado for a short while, and the comparison

inclined most critics to consider the Prado version as the original.

23 ⊞ ⊗ 57×116

Battle between Carnival and Lent
The Hague, Cramer Gallery
Grisaille copy of a lost work by Bosch, formerly in the Thyssen Collection in Lugano (1929-58, coming from Goudstikker in Amsterdam) (L. Ninane, *Le siècle de Bruegel*, 1963). In 1925 Friedländer discovered it on the Milanese art market, split into two pieces which were later reassembled, and stated it to be an original by Bosch (1927), later followed by Heinemann (1959). It was judged a copy by Glück (1932), who thought it might be the imitation of the *Lent and Carnival* by Bosch formerly in the Prado (see 141), by Tolnay (1937 and 1965) and by Swarzenski (BMB, 1951). Two variants painted in colour are in the Mayer van den Berghe Museum at Antwerp, and in the Rijksmuseum of Amsterdam; two others in private collections (Bax, 1949). This composition inspired the analogous subject by Bruegel the Elder. To judge from the style of the groups in movement, the original might have fallen within the period of *The Triptych of the Hay Wain* (21) but an aesthetic and chronological appraisal based on a copy is inevitably uncertain.

24 A   24 B   24 C

The Altarpiece of St Liberata

The triptych (Venice, Palazzo Ducale) illustrates the martyrdom of St Ontcommer, or *Virgo Fortis* (report by Father Gerlach, 1966 and Brabantia XVI, 1967, 189), and not that of St Julia of Corsica, as believed until now. It was seen by Zanetti (*Della pittura veneziana*) in 1771 in the same Ducal Palace 'inside the Hall of the High Tribunal'. In 1838 it was transferred to Vienna, where it remained until 1919; it then returned to its former location in Venice. Its authenticity is unanimously acknowledged (Frimmel, KC, 1896; etc.) while the dating is rather uncertain, because of the stylistic disparity between the panels. Tolnay, followed by Combe, set it between 1500 and 1505; Baldass (who judged it a late work in 1917), related it to the central part of *The Triptych of the Hay Wain* (1500 *ca.*) and thought it to have been repainted at the time of *The Altarpiece of the Hermits* (40). Infra-red rays used at the Rijksmuseum of Amsterdam, where the work was exhibited in 1958, revealed that each of the wings originally included a donor's figure (Baldass, 1959). Despite the fact that the painting suffered damage from fire, the central panel is of fine quality.

24 ⊞ ⊗ 104×28 1500-04

A. The City in Flames
Left wing, repainted at the time of the 'Hermit' altarpiece (40) with the Temptation of St Anthony illustrated against the background of a city in flames, occupied by demons, while the inhabitants flee through one of the gates. The subject is in no way related to the central scene of *The Martyrdom*; Baldass (1959) conjectured that the elimination of the figure

originally placed in the foreground may have resulted from a change in ownership.

24 ⊞ ⊗ 104×63 1500-04

B. The Martyrdom of the St Liberata
Central panel of the altarpiece, signed 'Jheronimus bosch' at lower left. It represents the saint crucified by order of her father, a pagan Portuguese king, who punished her thus for having successfully prayed that God would make her grow a beard, so as to remain a virgin. The legend of Ontcommer began in the southern Netherlands as an explanation of the iconography of the *Christ in Lucca (Holy Face)*, a copy of which had reached the region. The unusual icono-graphy of the Crucifix dressed in a long tunic led the faithful to believe that a woman was portrayed, thus creating the personage of the bearded virgin; it is worth recalling that her cult was widespread in 'sHertogenbosch and that an altarpiece was dedicated to her in the cathedral of that city. The saint is always portrayed with her dress tied round her ankles, but the detail of the beard is often omitted, as in the present painting. According to the old interpretation, the youth fainting at the foot of the cross was Eusebius, St Julia's defender; in the light of the new interpretation, he is one expression of the dismay that seizes five thousand converts made by St Liberata. No doubt, too, the swooning figure is an iconographic reminiscence of the fainting Virgin at the foot of the Cross. Baldass (1943 and 1959) noted reminiscences of Van der Weyden and the Master of Flémalle; Combe (1946 and 1957) referred to the grisaille Veronica painted on the right shutter of the Lisbon Triptych (43 B). According to Baldass, the central panel was

also touched up at the time of the re-painting of the wings, with the addition, among other things, of the strip of landscape on the horizon.

24 ▦ ✇ 104×28 1500-04 ▯ ⋮

C. The Harbour
Right wing, representing a disordered harbour with foundering ships. The two figures in the foreground were formerly thought to portray (Tolnay) the slave merchants who had sold St Julia to Eusebius. The background, as it is now, appears connected with that of the central panel. For repaintings, see above.

Triptych of the Flood

The view is unanimously held that 25 A and D (Rotterdam, Boymans-van Beuningen Museum) belong to the same triptych, of which the central compartment is lost. They were originally in the Chiloedes Collection in Madrid and subsequently went to the Koenigs Collection in Haarlem. They are painted on both sides, each with a scene on the interior and two tondi on the outside; the painting is carried out in grisaille, an unusual feature which Tolnay explained by assuming that the panels served as wings, not for a painted altar, but for one carved or in intaglio, like those which Bosch executed for the altar of the Brotherhood of Our Lady in the cathedral at 'sHertogenbosch (14). Their poor state of preservation hinders appraisal: the majority of critics agree as to their authenticity, except for Delevoy (1960) and Puyvelde

(1962). Variously dated to the period of *The Triptych of the Hay Wain* (Baldass, 1959) or to the full maturity after 1500 (Tolnay, 1965). The figures in the tondi are workshop productions according to Mrs Brand-Philip (1958).

The interpretation of the triptych's general concept is controversial. Baldass, referring to the Gospels, suggested an eschatological programme (man's destiny in the hereafter) the lateral scenes might be two prefigurations of the Last Judgement. Fraenger (1950) believed – without, however, providing any historical proof – that the triptych might have been dedicated by the Grand Master of the Free Spirit, Jacob Almaengien (Outline Biography, **1496**), to his wife and son, who were both drowned, and that the central part – now lost – represented the Flood; he identified it as the lost triptych *Sicut erat in diebus Noë* which, in 1595, belonged to the Archduke Ernest of Austria (92). Considerable light was thrown on the general interpretation of the meaning of the scenes by the Gospel passages variously utilised by Baldass, relating to the prophecy of the Kingdom of God and of the return of the Son of man (Luke XVII: 26–33; Matthew XXIV:15–18 and 37–39): 'And as it was in the days of Noah (*Sicut erat in diebus Noë*) so shall it be also in the days of the Son of man. They did eat, they drank . . . until that day that Noah entered into the ark; and the flood came and destroyed them all.

Likewise also as it was in the days of Lot; they did eat, they drank . . . But the same day that Lot went out of Sodom, it rained fire and brimstone from heaven, and destroyed them all. Even thus shall it be in the day when the Son of man is revealed. In that day, he which shall be upon the housetop, and his stuff in the house, let him not

come down to take it away; and he that is in the field, let him likewise not return back . . . Whosoever shall seek to save his life shall lose it; and whosoever shall lose his life shall preserve it'. The logical arrangement of the two wings (on the left *The Evil World*, on the right *The World after the Flood* (Tolnay; Fraenger; Bax, 1956; Linfert, 1959)), which takes into account the compositional orientation of the two scenes, was inverted by Baldass to abide by the sequence 'flood-days of Lot' of the Gospel text.

25 ▦ ✇ 69×36 1500-04 ▯ ⋮

A. The Evil World
Interior of the left wing (cut down at the top and a little also at the sides), representing a bleak landscape inhabited by monstrous beings, with cities on fire in the background, antediluvian animals, devils with animal heads and the 'grylli' characteristic of Bosch. The construction in parallel planes distributed from the bottom upwards follows a zig-zag course as in the wings of *The Triptych of Hay Wain* (21). The scene has been variously interpreted: as the world before the flood, peopled by the evil race of Nephilim (Fraenger, 1950); as the fall of the rebel angels (Bax, 1956); as an illustration of the Gospel passages quoted above, relating to the days of Lot and the ruins of Sodom, which in Bosch's day symbolised the Last Judgement (Baldass).

25 ▦ ✇ diam. 32,4 1500-04 ▯ ⋮

B. The Devil in the House
The tondo at the top of the reverse of the preceding panel portrays a woman fleeing from a bewitched house assailed by demons. Baldass referred to the

already-mentioned Gospel text (see above): 'In that day, he which shall be upon the housetop, and his stuff in the house, let him not come down to take it away'; E. Begemann Haverkamp (*Führer durch die Sammlungen des Museums Boymans*) related it to the story of Tobias.

25 ▦ ✇ diam. 32,4 1500-04 ▯ ⋮

C. The Devil in the Country
The tondo at the bottom of the reverse of the same panel (25 A) represents a peasant surprised by the devil in the open country. E. Begemann Haverkamp placed the theme in relation to the Gospel parable of the sower (Mark IV:4 and 14–15): 'And as he sowed some fell by the wayside, and the fowls of the air came and devoured it up . . .
The sower soweth the word . . . but, when they have heard, Satan cometh immediately and taketh the word away that was sown in their hearts'; Baldass again referred to the above-quoted passage from the Gospel according to St Luke; . . . he that is in the field, let him likewise not return back'.

25 ▦ ✇ 69,5×38 1500-04 ▯ ⋮

D. The World after the Flood
The interior of the right wing (cut down at the right) illustrates the ark on top of Mount Ararat with Noah, his sons and their wives, and the animals in pairs, leaving the ark. Better preserved than *The Evil World*, it is also more beautiful, with great imagination displayed in the depiction of the primeval landscape, which prefigures the outside of *The Triptych of the Garden of Delights* (representing

The Creation of the World; 30). The grisaille is refined and there is a graceful undulation in the composition. Baldass pointed out that the ark had originally been sketched larger and deeper, and inferred from this a proof favourable to the authenticity of the painting. The panel is interpreted as a prefiguration of the Last Judgement, in accordance with the Gospel passage quoted above: '. . . the flood came and destroyed them all' (Baldass); or as an allegory of the family tragedy of the Grand Master Almaengien (Fraenger).

25 ▦ ✇ diam. 32,4 1500-04 ▯ ⋮

E. Lost Soul
On the reverse side of the preceding panel, at the top, is a tondo representing a soul persecuted by devils, against a distant landscape. Concerning the monstrous toad at lower centre, Baldass (1959) drew attention to a preliminary drawing in the Kupferstichkabinett in Berlin, claimed to be a Bosch original. The enigmatic representation has been variously interpreted with reference to the passage in the Gospel according to St Luke (XVII: 33, and also IX: 24): 'Whosoever shall seek to save his life shall lose it' (Baldass); as the beginning of the parable of the Good Samaritan (Begemann Haverkamp).

25 ▦ ✇ diam. 32,4 1500-04 ▯ ⋮

F. Saved Soul
Placed below the preceding scene, this tondo portrays a soul kneeling before Christ (the soul of one who has died in a state of grace); in the background is the same soul, to whom an angel hands a white garment, within a broad, simplified landscape.

25 B & C Pl. XI A   25 A Pl. XI B   25 D Pl. X   25 E & F

Visions of the Hereafter

These four panels (Venice, Palazzo Ducale) must have constituted initially the wings of two small triptychs illustrating the Last Judgement and the Resurrection of the Dead (Baldass, 1959), flanked by the Ascent into the Empyrean and by Hell, the Garden of Eden and the Fall of the Damned; or perhaps of a single triptych, in accordance with a not unusual scheme whereby the lateral panels are superimposed, which appears, for instance, in the

according to Baldass (who in 1917 judged the paintings 'very archaic') close to *The Ship of Fools* (16); according to Tolnay, between the Lisbon *Temptation* and *The Delights* in the Prado (43 and 30). Bosch has surpassed the matter-of-fact medieval descriptions and realised instead a 'visionary' representation of the theme, in accordance with the visions of mystics such as Ruysbroeck and Master Eckhart (Combe; Tolnay). He went to the heart of

26 ⊞ ⊕ 87×40 1500-04 ⊟ ⋮

C. The Garden of Eden
Baldass attempted to trace the model of this scene to Dirk Bouts' *Garden of Eden* in the Lille Museum.
Souls of men and women, accompanied by angels and given over to innocent pleasures, move along the slopes of a wooded hill, crowned with the fountain of life. Tolnay noted that in the background, to the right, a cruel detail, presaging the corruption of this ideal existence, is introduced by the scene of the lion tearing to pieces another, unidentifiable,

Manichaeism, a duct through which souls and prayers enter the heavenly kingdom; for the flight of the souls, he drew attention to a Rhenish drawing of the late fifteenth century, now at the Kupferstichkabinett in Berlin. According to Combe, the panel illustrates a phrase from Ruysbroeck's *Ornament of Spiritual Marriage*, where God's irradiation is described as an 'abyss' resembling an 'immense effusion of essential light'.

The unusual device of representing the crowd at half length, and the slight foreshortening from right to left, with the vault in perspective, could be explained by the fact that the painting may have once been the background (left-hand corner) of a larger composition — known only through a sixteenth-century drawing at the Crocker Art Gallery in Sacramento (Swarzenski, B M B, 1955) — which Baldass (1959) judged a mixture of Bosch-like elements: it illustrates the Ascent of Calvary and, in the background, this Ecce Homo, the Suicide of Judas, and St John consoling the Virgin. The sinister chattering group at the top left are perhaps informers against Christ; the bunches of thorny twigs seem to refer to the flagellation; Christ is presented to the crowd by a fancy-dress Pilate in a grotesquely elegant costume. During the restoration undertaken in 1939, the panel was slightly widened along the central split, thus eliminating the damage caused by the badly executed joint and removing a third column, added between the two original ones probably in order to conceal the joint in question (*The Worcester Philadelphia Exhibition of Flemish Painting*, 1939).

A copy of the painting (oils on panel, like the original; 62·5 × 48.7 cm.) is preserved in the Clowes Fund Collection in Indianapolis. Tolnay, who had stated it to be authentic after a first inspection in 1940, is now inclined to consider it a workshop copy: in confirmation of this, suffice it to consider that the perspective effect, foreshortened from right to left, has completely disappeared. The copy was made after the third column had been inserted (here, it is placed closer to the central one) and the fragment cut away; a low wall was added in the lower part (in the Philadelphia work this is merely outlined), to transform it into an autonomous painting.

26 A

26 B PI. XIII

26 C

26 D PI. XII

altarpiece by Dirk Bouts in Louvain (Tolnay, 1965); Baldass thought that in such a case the left side included the Garden of Eden and the Ascent arranged one above the other, with Hell and the Fall of the Damned on the right. The exterior of the panels is coloured in marbled tempera, believed to be original (Baldass), in red for the Garden of Eden and the Fall of the Damned, in green for the Ascent into the Empyrean and for Hell. If the reconstruction into a single triptych is accepted, the effect achieved when the shutters were closed was one of diagonally alternated colour zones: green and red above, red and green below. They are thought to have come from the collection of Cardinal Grimani where in 1521, Marcantonio Michiel saw two works described as 'the canvas of Hell; the canvas of Dreams'. The panels appear to have been shortened; their state of preservation is not perfect, but they were restored in recent years and freed of the many repaintings. They were made known in 1886 (KC) and studied by Dülberg (*Früh-holländer in Italien*, 1905) who denied their authenticity, initially doubted also by Tolnay (1937), but generally acknowledged (Cohen, 1910; up to Tolnay, 1965). The panels were dated to the middle period:

the theme, solving the complicated iconographical problem of the divine spheres and the infernal rays; the floating upwards of the innocent, and the heavy fall of the damned.

26 ⊞ ⊕ 87×40 1500-04 ⊟ ⋮

A. The Fall of the Damned
This is viewed as an engulfing of the souls, pursued by demons, in the bottomless abyss. The number of the figures is quite limited compared to the preceding and similar compositions by Van Eyck, Bouts and Memling (Tolnay). As a possible model, Baldass suggested a panel by Bouts, now at the Louvre.

26 ⊞ ⊕ 87×40 1500-04 ⊟ ⋮

B. Hell
Apparently conceived as the anguished dream of the naked soul (Tolnay) who sleeps or meditates in the foreground, tormented by a devil. The infernal landscape with the rocks and the river, is crossed by sinister flashes reflected in the water, and animated by a few figures of devils and of damned souls, which accentuate the feeling of distress. Concerning the flaming water, Tolnay referred to the Apocalypse (XXI: 8).

wild beast; this may be compared with the similar episodes of the Eden panel of *The Garden of Delights*, where a wild boar frightens a mythical animal, and a big cat makes off with a mouse in the foreground.

26 ⊞ ⊕ 87×40 1500-04 ⊟ ⋮

D. The Ascent into the Empyrean
Of the four compositions, this is the most striking, with its strange luminous cylinder, formed by concentric rings, perhaps symbolising the celestial spheres (Tolnay), not unusual in late medieval iconography (Baldass referred to fifteenth-century miniatures) but which Bosch's art has transformed by the restrained relation of light to colour: the souls are literally absorbed by the divine rays shining out from the further end; they follow an upward zig-zag course, gradually losing their weight and leaving behind the accompanying angels until, alone, they reach the celestial light, a concept which Tolnay related to Dante's *Paradiso*. The souls' ascent is depicted in an entirely different style in the background of Bouts' *Garden of Eden* at Lille. As for the entrance in the shape of a luminous cylinder, Tolnay mentioned the 'column of glory' of

27 ⊞ ⊕ 50×52 1500-04 ⊟ ⋮

Ecce Homo
Philadelphia, Museum of Art (Johnson Collection)
This painting is generally attributed to Bosch except Boon (BM, 1960) and some doubts expressed by Baldass. Believed to be a work of the end of the first period by Baldass, who compared it to the Frankfurt *Ecce Homo* (10), and by Benesch (ML) who referred to the Vienna *Ascent of Calvary* (19); attributed to early maturity by Tolnay (1490–1500 *ca.*), by Linfert and by Combe, the latter suggesting that it be set at the period subsequent to *The Triptych of the Hay Wain* (21).

Copy of 27 (Indianapolis, Clowes Fund Collection)

28 ⊞ ⊕ 62,5×53 ⊟ ⋮

Ecce Homo
Switzerland, private collection
This came from the Rudinoff Collection in Vösendorf. A work of debatable authenticity, despite authoritative attributions by Benesch (ML), who dated it to the final period, suggesting as its model a woodcut of Dürer's *Great Passion*, and by Tolnay (1965) who held it to be a fragment of a larger composition from the last decade of the fifteenth century, perceiving in it the curves typical of late-Gothic style; he judged the inscription to be a later addition. We have no first-hand knowledge of the original, but the limpness of the modelling, the dry stiffness of the folds, the expression of the faces — reduced to a superficial, mechanical grimace, without that inner characterisation that is peculiar to Bosch's style — seem to refute the suggested authenticity.

29  60×40

A. St James of Compostela and the Sorcerer
Valenciennes, Musée des Beaux-Arts

The critics are not in agreement as to the authenticity of this work – painted on both sides (see 29 B) – thought by some (Tolnay, 1937 and 1965; Combe, 1946 and 1957) to be the copy of a lost painting by Bosch; Friedländer (1927) claimed it to be an original, Baldass (1943), the work of a follower. Combe related it to the style of the Philadelphia *Ecce Homo* (27), especially in the treatment of the black-ringed eyes, the accessories, the sorcerer's hat, the swollen column. According to Tolnay, on the other hand, the costumes are datable to 1510–20. The theme refers to the legend of St James the Greater (as told in the Golden Legend) who, having returned to Palestine after his fruitless preaching in Spain, converted the magician Hermogenes but was killed by the Jews; a small boat borne by angels carried his body to the location of present day Compostela. Portrayed here is Hermogenes ordering the demons to seize the saint, who is seen in the background. The saint is ordering the devils off – they are in submissive postures, cowed by the angel. It is interesting to note the development in the morphology of the demons, and the appearance of the alchemic egg, whose shell is burst by the limbs of the reptile inside.

29 60×40

B. The Temptation of Saint Anthony

On the reverse of 29 A. It represents the hut of the saint who prays on the threshold while beggars and cripples wander around. According to Combe, this is a mélange of elements peculiar to Bosch, but executed in a subsequent period. Tolnay and Baldass regard it respectively as a copy and an imitation.

The Triptych of the Garden of Delights

The second of the great triptychs that has come down to us in its entirety (Madrid, Prado). The painting may have been in the Brussels palace of Henry III of Nassau, Regent of the Netherlands, in 1517. A visiting Italian, Antonio de Beatis, described the palace and its treasures, and mentioned 'pictures' which sound very like the *Delights* – containing 'many bizarre details' such as the birds flying out of human behinds, etc. (see Gombrich, 1967). It became the property of Philip II after having been in the collections of Don

27

28

Fernando, prior of the Order of San Juan (he died in 1595), the illegitimate son of the Duke of Alba; mentioned in the inventory of the paintings sent by the king to the Escorial on 8 July 1593 ('una pintura de la variedad del mundo' – 'a painting of the variety of the world'); first described by Brother José de Sigüenza (1605), as the 'strawberry painting' and generally indicated by old Spanish writers as *la lujuria* (lust); Poleró's catalogue of the Escorial (under 129) carries the title *Los deleites terrenales* (the earthly delights). Authenticity was unanimously acknowledged (except for Dollmayr, 1898, who advanced the name of 'Master M.'), starting with Justi (1889). The dating, set at one point in the youthful period – about 1485 (Baldass, 1917) – due to the 'archaic' treatment of space – was moved forward by Tolnay (1937) to the time (1510 ca.) of *The Triptych of the Epiphany* at the Prado (62) on the basis of the painting's tonal refinement. Such a dating is now generally accepted by modern critics, albeit with some variations in the actual year. We would prefer to put it earlier than the Prado *Epiphany* and the last works such as the St Anthony paintings. The inscription on the exterior of the wings is an archaism which was to appear no more in the other works.

The prevailing interpretation is the moralistic-didactic one: on the exterior, we see as an antecedent fact, the third day of Creation; inside, in the left wing, the marriage of Adam and Eve, the authors of the ills of the world; at the centre, the illustration of carnal sins; on the right, the punishment — Hell. The painting's moral content was already perceived by Brother de Sigüenza (who wished that many copies could be circulated for the edification of souls); his interpretation was upheld, on the whole, by Baldass, Combe, Bax, Puyvelde. Combe (1946 and 1957) added the explanation of the symbols in the light of alchemy, the false doctrine which turns men away from salvation as does carnal sin, the former also resting on the union of the male (sulphur) and female (mercury) principles. Bax (1949) started from Tolnay's psychoanalytic

interpretation, to develop the search for erotic symbols, having recourse to Netherlandish folklore, to the various vernacular expressions, to the metaphors current in the poems of the early sixteenth century (published, however, only in 1524, after Bosch's death, in the *Refereynenbundel* of Jan van Styevoorts). Tolnay grafted a psychoanalytic explanation into the moralistic meaning: Bosch painted the dream of a mankind yearning to realise the repressed love impulses of the unconscious, and utilised as a source for the erotic symbolism Macrobius' theories on dreams, set out in the commentary to Cicero's *The Dream of Scipio Africanus*, and the 'keys to dreams' of the late fifteenth century, such as *Les songes de Daniel Prophète* (1482), whose ancient motifs crop up again in Freudian psychoanalysis and Jung's psychology of the subconscious. These interpretations are opposed by Fraenger's optimistic view (1947) that the triptych was commissioned by the Grand Master of the sect of the Free Spirit, as an illustration of the paradise of the Adamites (see Outline Biography, **1486–7**). Hell would thus represent a hell for heretics.

sinning against the doctrines of the sect: a hell which, however, contains the seeds of redemption. The theory, whose positive contribution is the thorough research on the symbols from a psychoanalytic viewpoint, was developed by Wertheim–Aymes (1957), who made of the right wing a 'purgatorium' from which the souls would go on to the centre, the heaven of the joys of love. These explanations, as Bax (1956), Puyvelde (1956 and 1962), Génaille (1965), Tolnay (1965), have pointed out, are devoid of any historical grounds: nothing proves that the heretics had a liturgical art, nor is the argument acceptable that a subject like *The Delights* could not have been commissioned for a church; whether the painting was intended for a religious body or for an individual, in Bosch's day the moralistic aim justified even the boldest representational means: this was confirmed by Brother de Sigüenza in his comments. Concerning the strange interweavings of the animal, vegetable and mineral worlds, Combe traced a probable source to some German woodcuts of the fifteenth century (notably the editions by Koberger of Nuremberg) where,

for example, rocks assume the bizarre appearances of crystals and tropical vegetation. A study of some of the iconographic elements of this triptych has recently been published in *Studia Muzealne* (v, 1966) by A. Spychalska-Boczkowska: the principal thesis of the study seems to be that the painting is to be interpreted in an astrological light, with emphasis on the Golden Conjunction of the sun and moon in the Constellation of Cancer on 6 June 1504. The fountain in Paradise represents the Sun and Cancer; the blue globe in the large lake, upper centre of centre panel, represents the moon and the round pool below with the bathing women the planet Venus. The centre panel would be given a favourable interpretation by this writer (but the article is not altogether clear), for astrologers throughout Europe expected great things of the Golden Conjunction; 1504 would then be a date *ante quem* for *The Garden of Delights*.

The triptych's state of preservation is not very good, especially in the large central panel, where the joints of the wood correspond with the flaking off of colour, now restored. Extant reproductions of this work include a Flemish tapestry of the sixteenth century in the Royal Palace at Madrid, and several partial copies, catalogued by Friedländer (1927) and by Tolnay (1965): three of the central panel (one was on the Berlin art market in 1927, coming from the Cardon Collection in Brussels; another with W. M. Newton in New York, in 1921; a third, on canvas, in the Budapest Museum). A copy of the exterior of the wings is in the Prado; one of the left wing was also in the Prado (part of the complete copy mentioned above). Copies of the right wing: one copy was in the Orloff sale in Paris (1920), various partial copies have been noted by Friedländer, there are also

29 A

29 B

99

four variants (different sales: De Fussac Fievez, Brussels 1923; Dorthmund, Christie's 1928; Vasto, Canessa of Naples 1928; Schulthess of Basel 1936), to which should be added the one in a private collection in Milan (A F, 1955).

30 ⊞ ⊕ 220 × 195 1503-04 ▤ ⫶

A. The Creation of the World

Exterior of the wings, forming a single composition: the world on the third day of creation, from a bird's eye view, inside a crystal sphere. This derives from the traditional representation of the created world as a crystal ball held in the hand of God or of Christ (Tolnay). At the top, on both panels, is a biblical quotation: *Ipse dixit et facta su(n)t, / / Ipse ma(n) davit et creata su(n)t (Psalms, 32:9; 148:5 (For he spake, and it was done / / for he commanded, and they were created). Concerning the representation of the world within a transparent globe, Bax (1949) referred to the reverse of a medallion by Pisanello; Tolnay, to the globe on which Christ sits, in Bosch's tondo representing the Last Judgement in *The Seven Deadly Sins* (2) and to a miniature in the *Livre des merveilles du monde* (1445) in the Pierpont Morgan Library in New York. In the upper left corner, floating in space sits God the Father, portrayed as an old man with tiara and beard. The episodes of the creation within a tondo, with the divine hand outside, in the place of the Creator, were traced by Combe (1946, 1957) to the engravings of Schedel's *Liber chronicarum* (Koberger, Nuremberg 1493); the earth surrounded by water to the paradise of Paul Limbourg's *Golden Book* for the Duc de Berry. Bosch also treated the theme of the creation of the world in a lost painting, executed for the cathedral of 'sHertogenbosch (see 105). The animals have not yet appeared on the earth, but plants and strange vegetable-mineral formations are burgeoning, which already suggest the abnormal luxuriant growth and the intermingling of worlds displayed in the interior of the panels. Bax (1956) saw sexual symbols in the vegetable forms. The iconography of the theme appears altogether fresh (Tolnay): the Creator is relegated to a corner, the globe becomes the main subject. The refined conception has some parallel in *The World after the Flood* (25 D).

30 ⊞ ⊕ 220 × 97 1503-04 ▤ ⫶

B. The Garden of Eden

Interior of the left wing, illustrating the Creation of Eve. The usual arrangement: creation, original sin, expulsion, has not been followed. The iconography is also quite unusual in painting (though not in miniatures [Tolnay, 1965]): Adam is already awake, and the Maker

presents Eve to him. Bosch has here used a careful realism, in the Eyckian tradition, when rendering the naked body, especially in the case of Adam. The image of the Creator portrayed as Christ is linked to the ancient tradition (Combe, 1946 and 1957 and Spychalska-Boczkowska 1966), neglected by the artists of the fifteenth century but taken up by Bosch, according to which God created the world through His Word (Logos). In the Garden of Eden there are exotic plants and animals, such as elephants and giraffes (taken perhaps from medieval bestiaries); some of these are beginning to devour each other. In the background, four fantastic rocks in geometric-abstract shapes serve as a dwelling-place for birds (see Spychalska-Boczkowska for a discussion of the birds). Concerning the cactus placed behind Adam and considered to represent the Tree of Life, Combe called attention to the tree of Paradise in an engraving of Schedel's *Liber Chronicarum* (Koberger, Nuremberg 1493); Dvořák (1924) to that of *The Flight into Egypt* engraved by Schongauer. The palm-tree with the serpent coiled around it is the tree of the knowledge of good and evil (Combe, again calling attention to the *Liber Chronicarum*) which bore the tempting fruits offered by woman (the senses) to man (superior reason), according to Ruysbroeck's *Ornements des noces spirituelles*. Among the alchemistic elements (Combe) are the three-headed dragon on the edge of the pond and the rocky egg, dwelling place of the ravens. The exact centre of the composition is formed by the Fountain of Life, a strange flamboyant Gothic monument of crustacean appearance. At the top it bears a crescent (interpreted variously); at the centre of the base disc a circular opening with a perching owl (according to Bax, 1956, a sexual allusion to the multiplication of the species; to Fraenger, the ancient bird of wisdom, as maintained by Brother de Siguenza). Fraenger believed the disc, the hole and the owl to form one of the 'points of concentration' used by the mystics to attain a state of ascetic exaltation; furthermore, he indicated as a source for the landscape an edition of the *Letter of Alexander to Aristotle*, by Eusebius. It must be pointed out that a convincing interpretation of this panel, and of the whole triptych, has so far eluded everyone. The many ingenious attempts are of interest in so far as meanings are suggested for individual symbols (Tolnay 1965 pp. 360-3 provides many bibliographical references); but the relation of all the symbols to each other and thus the meaning of the whole is still mysterious.

30 ⊞ ⊕ 220 × 195 1503-04 ▤ ⫶

C. The Garden of Delights

Central panel of the triptych,

representing nudes of both sexes, among them also negroes and negresses, joined in couples or in groups within odd vegetable or mineral formations who give themselves over to sensual pleasures. Tolnay (1937 and 1965) proposed as a literary source the description of the fourth heaven in Baruch's *Apocalypse* X, which includes the plain, the pond and the large exotic birds. Combe (1946 and 1957) referred to the dream-like atmosphere to the 'sleep of the souls' dimmed by sin. Fraenger (1947), on the other hand, viewed it as a description of the Adamites' sublime and innocent *ars amandi*. The gentle and ambiguous intertwining of the nudes is perhaps not devoid of an inspiration from real life, drawn from the *stoven*, the gay and ill-famed baths of the period, mentioned by Dorfles (1953), but the figures possess the preciosity of fifteenth-century Flemish miniatures. At the centre of the composition is the cavalcade of lust (?) around the fountain of youth (?) (Combe underlined the alchemic motif of the elixir of life), in which women bathe, bearing on their heads ravens, peacocks, ibises, all of which have been given conflicting interpretations. The animals in the cavalcade — leopards, panthers, bears, lions, bulls, unicorns, deer, boars, donkeys, goats, griffins, camels — borrowed from the bestiaries and from mystical writings, might be symbols of lust (Bax) and of other sins (Baldass), or of the Saviour (Combe), as an allusion to man who mortifies his divine nature; the griffin in the centre foreground may have been borrowed from one of Schongauer's engravings (Dvořák, 1924). At the back, four streams, perhaps from the four corners of the Earth (the four fantastic rock-formations) flow into a lake in which floats a huge grey-blue globe. Acrobats are performing on it (in this connection, Tolnay drew attention to *The Garden of Love* and the illustrations of the *Roman de la Rose*, already mentioned by Kuhn J K S, 1913; see, too, Spychalska-Boczwoska 1966). The four strange rocks are inhabited by lovers. The mineral-vegetable outgrowths of all these monuments, based on horns, palmettes, cones, cylinders, and half-moons, are male and female sexual symbols (Fraenger; Bax); the transport tubes strewn on the grassy ground are female symbols (Fraenger) or of Mercury (Combe), the female principle in the alchemic creation known as the 'great work'. The glass, like the bubbles, egg-shells and brittle fruit-shells, emphasises the idea of fragility and transience which seems so manifest in this panel. The heads of the lovers are crowned with dewy fruits, strange vegetations bloom from naked bottoms, gigantic bushes blossom from the hard coral. Fruits, fishes, birds, convey an erotic symbology of oneiric, alchemic, mystic, or

more generally popular origin. Tolnay noted that cherries, strawberries, raspberries, grapes — with which the lovers delight themselves — stand for voluptuousness in the ancient 'keys to dreams' quoted by Artemidoro (*Les jugements astronomiens des songes*, Troyes 1634), which includes the plain, the pond and the large exotic birds. Combe (1946 and 1957) referred the dream-like atmosphere to the *Songes de Daniel Prophète* (1482); salt-water fishes signify voluptuousness (Artemidoro), anguish (*Songes de Daniel*), the pleasures of past joys, according to the mystics. The mollusc valve (here enclosing two lovers) is a common popular feminine sexual symbol (Tolnay), or a depiction of adultery according to Bax, who identified the bearer as the cuckolded husband. The transparent bubble around the huge strawberry and another couple, was stated by Baltrusaitis (1955) to have been borrowed from Oriental representations, by Bax to indicate adultery, by Combe to represent the nuptial chamber for the alchemic union of the male and female principles, as do the gourds, the corals, the eggs that shelter lovers, all symbols of the alchemist's crucible where the 'great work' is accomplished: it is significant that the geometric centre of the painting should be marked by an egg, balanced on the head of one of the horsemen.

Concerning the transparent bowl and the glass bells sheltering other nudes, among them an ambiguous trio on the right, Tolnay recalled the Flemish proverb 'happiness is like glass, it is soon shattered'. The robins and the other birds are popular symbols of lasciviousness; the butterflies,

of flightiness; the little owl, of heresy; the raven (incredulity, for the mystics) was for the alchemists' matter blackened at the first stage of the 'cooking'; the mouse (inside a glass tube on the left, under the transparent bubble), is always an evil symbol. The gigantic birds going into the pond on the left are drawn from alchemy and the bestiaries (Combe); the hoopoe feeding on refuse stands for the soul rejoicing in false doctrines; the kingfisher, for hypocrisy. Also alchemistic are some of the colours, such as orange (the effulgence preceding white, second stage of the 'cooking'), red (the high point of the creative process), while azures and blues are the colours of deceit and evil. The group including a clothed man, in the cave at lower right, has been variously interpreted by scholars: Tolnay claimed it to symbolise original sin; Bax viewed it as portraying Adam, Eve and Noah; Fraenger, as the painter himself, the second Eve and Bosch's heretical patron Almaengien; J. Mateo Gómez (AEA, 1963), as Eve, the Baptist — who was to wash sin away through baptism — and Adam: Further groups and individuals have been also analysed.

30 ⊞ ⊕ 220 × 97 1503-04 ▤ ⫶

D. Musical Hell

Interior of the right wing, illustrating the punishment of sins. Among the literary sources suggested is *The Vision of Tondalus* (Tolnay; see also Outline Biography; **1482**), especially for the hell of ice and fire, the monster swallowing the damned, the bridge on the

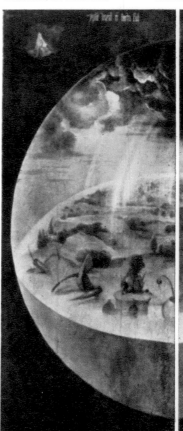

30 A

river; also the *Grand calendrier des bergers* for 1493 (Baldass, 1959). Tolnay, Bax and Fraenger attributed a sexual meaning to the various elements (vase and lantern: female emblems; knives and skates: male emblems; climbing and ladders: sexual intercourse); Combe (1946 and 1957) referred to the Bible as well as to alchemy (to which are connected the cold colours, black and azure, of the murky wells of hell). Tolnay interpreted this hell as a frightening dream of the painter, identified as the little man leaning on the edge of the hollow egg; Fraenger (1947), as the testimony of universal restoration by means of the three instruments hurled from heaven with Lucifer, which will redeem sinners through the musical revelation of the Trinity; Combe cited Ruysbroeck's threat to sinners, who will freeze for having despised true love, and burn for having worshipped false love instead.

Stylistically and iconologically, this is a development of the theme of Hell as it is illustrated in *The Triptych of the Hay Wain* (21) and, according to Baldass, also of that in the Vienna *Triptych of the Judgement* (50). The chief figure is that of the central monster, the alchemic man (Combe): the colours (from bottom to top, black, white, red) reflect the stages of the 'cooking' of mercury; the legs in the shape of a hollow tree (allusive to the alchemist's crucible and to nature's womb; see also 43 D) rest within the two vessels 'of art and of nature' which lead to the 'great work' (Tolnay, on the other hand viewed them as the 'blue

boats' of destruction; see also 16); the body is the alchemic egg (according to Fraenger, the corrupt universal egg; to Bax, a beheaded giant goose, a reference to a barbarous local pastime); inside the hollow, a diabolic tavern at the obscene sign of the bagpipe; the servant witch, wearing a crescent-shaped head-dress, recalls the 'Popess' of the Tarot cards (Combe). The monster's head is possibly a self-portrait (Benesch), an example of the theme of the thoughtful 'eye-witness' which recurs in many painters' works (see for example, 19). It bears a round target supporting a pink bag-pipe (female and male emblems [Bax]) on which revolve witches, demons and sinners. A first suggestion of the tree-man is found in the rather youthful sketch portraying *St Anthony*, in the Kupferstich-kabinett in Berlin, the reverse of which bears *The Concert in the Egg* (7); a drawing with variants, believed to be authentic (Tolnay; Baldass; Combe) is at the Albertina in Vienna; a variant is at the Kupferstichkabinett in Dresden (Tolnay judged it to be by an imitator; Bax, 1949, authentic). The harp, the lute and the barrel-organ of the musical hell, turned into instruments of torture and surrounded by damned souls and devils singing from the score, were interpreted by Tolnay and Bax (on the basis of Freud's theories) as sexual symbols of the punishment of carnal sin; by Combe, as biblical instruments of praise to the Lord, neglected by the sinners during their lifetime; by Fraenger (contradicted by Lenneberg, 1961), as reminis-

cences of the harmony of Heaven: the score is said to bear an Adamitic wedding march. The player turning the organ's handle is a beggar, recognisable as such (Bax) by the string with a lead mark hanging from his bowl, a brand imposed by a decree of 1459. The enthroned monster with a bird's head and his feet emerging from the devil's pitchers, is Satan (Combe; Fraenger; Tolnay): he swallows the damned and discharges them as excrement through a transparent bubble (an un-pleasant echo of the voluptuous bubbles in *The Garden of Delights*); on the edge of the sewer, the damned soul defecating gold coins perhaps alludes to the heresy of alchemical transmutation; the one who vomits, to the first stage in the 'cooking' (black), also called 'vomit' (Combe). Around these groups are multiplied the punishments, partly identifiable by a comparison with *The Seven Deadly Sins* (2). At lower left is the torture of the wrathful man, transfixed by a sword, set within the wider scene of a fight between a group of dice players behind him, assaulted by devils (Combe; Baldass); the man torn apart by dogs symbolises envy (Baldass); on the right, the scene of the covenant with the Devil (Combe) which one of the damned is induced to sign by a sorcerer with a pig-like head and a monastic veil, and by another with a toad depicted on his shoulder, holding Egyptian alchemical texts: the monster proffering the pen carries a hanging, severed foot, the alchemic symbol of the fixing of mercury ('cutting of the foot');

Preliminary drawing for the tree-man in 30 D (Vienna, Albertina)

according to Bax, on the other hand, this portrays a scene of lasciviousness — the severed foot being a symbol of the male organ; for Fraenger it is a scene of polemics against the avarice of the clergy. On the frozen pond are sinners with skates, sexual emblems like the knives (Combe viewed knives, arrows, spears as the symbols of fire in the alchemist's crucible). The letter 'M' incised on the two gigantic knives, which also appears in other works (see 50 D and 51 D), was variously interpreted as the signature of Jan Mandyn (Glück, ZBK, 1895), of Jan Mostaert (Dollmayr, 1898), of a cutler from 'sHertogenbosch whom Bosch placed in hell (Frimmel, 1898; Glück, 1904; Gossart, 1907); as the initial of 'Mundus', a sign of universality, or as referring to the masculine emblem of the knife (Tolnay); as the letter of the zodiacal sign of Scorpio; the symbol of male organs; as connected to the letter of sulphur, the

alchemic male principle (Combe). The huge ears pierced by an arrow are thought to represent unhappiness (Tolnay, pointing out the prototype in a miniature of the *Livre des merveilles du monde*), or the deafness to the Gospel warning 'he that has ears for listening, let him hear' (Combe); again, ears and knife together allude to the male organ, as most critics point out. The key hanging from a stick held by a monk (on the bucrane on the left) was interpreted: as a sexual symbol (Bax), as conjugal desire forbidden to the clergy (Tolnay), as the key of knowledge disregarded by the doctors of the law (Combe). On the right, next to the huge lantern, is portrayed avarice or, according to Baldass, a sacrilegious thief. In the background, the vision of the hell of fire: Fraenger perceived in it the symbology of the four elements (village: earth; infernal river: water; windmill with luminous blades: air; volcano: fire). Bax maintained that the walled-in area represented Purgatory; Combe pointed out the theme of fire as symbolising the union of sexual and heretical natures (punishment of Sodom and Gomorrah). It is not possible to summarise briefly the interpretation of this panel by N. Calas (*Harvard Art Review*, Winter 1967, pp. 15–20). He bases his theory on Augustine's comment-aries on the Psalms of David, and his feud with St Jerome; the attempt to fit Bosch's symbols (in the 'Prodigal Son' and Vagabond paintings (61 and 21 A) also) to the words of Augustine unfortunately seems too contrived and artificial to carry any conviction.

31 ⊞ ✦ 27×40,6

The Garden of Eden
Chicago, Art Institute (R. A. Waller Fund)
A composition generically inspired by *The Garden of Eden* illustrated in *The Triptych of the Garden of Delights* (30), with *The Creation of Eve*, *Original Sin*, and *The Expulsion of Adam and Eve*. Judged authentic by Friedländer (1937), it was displayed as such in the 1936 exhibition at Rotterdam (Boymans Museum), with a dating prior to 1500, and at the 1939 exhibition of Flemish painting (Worcester, Art Museum); in the catalogue of the Chicago Art Institute it is also ascribed to Bosch, and dated to 1509. Tolnay (1937

31

and 1965) rejected the attribution, together with other scholars, and dated the work to about 1520.

32 ⊞ ✦ *250×305* 1504*

The Last Judgement
Lost work, commissioned in 1504 by Philip the Fair (see Outline biography). The various proposed identifications (e.g. with the Vienna Triptych, n. 50 [Hymans, 1884], or with the Munich fragment, n. 48 [Buchner and Tolnay]) are merely hypothetical.

33 ⊞ ✦ 63×43,3 1504-05

A. St John on Patmos
Berlin-Dahlem, Staatliche Museen
According to Baldass, the panel – painted on both sides – should be connected to *St John the Baptist* in the Lázaro Galdiano Museum in Madrid (34), as the right wing of a diptych or triptych; it was bought in 1907 in England, where it was part of the W. Fuller Maitland Collection in London, and it is signed 'Jheronimus (Bosch)' at lower right. Its authenticity has been unanimously acknowledged, from Cohen (1910) onwards; the date is put between 1485–90 (Tolnay) and 1490–1500 approximately (Baldass), and a later period (Combe), on the basis of the affinity of the delicate external grisaille to the landscape of *The Epiphany* of the Prado (62). To our mind, it forms one of the stages in a departure from the highly-charged imagination of *The Delights* (30), a return to a calmer and simpler vision of nature. With a wonderful delicacy of touch, Bosch portrayed the saint on Patmos, at the moment when, according to the Apocalypse, he interrupts the writing on which he was intent, because of the apparition on the mountain of an angel (the wings still display the peculiar vegetable-mineral composition in the manner of *The Delights*) pointed out to him by the Virgin (upper left, against the solar disc). In the right foreground a 'gryllo' recalling the locust-demons of the Apocalypse (IX, 10), with a bespectacled human head, locust wings, paunchy body, scorpion tail (according to Fraenger, this is an anti-clerical allusion), strives to get hold of the fallen ink-pot, but is held at bay by the eagle, the symbol of the Evangelist (according to Redslob (*Gemäldegalerie-Dahlem*, 1964] the bird is instead the saint's tame partridge, as described in *The Golden Legend*).
The theme of the saint recalls the analogous subject in an engraving by Schongauer (Dvořák, 1924). It is one of the first paintings of Saints by Bosch known to us (but see 35), and was undoubtedly preceded by others now lost, as can be inferred from a drawing of the period of early maturity representing *St Anthony*, now at the Kupferstichkabinett in Berlin, on the reverse of *The Concert in the Egg* (7). Fraenger conjectured a revolving painting for the meditations of the sect of the Free Spirit, on one side of which (33 B) were represented the three eras of the world according to Gioacchino da Fiore (the dark background with demons being the symbol of the Kingdom of the Father; the Passion, that of the Son's; the pelican, that of the Holy Ghost's; the saint, depicted on the other side, might be a portrait of Grand Master Almaengien, see Outline Biography, **1496**).

33 ⊞ ✦ 63×43,3 1504-05

B. Story of the Passion of Christ
On the reverse of the preceding painting, a grisaille tondo with scenes from the Passion, against a dark background with demons: it is the theme of the world reflected in the iris of the divine eye (Combe): in the pupil, the pelican feeds its young on its own blood (theme of the redemption through Christ). The episodes, delineated with a delicacy that is reminiscent of the grisailles of *The Triptych of the Temptation of St Anthony* (43), illustrate, starting from the right, the Prayer in the Garden of Olives, the Kiss of Judas and the Seizing of Christ, Christ before Pilate, the Flagellation and the Crowning with Thorns (within domed buildings) and, in the vast background toward the top, the Ascent of Calvary, the Crucifixion, and the Deposition.

34 ⊞ ✦ 48,5×40 1504-05

St John the Baptist in the Wilderness Madrid, Lázaro Galdiano Museum
According to Baldass (1943 and 1959), the panel was cut at top and bottom by a total of some thirteen centi-metres, and originally constituted the left wing of a polyptych together with *St John on Patmos* (33); this last theory was opposed by Tolnay (1937 and 1965), because of the marked differences in treatment and colour discernible in the two works; moreover, the panel in question is painted on only one side. Its authenticity is unquestioned; the dating varies between 1490–1500 (Baldass set it at the period of *St John on Patmos*) and the period of *The Triptych of the Garden of Delights* (30); Combe (1946 and 1957) considered it the link between *St Jerome* in Ghent (39) and *The Delights* (30); Tolnay gave as terms *post* and *ante quem*, *The Altarpiece of the Hermits* (40) and *St Christopher* in Rotterdam (36); at any rate, the last two critics classified it as a work of the late period. In our opinion, it is to be placed at the beginning of the late maturity 1504–05. There are echoes of the phantasmagoric world of *The Delights* (Bax, 1949 interpreted the landscape elements as alluding to the evil reigning over the world), in the jagged tower-rocks (according to Fraenger, 1948, the saint's prison) and the exotic plant of sinister beauty (which Devoghelaere [AV 1936] interpreted as the tree of Jesse). The open fruits from which birds peck the seeds (the fruit in the foreground was somewhat restored) indicate, according to Tolnay, who suggested a dream of the saint, the temptations of the senses which divert the Baptist from his meditation and the symbol of the lamb (the Saviour) to which he points with one finger. More simply, one might suggest that the fruit is meant to be a pomegranate, signifying both the Church and the hope of Redemption. This is one of Bosch's most beautiful paintings, saint and landscape suffused with a golden calm which is undisturbed by the occasional dream-like details, never quite absent in a work by Bosch.

35 ⊞ ✦ 41,25×26,25

The Temptation of St Anthony
New York, Chrysler Collection
The panel, of which the top part is missing and which was probably also cut down at the bottom, was ascribed to Bosch by Tolnay (*Art in America*, 1944; and 1965), who judged it a relatively youthful work, prior to *St John on Patmos* (33) which he dated to 1485–90, divining in the range of the light colours, subordinate to the greys and browns, a precedent to the colour developments of the Lisbon Triptych (43). The figure resembles the youthful drawing at the Kupferstichkabinett in Berlin, on the reverse of *The Concert in the Egg* (7), while

34 Pl. XLI

35

the female nudes recall *The Triptych of the Garden of Delights* (30), as does the motif of the mollusc valve closed on a figure and borne on another's shoulders (a symbol of lust). The house in flames in the background may allude to the saint himself, whose emblem is fire. Opinion here can only be given on the basis of the photograph, but a certain dullness in the figure and in the characterisation of the little monsters, and the presence of both early and mature motifs suggest that it is a workshop product, to be included in the period of the 'ascetic' paintings of saints (40, etc.).

36 ⊞ ✦ 113×71,5 1504-05

St Christopher
Rotterdam, Boymans-van Beuningen Museum
Formerly in the Koenigs Collection in Haarlem, to which it had passed from an Italian

33 A

33 B

36 Pls. XXXVIII–XXXIX

collection (Baldass, 1943 and 1959); it entered the museum in 1940 with the Van Beuningen donation. Signed at lower left: 'Jheronimus bosch' (though the inscription is barely visible). The upper part, now slightly rounded, was initially a semicircle according to Tolnay. Its authenticity is unquestioned; the dating, on the other hand, is controversial: it was stated to be a work of the early maturity by Baldass, who related it to *St John on Patmos* (33), and of late maturity by Tolnay, who placed it after *The Altarpiece of the Hermits* (40); according to Combe, it is datable between *St John on Patmos* and *The Delights* (30). Mosmans believed, without sufficient grounds, that it was a painting executed for the altar of St Christopher in St Anne's chapel

in the cathedral at 'sHertogenbosch, begun in 1498 and dedicated in 1510. The iconography is fairly faithful to the tradition found in engravings and miniatures. The theme is borrowed from a popular version of *The Golden Legend* and from a German elaboration of the fourteenth century (Bax, 1949): the giant Christopher abandons the Devil's service (the dragon pursuing the naked man on the far bank) and bear hunting (on the left) after his conversion by a hermit (to the right, on the bank) and takes up the task of ferrying travellers across a river. One night, Jesus appears to him in the guise of a small child who wants to cross the river. The saint willingly takes him on his shoulders, but finds in midstream that the little child is a burden of immense weight. He has been carrying the whole world on his shoulders (the child is usually shown with a globe in his hand) as he learns when he at last reaches the shore and the child reveals Himself to him. The fish would be a symbol of Lent (of repentance [Tolnay]) or of Christ (Bax). The dove-cot and the pitcher hanging from the tree which serves as a dwelling for hermits who feed on honey (the world of the senses), would allude to temptations (especially to lasciviousness [Bax]) or to the corruption of the clergy (Combe).

37 ▦ ✪ 45×20 🗄 ⠆

The Small St Christopher
Madrid, private collection
First published by Diego Angulo (BM, 1940); Tolnay (1965), supporting the attribution, advanced the theory that the panel was reduced at the sides and, although without first-

37

Autograph drawing of a Temptation of St Anthony referable, as a precedent, to 35 (Berlin, Kupferstichkabinett)

hand knowledge of the work, dated it to the end of the middle period of activity, close to *The Altarpiece of St Liberata* (24). There are affinities between the landscape represented in this *St Christopher* and that of the right wing in the Venetian altarpiece (40); Tolnay referred, moreover, to *The Epiphany* of the Prado (62) for the amplitude of the background with a raised horizon, and to German engravings for the type of the saint. Jesus is represented within a crystal globe (the world), surmounted with the cross and the banner of Resurrection. The appearance of the troop of devils, whose crescent-bearing flag waves at lower left, is an innovation. Despite Tolnay, some doubt may be felt as to the autograph nature of this work.

38 ▦ ✪ 23×36 🗄 ⠆

St Christopher
Winterthur, Reinhart Collection
Published for the first time as one of Bosch's original works by Pfister (1922), then by Friedländer (1927); Tolnay (1965) refuted its authenticity, dating the painting to about

38

1540 on the basis of the brown-monochrome colour range. The quantity of demons and grotesques clearly reflects a 'Boschian' taste; a copper-plate engraving by De Hameel (Amsterdam, Rijksprenten Kabinett) signed

bosche' of the same subject shows the same swarm of figures. These swarms are characteristic of imitators of the Bosch manner.

39 ▦ ✪ 77×59 🗄 ⠆
1505*

St Jerome in Prayer
Ghent, Musée des Beaux-Arts
This work came to the museum in 1908 with the Hulin de Loo purchase; it is unanimously judged authentic and dated to a more or less late period of maturity. Baldass (1917) set it at a moment between youth and maturity, very close to *The Lisbon Triptych* (43); Combe related it instead to the later period of *The Triptych of the Garden of Delights* (30), in view of the crystalline brush-point technique, specifying that it is

probably subsequent to the triptych, given the serenity of the landscape. The saint is not portrayed kneeling (the usual iconography), but lying face downwards, projected forward with the crucifix

between his arms and his hands joined in ecstasy. Jerome's body straddles a little stream which becomes a pool in the foreground. Combe thinks the scene illustrates a passage from Ruysbroeck's *Spiritual Tabernacle*, where an allusion is made to Moses saved from the water (Moses to be identified with the saint) and, symbolically, to the need for casting off the vanities of this world, as mutable as water, to deprive memory of sensory images and the mind of intellectual ones, and to prepare two stone tablets to be carried to Mount Sinai, which signifies the 'escape from temptations'. The stone slabs appear on the rock on the left.

39

40 A   40 B   40 C

The Altarpiece of the Hermits

This triptych (Venice, Palazzo Ducale), portraying St Jerome at the centre, St Anthony and St Giles at the side, was reported to be in its present location by Zanetti (*Della pittura veneziana*, 1771). In 1838 it was at the Kaiserliche Galerie in Vienna, from which it was transferred to the Kunsthistorisches Museum (1893), later to return to Venice in 1919. The two upper corners are a later addition: originally, the panel probably had a rounded or keel-arched ending. Its authenticity is unquestioned (Frimmel, K C, 1896; etc.), and it is placed soon after *The Lisbon Triptych of the Temptation* (43) (Tolnay; Combe) or soon before (Baldass). According to Tolnay, the altarpiece was inspired by Ruysbroeck's *Book of the Supreme Truth*, wherein the hermits Anthony, Jerome and Giles embody the three degrees of the soul's mystical elevation. The painting has been extensively damaged, probably by fire (Friedländer, 1927).

40 ⊞ ⊗ 86,5×29 1505* ▤ ⦂

A. St Anthony

Left wing: St Anthony is portrayed in a nocturnal land-scape with a village on fire in the background, walking toward a pond to draw water with a pitcher. Fire recurs in the representations of the saint as his own attribute, referring to the illness known as 'St Anthony's fire', or to his power of protecting from the flames. All around him teem the evil visions that trouble his ascetic meditations: the principal motif is the nude woman in the water near the hollow tree with a cloak draped over it. A similar episode is represented in the right wing of *The Lisbon Triptych*; in the latter, however, the woman is portrayed together with a man. According to Combe, the group symbolises the heretical-alchemistic coupling, as do the water and fire elements; Baldass thought

the theme to have been inspired, as in the Lisbon work, by a tale from the *Vitae patrum*, in which St Anthony meets the Devil who is in the shape of a queen bathing. Below the woman are a fish-demon pouring wine from a jug, a dwarf-demon reading a missal, a peacock-demon spreading its tail, and a gryllo formed only by a head and legs, with an owl's nest as a head-piece.

40 ⊞ ⊗ 86,5×50 1505* ▤ ⦂

B. St Jerome

In the central panel, signed 'Jheronimus bosch' at lower right, the saint is portrayed not in the traditional manner as a scholar in meditation, but as a penitent ascetic kneeling among

41

the ruins of a pagan building before an ancient throne serving as an altar, on which stands a crucifix. The raised platform, the ruins and the altar with reliefs recall the central compartment of *The Triptych of the Temptation of St Anthony*. The reliefs on the throne, representing Judith beheading Holofernes (symbol of the soul's victory or, according to the *Speculum humanae salvationis*, a prefiguration of the Virgin's victory over the Devil [Tolnay]), and a horseman (chastity and faith) bestriding a unicorn (another Marian symbol [Baldass]) refer to the triumphs of virtue; the pagan idol falling from its pedestal behind the

saint is a common theme: it frequently occurs in the icono-graphy of the Flight into Egypt, where an idol falls down as the Holy Family goes by. The evil elements, on the other hand, include the hut in the back-ground with abnormal vegeta-tion sprouting on the roof, simulating a chimney and a wreath of smoke (Tolnay); the plinth of the idol, bearing the figure of a sun and moon worshipper, and with a cavity containing an owl; and the relief on the lower part of the throne, representing a man diving into a beehive and coating himself with honey (a drawing by Bosch, with a similar motif on one side and a preliminary sketch on the other, is now at the Albertina in Vienna). According to Bax (1949) the scene alludes to carnal love, and Tolnay (1937) noted that this was the interpretation of beehive and of honey found in many moralising works of the Middle Ages, going back to Freidank's *Modesties*; Combe referred to the alchemistic identification of honey and mercury, with the same meaning of sexual union; the birds which come out of the honey-thief's posterior (as they do in the Albertina drawing and in the central and right-hand panels of *The Delights*) are inter-preted by Bax (1949) to mean extravagance. The general atmosphere of decay and dere-liction — dead trees and twigs, crumbling masonry, animal skeleton — in which the saint contemplates the crucifix, may refer to the death of the old pagan world. The state of preser-vation is mediocre: considerable repainting in the landscape and in the sky and retouching in the saint's head and breast.

40 ⊞ ⊗ 86,5×29 1505* ▤ ⦂

C. St Giles

In the right wing, St Giles is shown praying in a cave before a slab from which hangs a scroll; the representation is related to *The Golden Legend*, according to which the scroll, deposited by an angel during Sunday mass, bears the names of those who shall be saved through the saint's intercession

(Tolnay). Still according to the *Legend*, the arrow that strikes the saint's breast was directed by the hunters at his doe, crouching on the ground. The cave setting recalls those on the exterior of the wings of the Anderlecht Triptych (63) (Baldass). In this scene the landscape is calm and fertile but not without one or two jarring motifs: the porcupine, symbol of fleshly desires, the bird feeding on a carcase, the skull. The saint is set apart from these signs of the tribulations of mortal life.

41 ⊞ ⊗ 38,4×24,3 ▤ ⦂

The Temptation of St Anthony

Kansas City, Gallery of Art
The motif of the kneeling saint drawing water from a stream with a pitcher is patterned after the left wing of *The Altarpiece of the Hermits* (40) (Tolnay, 1965). The painting, published by A. H. Barr, jr. (*Fantastic Art, Dada, Surrealism*, 1936) and containing Bosch-like elements, is not considered authentic by Tolnay.

Triptych of the Patience of Job

This work (Bruges, Musée Groeninge) came from the

church at Hoeke, in the province of Bruges, and its authenticity is variously regarded. Friedländer (1937) and Boon (H, 1953) believed it to be a heavily restored original; Hosten and Strubbe (*Stedelijk Museum van Schone Kunsten*, 1938), the work of an imitator; Tolnay the copy of a lost work. The imitation of elements from *St Jerome* in Ghent (39) and from the right wing of *The Altarpiece of the Hermits* (40 C) suggests it might well be a product of the workshop: a proper appraisal is hindered by its poor state of preservation and by repainting. The peculiar arrangement of the wings, which causes the hermits to turn their backs to the centre, has led to the assumption (Bisthoven, 1959) that they might have been imitated from another triptych of which they occupied the exterior, so that the original position was reversed and the figures faced each other. The outer wings of this triptych bear a marbled ornamentation and two coats-of-arms each, of which the one at far left was identified as that of the Vervoort family (Bisthoven). The shape of the shields does not appear to be prior to the second half of the sixteenth century.

42 ⊞ ⊗ 98,1×30,5 ▤ ⦂

A. The Temptation of St Anthony

Left wing: St Anthony inside a cave kneels before an altar with an embroidered cloth (an unusual element in Bosch's iconography). Around him, the usual proliferation of little monsters, among which a child

43 A   43 B

104

inside a gourd, which might be an allusion to the crucible and to the 'child of alchemy'.

42 ▦ ⊛ 98,3×72,1 ▤ ⦙

B. The Tribulations of Job
The central panel portrays Job sitting half naked with a red cloak on his shoulders, in the act of looking away from a group of musicians, one of whom uses an animal skull as a stringed instrument. According to tradition they seek to divert Job, but the hypothesis was also formulated, for this work in particular, that they may have come to taunt him (Denis, RBAH, 1952). On the right, four figures emerge from a tumble-down house, among them a fox dressed as a monk. In the background, Job's house is on fire. The theme of Job was treated by Bosch in a lost work, bought in 1523–4 by Damião de Góis (see Outline Biography and 109). It was a subject often treated by Bosch's follower and imitator, Jan Mandijn.

42 ▦ ⊛ 98,8×30,2 ▤ ⦙

C. St Jerome Penitent
Right wing: St Jerome is praying before a crucifix placed on an altar-throne; the representation appears to be an imitation of that at the centre of *The Altarpiece of the Hermits* (40 B); the rock concretions, the vegetables and the stone slabs on the roof of the structure are derived from *St Jerome* in Ghent (39).

The Triptych of the Temptation of St Anthony

This is the third of Bosch's great triptychs to have come down to us in its entirety (Lisbon, Museu Nacional de Arte Antiga); it relates to the theme of St Anthony tempted, through which the artist could illustrate the thought that obsessed late-medieval society: Satan's rule over the world and the struggles of the soul. According to an undocumented tradition (Bax, 1959; Vieira Santos BMNA, 1958) and letters from the museum's directors (1966), the painting is said to have been bought between 1523 and 1545 by the Portuguese Humanist Damiao de Góis (see Outline Biography **1523–24**); it is therefore difficult to identify it, as was suggested, with one of the three *Temptations* sent to the Escorial in 1574 by Philip II (Justi, 1889), which the king would then have allowed to go to Portugal; we know, on the contrary, that Philip II constantly sought to secure the best Flemish paintings then in Lisbon (Vieira Santos). The first certain document relates that around the middle of the nineteenth century the complete work was in the Real Palácio das Necessidades (Palácio Ayuda), from which King Ferdinando II sent it to Germany to be restored; there, in accordance with the custom of the time, a thick varnish was spread over it, which made its

42 A   42 B   42 C

surface bituminous. This was removed only in 1911, after the painting had been given to the museum by King Manuel. A new restoration was carried out on the occasion of the 1958 Amsterdam Exhibition.

The painting's authenticity is unquestioned (Dollmayr, 1898; etc.); the dating, moved up at one point to the final period (Baldass, 1917), was rightly put back by Tolnay (1937) to the middle period in view of the late-Gothic flamboyant style which was widespread throughout Western Europe at the turn of the fifteenth century. Tolnay suggested the years 1490–1500, Combe 1500 *ca.*, Baldass (1959) 1490–1505, Cuttler (AB, 1957) 1500–05; in our opinion, it is datable to 1505 or soon after, chiefly because

the ideas behind this picture – man assailed by the devil in every sort of disguise, intellectual as well as fleshly – are expressed with a subtlety and depth of understanding that seems to belong to a period after, rather than before, the other great triptychs (21 and 30). The presentation of the saint and Christ as insignificant, scarcely noticeable figures in the midst of Pandemonium is analogous to the late Ghent *Carrying of the Cross* (70) It is signed on the left of the central panel. Over fifteen partial or complete copies of this work are known, as catalogued by Friedländer (who considered excellent the imitation of the central panel, formerly Goudstikker, now in the Rotterdam Museum) with

additions by Tolnay (1965). Four of the copies are signed (Brussels and Bonn, complete copy; Prado, only the two wings, of which the right one is signed; Antwerp Museum, only the central panel); the best is that in Brussels, the only one in the dimensions of the original.

It was conjectured (Bax, 1949) that the triptych was originally destined for a hospital of the Order of the Anthonites where the dreadful 'fire of St Anthony' and the exceedingly widespread venereal diseases were treated: the patients are assumed to have been carried before the painting in the hope of a miraculous recovery worked by the saint who turns to bless while gazing at the viewer. On the other hand, the considerable

43 C Pls. XLIV & XLV A   43 D Pls. XLII–XLIII, XLV B & XLVI B   43 E Pls. XLVI A & XLVII

diffusion of paintings and sculptures on the theme of the Temptation, linked to the mystical idea of the struggle between deception and contemplation, between Satan and Christ does not really require such a hypothesis. The most striking element in the triptych is the extraordinary proliferation of monstrous figures, in a theme that is neither a Hell nor a Last Judgement. A fairly elementary repertory of demons – lions, dragons, serpents, bears, wolves – and of the torments inflicted by them on the saint during his retreat into the Egyptian desert had already appeared in the life written by St Athanasius and was taken up in the *Vitae patrum*, published also in Dutch (Vaderboek, Zwolle 1490): these were, together with *The Golden Legend* (translated at Gouda in 1478), Bosch's primary literary sources (Bax, 1949). This triptych has proved as fertile in modern inter-pretations as *The Garden of Delights*. Bax (1948) would like to see in it a depiction of mortal sins; he points out in particular the brothel (formed by the earth-man on all fours) in the left-hand wing, and the table of gluttony in the right-hand wing. Tolnay sees the saint surrounded by the inventions of the Devil, the worst of which is the Black Mass as he considers the episode on the saint's left in the central panel. Combe's explanation is alchemical. For both these latter writers the figure of the man (central panel) who sits with his back to the spectator, wearing a top-hat is of paramount importance. He is a sorcerer; to his left, there is a circle marked out on the ground, with the signs of the zodiac drawn round its circumference (very faint in the Lisbon picture; clearly visible in the Brussels example). Cuttler, in his 1957 studies of this painting, confined the witchcraft element to the airborne creatures on the right and left-hand wings, and the sinister group in the background of the left wing. He would like to see in the triptych a wide variety of references – to the planets, the four Elements, the Apocalypse, the Deadly Sins, – thus emphasising the nearly universal sway of the Devil, and the uniquely heroic character of St Anthony, who triumphs over the swarming forces of evil.

43 131,5×53 1505 - 06

A. The Seizing of Christ
Painted in grisaille on the exterior of the left wing. This episode and the subsequent one are framed by a sort of pointed-arch 'window' (Baldass, 1959) against a brown ground, perhaps repainted; in lieu of this ground, the Brussels copy has an architectonic frame which probably reflects the original appearance. The composition is divided into an almost bare foreground where St Peter is shown cutting off Malchus' ear, and a middle distance wholly taken up by the soldiery around

Christ. On the left, Judas walks away with his pieces of silver after the kiss of betrayal. On a rock to the right, in the background, appears the chalice, a reference to Christ's agony on the Mount of Olives (Tolnay).

43 131,5×53 1505 - 06

B. St Veronica
Exterior of the right wings, St Veronica offers Christ a veil with which to wipe his face; in the foreground, the good thief makes his confession, while the bad one refuses the comforts of religion: the latter is blindfolded, possibly as a symbol of his moral blindness. Among those following the cross-bearer—as yet another element of human unfeelingness translated into a *genre* note – stands out the figure of the fat burgher leading his two small children to watch the show. The theme of the bad example set for the young was often treated by the humanists of the period (e.g. Erasmus), and Brant dedicated to it a chapter of his *Ship of Fools*.

43 131,5×53 1505 - 06

C. St Anthony's Aerial Torment and his Return to his Retreat
On the interior of the left wing St Anthony is dragged in flight by devils, and supported back to his retreat by his companions, substantially as described in the Life by St Athanasius and in *The Golden Legend*. An engraving (1471–3) by Schongauer (Dvořák, 1924) already displays the diabolic flight of the saint, but with an entirely different expressionist graphism, within a compressed space; Bosch's creation emphasises the contrast between the figure of the saint resisting through prayer, and the whirl of the demons who drag and torment him: a winged toad, a fox holding a scourge, a rat. Nearby are a merman with two fishes and a ship with a naked devil on board, borne by a monster; concerning the latter, references have been made to medieval illustrations of the animals of the Zodiac and of

bestiaries (Bax; Cuttler, AQ, 1957). Below, on the small bridge that spans a frozen torrent, the saint is supported by two Anthonite brethren and by a lay figure, described in the life written by St Athanasius as 'the friend', and sometimes identified as Bosch's self-portrait (Bax, 1949; Baldass, 1959; Tolnay, 1965). A bird-demon, skating on the frozen water, makes his way toward the small bridge with two little monsters and bears in his beak a note with an illegible inscription; Tolnay assumed it to be a 'brief' of indulgence; Combe read in it the word 'fat', alluding to the cleric 'fattened' by his trading in indulgences; Bax saw it as the reflection of a false *protestatio* to mock the Devil, represented in a theatrical work of the sixteenth century. The bird that swallows its new-born chicks as they break out of the egg might be an 'anti-pelican' (the self-sacrificing pelican being a symbol of the Saviour) (Bax; Cuttler, AB, 1957) and the egg an allusion to the alchemist's crucible (Combe). Farther back, the saint's hut (according to Bax and Cuttler, a brothel) is strangely transformed by the forcible entry of a giant who forms a door-way with his hindquarters, holds up the roof and comes through with his head, into which is driven an arrow, symbol of insanity and of self-destruction (Tolnay). A procession of devils – one wearing a mitre and carrying a crosier with a crescent – is moving toward the hut. The critics have tended to apply an erotic interpretation to the various symbols: the giant in the hut would thus represent onanism (Tolnay); the little monster playing the bagpipe, sodomy (Bax); the animals in flight sexual temptation (Bax); the fish-monster on the left, with a scorpion's tail, swallowing another fish and bearing a phallic symbol on his back, perverse lust (Tolnay), envy (Cuttler), hypocrisy (Bax). Puyvelde (1962) denied all this symbolism, and judged the demons to be merely fantastic inventions by Bosch: the work's

title to mean not 'temptations', but 'torments', that is to say, the Devil's revenge for the saint's unshakeable faith.

43 131,5×119 1505 - 06

D. The Temptation of St Anthony
Central panel, signed 'Jheronimus bosch' at lower left; at the centre of a complex scene, the kneeling St Anthony turns toward the viewer with his hand raised in blessing (Bax, 1949), or drawing attention to the chapel in the background, where Christ appears, illuminated by a divine ray, and points out the crucifix. The letter 'T', discernible on the right sleeve of the saint's habit, recalls the coat-of-arms of the Anthonites bearing the emblem of the crutch. All around seethes the diabolic whirl, interpreted (Tolnay, 1937 and 1965; Castelli, 1952; Baldass, 1959) as the witches' Sabbath, or (Bax, 1949) as the feast of the temptations, with personifications of the various sins, which were originally more numerous: the radiograph taken in 1944 has, in fact, revealed the existence of figures later eliminated by Bosch, among which one holding a looking-glass (Pride ?) in the group behind the saint (Tolnay). The group on the saint's left is thought by Tolnay and Baldass to be participating in the Black Mass. Referring to the woman offering a cup to the swine-man, Fraenger referred to Deuteronomy XXXII. 'Their wine is the poison of dragons and the cruel venom of asps'. The negress to the left holds up a dish on which stands a toad bearing an egg; toad and egg are interpreted as either, magic and a parody of the Host, or, alchemically, sulphur and the crucible (Combe). Behind the saint, an elegant lady hands a bowl to a nun, beside whom sits a 'gryllo'. Brion (1938) thought it a self-portrait. Below this group a magician with a top-hat and wand crouches near a low wall: he is orchestrator of all the horrific apparitions according to Tolnay, 1937 and 1965 and

Combe, 1946; next to him, on a cloth, a severed foot (an alchemistic or erotic symbol); it appears in *The Musical Hell* (30 D). Cuttler interpreted the central group in an astrological key, with reference to the seven deadly sins and to the planets, basing himself on Florentine engravings of 1460, representing the children of the planets. Bax (1949) believed the scene inspired by an episode from the *Vitae patrum* (not found in St Athanasius), where a spell is cast by a

46

beautiful queen (the Devil) who meets St Anthony near a river and takes him to her castle, where she offers a banquet of false charity to the poor and the sick. To the right, on the same level as the sorcerer, a diabolical priestly figure, whose robe is torn to show the skeleton and rotten entrails beneath, reads from a book: perhaps he officiates at the Mass (Tolnay), or perhaps he has got hold of the saint's Bible (Cuttler). Around the main scene are distributed four demonic groups. The troop drawing near on the left, with fierce monsters and a woman wearing a helmet in the shape of a hollow tree, personifies blood-thirsty violence (Bax; Baldass). The enigmatic group in the water on the right is interpreted as a diabolic parody of the Flight into Egypt and of the Adoration of the Magi (Bax; Cuttler), or as an alchemistic representation (Combe): the woman riding a rat (false doctrines), holds in her arms the 'child of alchemy'; the winged hunter with a head in the shape of a thistle flower (in St Bonaventura the thistle is the temptation that stimulates the dreams of the lazy man [Combe]), mounts a horse with a pitcher-shaped belly (Satan's pitcher, but also 'the horse's belly' a stage in the 'cooking' of mercury). From a gourd on the left (another alchemistic crucible, 'gourd of the sage') emerge some demons, one of which desecrates the angelic harp. The fourth diabolic group is formed by the boat-fishes: the sail of one displays a ray (a scaleless fish, therefore impure); in the other, monkey-like demons attend to the Devil's fishing. Strange bas-reliefs (according to Tolnay, they are projections of the saint's visions) ornament the cylindrical tower: the return of the sons of Hebron with the vine of the promised land (a prefiguration of the baptism of

44

45

Copies of the Temptation of St Anthony *(47); (left) Amsterdam, Rijksmuseum and (right) Madrid, Prado*

Christ, according to the *Biblia pauperum* [Baldass; Tolnay]) ; the sacrifice of a swan to a pagan god; the dispersal of the worshippers of the golden calf and Moses being entrusted with the tables of the law (prefiguration of the descent of the Holy Ghost). Behind, a covered bridge surmounts a pool with nude bathers, and leads to an egg-shaped tower: interpreted by Bax as a brothel; by Combe, as an alchemic symbol.

43 131,5 × 53 / 1505 - 06

E. The Meditation of St Anthony
Interior of the right wing: the saint isolates himself, through meditation, from the snares that surround him. The theme of the naked woman in the hollow tree, derived from the tale by St Athanasius, recalls the left wing of *The Altarpiece of the Hermits* (40 A); a toad-demon holds the draperies open, and offers a cup to an old woman with a diabolic nimbus, who pours him a drink (Temptation of the illicit creation of the homunculus [Castelli, 1952]). Bax (1949), going back to the source of the *Vitae patrum*, explained the scene as the meeting of the saint with the queen bathing in the river; in the background, the wondrous city to which she leads the saint. The other temptation concerns gluttony (Bax, 1949; Cuttler, 1957): the magic table supported by nude demons, on which are a loaf of bread and a jug with a pig's trotter stuck in it, an evil symbol. Other perturbing elements are the 'gryllo' formed by a huge belly with a knife in its navel, topped by a red hood that leaves the ear uncovered (for Castelli, a symbol of the 'listening' to the lowest stimuli) and the old man-child on the right in the baby-walker (according to Combe, the homunculus or Child of Alchemy); according to Cuttler he is the Fool, characterised as a child. In the sky fly two demons, man and woman, astride a big fish. Cuttler derives these figures from a miniature in a tract against witchcraft, now in the Bibliothèque Royale, Brussels (Ms. 11209). At the back, a city with oriental-looking towers, surrounded with a moat where a nude man fights a dragon, while a crowd looks on from the terrace.

44 150 × 94 / 1505 - 07

The Ascent of Calvary
Madrid, Royal Palace
Formerly in the Escorial, where Philip II sent it with other paintings in 1574 (see Outline Biography). Its authenticity is unanimously acknowledged (Justi, 1889; etc.); the dating is set at late maturity by Tolnay and Baldass, on the basis of the solidity and weight of the figures, close to those of *The Crowning with Thorns* at the Escorial (58) and of *The Epiphany* of the Prado (62 C). Combe suggested a time between the youthful and the early-mature periods, drawing it nearer to the date of *The Ascent of Calvary* in Vienna (19 A). Note that, in both pose and expression, the Christ rather resembles the St Anthony of *The Lisbon Triptych* (43 D). The compositional scheme consitutes an intermediate stage between the Vienna painting, with the figures on two levels, and the late *Christ Bearing the Cross* in Ghent (70), reduced merely to heads around the central fulcrum of the cross. As in the drawing at the Crocker Art Gallery in Sacramento, representing *The Ascent of Calvary* in the foreground and, in the background, the same theme as the Philadelphia *Ecce Homo* (27), the sorrowing group of Mary and John appears on the right in the landscape; Jerusalem with its towers closes the horizon. The palette is quite sober, almost monochromatic, the shapes delineated with remarkable breadth: Carel van Mander (1604) recalled that he had seen in Amsterdam a *Christ Bearing the Cross* (102)

where Bosch had applied more 'grandeur' than usual (Baldass), from which it can be inferred that the style of this painting was not an isolated case.

45 88 × 72

The Temptation of St Anthony Madrid, Prado
Made known by G. van Camp (RBAH, 1955), exhibited in Bruges in 1958 and in Brussels in 1963. Given to the Prado in 1964 by Mrs van Buuren from whose collection in Brussels it came. It is thought that it might originally have been one of the three *Temptations* belonging to Philip II, mentioned among the works sent to the Escorial in 1574 (Justi, 1889). It was connected, possibly as part of a same triptych, to the two lateral panels of the Prado, formerly at the Escorial, which are copies of the wings of *The Lisbon Triptych* (43). Van Camp made comparisons with the left wing of the *Altarpiece of the Hermits* (40) and noted that the design of one of the monsters (the one on the left, with wheels) is to be found on an autograph sheet at the Ashmolean Museum in Oxford, and was not utilised in other known works by Bosch. We have no first-hand knowledge of the painting, but we do not feel that the somewhat casual assemblage of elements from Bosch's repertory – 'grylli', monsters, nude women in the water, infernal vision in the background – favours authenticity.

46 26 × 19,3

The Temptation of St Anthony Nashville

(Canada), Private collection
Formerly in Haarlem, Gutman Collection
This panel was maintained as authentic by Friedländer (1927) who indicated its provenance from Spain – it was displayed at the Bosch exhibition of the Boymans Museum in Rotterdam (1936). Tolnay (1965) denied its authenticity, because of the thin strokes of the brushwork and of the palette dominated by yellows and blues. The motifs – woman in the water, 'gryllo' with a monk's hood, birds coming out of the posterior of the man with his foot in the jug, boat-toad – are usual in Bosch's workshop, as is the motif of the house attacked by demons with ladders. The group of the duck with its ducklings also appears in the Vienna *Judgement* (59 D).

47 ——

The Temptation of St Anthony Half-length
Two copies of a lost work, datable (Combe, 1946 and 1957) considerably earlier than *The Lisbon Triptych* (43). One (63 × 82, see Bosch Cat. 1967, n. 6), is now at the Rijksmuseum in Amsterdam, originally from the Schmidt-Degener Collection in the same city (Friedländer, 1927); it bears the inscription 'Jheronimus bosch' at lower right and was judged by Glück (JKS, 1935) to be a copy of the *Temptation* which, in 1516, was the property of Margaret of Austria (see Outline Biography and 35). The other copy is at the Prado in Madrid (Brans, GBA, 1952) and was bought in 1838, at the time of the expropriations of the convents; it measures 70 × 100 cm. and seems of slightly higher quality, although it is also considered as a copy of the early sixteenth century. The physiognomy of the saint closely resembles that of the Lisbon painting, to which are also related the flying fish, the nude woman, the hut completed by a human element: here, the head of an old woman with a dove-cote for a head-piece. Other elements, such as the projecting sign of the swan, appear in *The Prodigal Son* in Rotterdam (61); Brans inferred from this that it is not a

copy, but an imitation in the manner of Bosch. Bax considers the house to represent a brothel, an echo of the house in *The Prodigal Son*.

48 60 × 114 / 1506 - 08

The Last Judgement
Munich, Alte Pinakothek
The fragment passed from the Staatliche Galerie (1822) to the Germanisches Nationalmuseum in Nuremberg (1822–1920), then to the store-rooms of the Munich picture-gallery, where it was re-discovered by Buchner (MJ, 1934–6) who proposed that it be identified as the *Judgement* commissioned in 1504 by Philip the Fair (see Outline Biography) suggesting that the original width was approximately two and a half metres. It was restored in 1935. Its authenticity is not questioned; the dating, leaving aside Buchner's hypothetical identification, is set at the late period, after *The Delights* (30). This panel was probably the lower right-hand corner of the original panel: in the lower left corner appears a train, believed to be the edge of the cloak worn by St Michael, the weigher of souls (Baldass). The subject is the Resurrection of the Dead: Models for two of the figures (the demon with a scorpion's tail, seen from the back on the right, and the 'gryllo' lying down on the ground, formed by a hooded head and very long legs) are to be seen on a sheet of sketches at the Ashmolean Museum in Oxford.

48

49

49 59 × 51

The Temptation of St Anthony 'sHertogenbosch, Fr. van Lanschot Collection
Made known by Friedländer (1927) when it was on the Munich art market; it passed to the collection of Count Dohna-Schlodien in Silesia, then to the Thyssen Collection in Lugano, and from there to 'sHertogenbosch (1965). Tolnay (1965) does not consider it authentic; rather, a composition made up from studies of monsters, and elements from the paintings. The Ashmolean drawing could be a source.

107

The Triptych of the Last Judgement
Vienna, Akademie der Bildenden Künste

The triptych represents at the centre the Last Judgement and the punishments of the damned, at the sides Original Sin and Hell, on the outside St James of Compostela and St Bavon. It was originally in the picture-gallery of the Archduke Leopold Wilhelm of Austria and is listed as an authentic work by Bosch in the 1659 inventory. At the end of the eighteenth century it was in the collection of Count Lamberg-Spritzenstein, from which it came to its present location as part of a bequest. In the seventeenth and eighteenth centuries it was subjected to several repaintings, now partly removed. Its authenticity was denied by Dollmayr (1898) who ascribed it to 'Master M' (perhaps Jan Mostaert), Glück (1904), Tolnay (1937 and 1965), Combe (1946 and 1957) and Delevoy (1960). Glück held it to be a reduced copy of the *Last Judgement* commissioned in 1504 by Philip the Fair (see Outline Biography), brother of Margaret – the latter was regent of the Netherlands – and son-in-law of Isabel of Castille, which would explain the presence of James of Compostela and St Bavon, patron saints of Spain and of Flanders respectively. Its authenticity was upheld by Hymans (1884), who identified it as the painting executed for Philip the Fair, disregarding the difference in dimensions with respect to the latter work; by Friedländer (1921 and 1927); by the authors of the catalogues of the Vienna Academy (Eigenberger, 1927; Münz, 1957; Poch-Kalous, 1961); by Baldass (who considered it a copy in 1917, before the restorations); and by Puyvelde (1962). These scholars based their judgement on the results of the cleanings which revealed many corrections and second thoughts – unlikely in a copyist – and on the quality of the exterior of the wings which are, however, in the opinion of the present writer, far removed from the vibrant brushwork of Bosch's grisailles. The painting so impressed Cranach that he made a copy of it in the same dimensions, during his visit to Flanders; it is now preserved in the Berlin Museum. The dating varies between the youthful period (Puyvelde) and the beginning of the late period (Baldass) whose view is based on the analogy of the external figures with *The Prodigal Son* in Rotterdam (61), of the more complex vision of the *Hell*, of the spatial conception of the *Garden of Eden*, similar to the *Epiphany* of the Prado (62); it is generally set at the mature period (by Tolnay, after the Lisbon *Temptation*; by Combe and Poch-Kalous, immediately before it). To our mind, this is a workshop product of high quality, utilising, often rather limply, elements derived from *The Delights* (Christ as the creator of Eve) and from *The Lisbon Triptych* (the severed foot on the cloth): and therefore subsequent to either of these works; the monogram 'M' on the chipped knife (from *The Delights*) is a recurrent motif in Bosch's workshop (see the Bruges complex, 51). The colours do not glow, the metallic light-blues and the orange-reds are all foreign to Bosch; unity is lacking between the centre and the wings, as well as a good balance of all the elements.

50 ⊞ ◉ 167,7×60 ▤ ⦂

A. St James of Compostela
Exterior of the left wing, painted in grisaille; it bears a full-length portrayal of St James walking. It is the usual theme of the journey through the evil world (Baldass), alluded to by the group of the blind man and of the paralytic in the background on the left, and by the assault on the right. The outline of the man hanged from the tree on the hilltop recalls *The Golden Legend*, according to which the saint revived a man hanged in punishment of a crime which he had not committed. The painting, restored in 1957, is now said (Baldass) to reveal the pictorial quality of *The Prodigal Son* in Rotterdam (61). Glück, on the other hand, inferred from the bare shield in the lower part that this is a copy (intended for another patron), of the *Judgement* executed for Philip the Fair.

50 ⊞ ◉ 167,7×60 ▤ ⦂

B. St Bavon
Exterior of the right wing, painted in grisaille, portraying St Bavon, patron saint of Flanders, as a young knight with a falcon on his left wrist, distributing his money to the poor before retiring into a monastery (Bax, 1949; Baldass, 1959). The motifs of the mummified foot and of the bowl balanced on the infant's head also appear, with a sinister meaning, in the central panel of *The Lisbon Triptych* (Combe, 1946 and 1957) and, the foot alone, in the Musical Hell of *The Delights*. But Puyvelde (1962) noted that the foot was the usual exhibition of cripples, intended to arouse compassion. As for the old woman seen in profile with the child on her shoulders, Baldass called attention to a drawing attributed to Bosch, now in a private collection in San Francisco. The paint was restored in 1957. Concerning the empty shield and opinions on the authenticity of the work, see 50 A.

50 ⊞ ◉ 167,7×60 ▤ ⦂

C. Original Sin
Interior of the left wing, illustrating, from the bottom upwards, the Creation of Eve, Original Sin, the Expulsion from the Garden of Eden, within a continuous landscape crowned by the apparition of God the Father among the clouds, and by the Fall of the rebel angels transformed into insects. The themes recall the left compartment of *The Triptych of the Hay Wain* (21), though here they are distributed in a reversed sequence and treated with stiffness both in the landscape and in the figures; the figure of Christ creating Eve seems particularly vacuous, so that it cannot be taken to be a preliminary stage for the same motif in *The Delights*, as claimed by Baldass (1959). At any rate, the repaintings, not yet removed, seriously hamper a stylistic appraisal. As concerns one of the details – the fox watching a fowl – Combe drew attention to the reverse of a drawing bearing Bosch's apocryphal signature, preserved in the Rotterdam Museum.

50 ⊞ ◉ 163,7×127 ▤ ⦂

D. The Last Judgement
The central panel was cut down by a few centimetres in its upper part; it was restored in 1927. It represents the Judgement at the top, in accordance with the description in Revelation with Christ the Judge between the Virgin Mary and St John, apostles and angels; and with some barely suggested details of the ascent of the redeemed souls (on the left among the clouds). Below is the punishment of the damned, the actual core of the painting, of which it takes up three quarters, continuing in the right wing with the Hell. The setting of the two groups of episodes is also similar: those in the foreground are depicted in a strong light that grows gradually fainter until it dies out into a distant landscape burnt with fires. The 1659 inventory specifies that the panel represents the Judgement and Hell with the punishment of the seven deadly sins (Baldass, 1959): but, in addition to these, many other faults are punished, so that the composition appears as a true kaleidoscope of torments, with complicated machines and contrivances handled by a motley crowd of demons.

As in the case of *The Seven Deadly Sins* in the Prado (2), to which correspond the punishments for gluttony, sloth, lust and avarice, the literary sources are *The Vision of Tondalus* (see Outline Biography, **1482**) and the *Calendrier des bergers* (1493). The former provided the infernal valleys, the bridge bristling with nails, the slothful pounded at by the devils on the anvil, the homicides cooked over a slow fire in a frying-pan, the misers turned on a spit. The *Calendrier* specified the punishment of the glutton, made to sit at a table and forced to swallow a filthy drink; that of the wrathful (Tolnay), hung from butcher's hooks, and of the proud, broken on the wheel. The nude woman wreathed with coiled serpents and followed by a demon (in his turn impersonating a maid-servant) is a symbol of lust (Bax, 1949; Baldass, 1959), in connection with which Combe (1946, 1957) referred to the nude of *The Love Potion* at the Leipzig Museum, a Rhenish work of the latter half of the sixteenth century. The motif of the bad assaulted by demons is also to be found in *The Seven Deadly Sins* of the Prado. According to Baldass, wrath is illustrated in the central group, with the knight in armour and the devil wounding a sinner. A great number of sins are punished by piercing the damned with swords, knives, spits, arrows. Bax (1956) attributed an erotic meaning to many of these scenes: the adulterer, tried and executed, is said to appear on the bridge; the millstones to be the male and female emblems; the naked fat man in the centre foreground with a wound in his stomach, to represent lewdness; the motif of the plucked partridge with its young was taken up by Bruegel in his engraving of Lust. Combe, in his turn, thought the chipped knife with the incised 'M' to be a sexual symbol linked to the zodiacal sign of Scorpio; Tolnay also interpreted it as a male symbol countersigned by the initial of *Mundus*, while others viewed it as the mark of a cutler, or the signature of a painter (see 30 D). Concerning the three men impaled to the right of the bridge, Combe referred to German woodcuts and paintings of the fifteenth century, inspired by the atrocious impalement of *The Martyrdom of the Ten Thousand Knights*. Bosch probably contributed to the lower central part; on the whole, these horror scenes lack conviction.

50 A

50 B

50 ⊞ ⊕ 167,7×60 ▤ ⦂

E. Hell

Interior of the right wing, representing Satan enthroned and the souls of the damned being led toward him; he sits below a tower with a porticoed entrance framed by a frieze of toads. Bax (1956) perceived in this episode of infernal judgement reminiscences of the contemporary theatre, and explained almost all the motifs as punishments of carnal sin in its various forms. To Satan's left is the group of lust (Baldass, 1959); a nude woman with musician demons, among whom one with the bagpipe, a sexual symbol, and above them a demon throwing a harp from the window. Farther back, a nude damned soul tormented by toads and serpents and turned into a human target (which Bax interpreted as a sexual allusion). The oven-shaped structure may have been inspired by the *Vision of Tondalus* (Tolnay), from which were also borrowed the figures of giants that people the middle part of the painting, looming against the fiery landscape: in these images Tolnay saw a prefiguration of the vision of Hell in *The Triptych of the Garden of Delights*. The panel is still covered with eighteenth-century repaintings.

The Triptych of the Last Judgement
Bruges

Formerly in the E. Gravet Collection and later in the Seligman Collection in Paris; later bought by A. Beernaert (1907) who donated it to the city of Bruges (L. Ninane, *Le siècle de Bruegel*, 1963), where it is still located (Musée Groeninge). The upper part is arched. It was restored in 1936, and a further cleaning in 1959 revealed that the exterior of the shutters painted in grisaille represented a *Crowning with Thorns* of high quality, which recently induced Pauwels (*Catalogue of the Groeninge Museum*, 1960) to consider the triptych an authentic work, followed by Tolnay (1965) who took up Friedländer's old hypothesis (1927), although in 1937 he had expressed a negative opinion. The rest of the

critics (writing before the recent cleaning) consider it a 'pastiche' of Bosch-like elements (Combe, 1946; Bober *Speculum*, 1952) executed by an imitator (Baldass, 1943) or in the workshop, though it is of good quality (Held, CAJ, 1952; Bisthoven, *Corpus*, 1959). Various elements seem derived from *The Seven Deadly Sins* (2). *The Hay Wain* (21 C) and *The Delights* (30), that is to say from works of the most diverse periods; but new themes also appear, which may have stemmed directly from Bosch. Nevertheless, a negative impression is produced by a certain mechanical repetition of the motifs (for instance, the complex of ladders) and the odd empty spots in the fabric of the composition.

51 ⊞ ⊕ 199×57,3 ▤ ⦂

A–B. The Crowning with Thorns

The exterior of the wings forms a single composition, painted in grisaille (regrettably, in a very poor state of preservation), portraying, on the left, Christ crowned with thorns, and a group of soldiers on the right.

51 ⊞ ⊕ 99,5×28,3 ▤ ⦂

C. The Elect

Interior of the left wing, representing the Elect arriving in Heaven in a vessel; at the back, the fountain of life, less elaborate than that of *The Delights*. Heaven is represented here as an earthly paradise.

51 ⊞ ⊕ 99×60,3 ▤ ⦂

D. The Last Judgement

Central panel, bearing at lower right the inscription 'jheronimus bosch', and representing the Last Judgement, but in fact almost completely taken up by infernal punishments, as in the Vienna *Judgement* (50). Above, Christ within a tondo with his feet on the globe, surrounded by trumpet-blowing angels, apostles and saints: the figures of the Virgin and St John as intercessors are lacking. In the middle and lower zones reappear some motifs from *The Delights* (the musical

hell, the platform with the bagpipe, the knife with the 'M'), from the Vienna *Judgement* (the damned soul on a spit, the barrel out of which flows a foul liquid), together with other new ones. Particularly effective are the portrayals of the 'grylli', notably those in the foreground in which we divine an autograph intervention.

51 ⊞ ⊕ 99,5×28,5 ▤ ⦂

E. The Damned

Interior of the right wing, representing the gates of hell, a group of demons with ladders assailing the walls, and a man transfixed by a sword, who rides an ox and holds a chalice (imitated from Hell in *The Triptych of the Hay Wain*), pulling a wheeled platform that bears various damned souls inside a cauldron.

50 C

50 D Pls. XLVIII–IL

50 E

51 A   51 B   51 C   51 D   51 E

52 ⊞ ⊗ 83,5×93,5 ▤ ⋮

The Last Judgement
Baytown (U.S.A.), Princess
Kadjar Collection
This work came from the
E. Pacully Collection in Paris,
and bears at lower left the
inscription 'Jheronimus bosch'.
It appears to be an imitation,
though with variants from
engravings on the same theme,
executed by Allaert de Hameel
and Hieronymous Cook
after a prototype by Bosch.
It is judged an imitation or
workshop copy by Friedländer

53 ⊞ ⊗ —— ▤ ⋮

The Vision of Tondalus
Wood, 54 × 72 cm. Madrid,
Museo Lázaro Galdiano
Tondalus (See Outline
Biography **1484**) is sitting at the
lower left of the picture and
dreaming his dream under the
inspiration of the angel beside
him. The vision is of a hell which
bears many Boschian features,
e.g. the occupant of the bed
(upper right) surrounded by
monsters (see 2 and 13 B);
the Hell scene of the Madrid
table-top; the hanged man

Allaert de Hameel, The Last Judgement, *engraved copy
of a lost original by Bosch*

white and not blue (Tolnay).
In the background on the
right, is the annunciation to the
shepherds; on the left, two
shepherds are cooking over a
fire. Fraenger (1950) believed
St Joseph to be a portrait of
Jacob de Almaengien (see
Outline Biography, **1496**). Two
other copies of the work, with
variants, are in the Brussels
Museum and in a Dutch private
collection (Tolnay).

55 ⊞ ⊗ —— ▤ ⋮

The Crowning with Thorns
Work known through a good

52
(1927), an excellent copy by
Tolnay (1965); according to
Combe (1946 and 1957) it is a
'pastiche' derived, in addition to
the above-mentioned engraving,
from *The Last Judgement* in
Vienna (50), with elements from
The Lisbon Triptych (43) — the
nude woman in the water, the
hollow gourd in the foreground
— and from Hell in *The Triptych
of the Hay Wain* (21), such as
the trumpeter demon on the
gourd.

against the distant blaze (Venice
Last Judgement 26; *Hay Wain*,
21 D); the glutton forced to
drink (Vienna *Judgement* 50
D); the horrible advances of a
nun-like creature (Hell of *The
Delights* 30 D); creature blowing
its trumpet-nose (frequent
motif, e.g. devil on top of *Hay
Wain* (21 C), Vienna *Judgement*
(50 D) and so on. The misers in
the vat full of coins are described in the *Visio Tungdali*.
These words are, by the way,
written under the figure of the
sleeping visionary.

54 ⊞ ⊗ 66×43 ▤ ⋮

**The Adoration of the
Child**
Cologne, Wallraf-Richartz
Museum

54

One of the most imaginative
features of the picture is the
great mask whose hollow eyes
stare at the spectator: out of his
vegetable ears grow trees, and
on his crown lies a soul being
tormented by a monster, an owl
and a monkey. The mask echoes
the great white face of Hell of
The Delights (30 D). Bax
(1948), Castelli (1952) and
Tolnay (1965) have considered
this picture; it is relegated by
them to Bosch's School.

The authenticity of this work
was upheld by Justi (1889)
and Puyvelde (1962), who
related it to the Flemish Primitives, considering it a youthful
work. Tolnay (1965), considered as original only the
principal figures, on the basis of
the drawing technique which
shows through under the colour
for which he referred to *The
Crowning with Thorns* in
London (57). Friedländer
(1927) doubted that the work
could be an original; and it was
considered a copy of a lost work
from the late mature period by
Combe (1946 and 1957), who
judged it to be slightly subsequent to *The Ascent of
Calvary* in Madrid (44), and by
Baldass (1943 and 1959) who,
in 1917, had held it to be the
copy of a late work; Delevoy
(1960) also denied its
authenticity. The expanded
style of the figures recalls the
period of late maturity, and the
Virgin's face displays analogies
to *The Epiphany* of the Prado
(62); but the stiff rendering, the
mechanical smile of the on-
looker behind the curtain, the
style of the animals, bear out the
theory that it is a copy. The
colours, however, are delicate.
Contrary to traditional iconography, the Virgin's mantle is

*Copy of 55 (Berne,
Kunstmuseum)*

*Copy of 55, with variants
compared to the one in Berne
(Antwerp, Musée Royal des
Beaux-Arts)*

copy, now at the Kunstmuseum in Berne (oils on panel, 82 × 60 cm.; it came in 1846 from the Hallwyl Collection); another one, identical except for variants in the faces and in the colours, belongs to the Philadelphia Museum (65 × 57 cm.; from the Paterson Collection in London), and a third, also of high quality, with the figure of a donor on the left, to the Antwerp Museum (Combe, 1946 and 1957) (83 × 68 cm.; from the Kaufmann Collection in Berlin, 1895). The lost original is chronologically set

56

57 Pls. L–LII

(Combe) before the Madrid *Ascent of Calvary* (44) and, at any rate, before *The Crowning with Thorns* in London (57) (Baldass, 1943; Tolnay, 1937 and 1965). Four other copies of the painting were catalogued by Friedländer (1927) and yet another is in a Milanese collection (A.F., 1955). The pose of the soldier resting his foot on the parapet is repeated in the *Crowning* now at the Escorial (58); the head is also similar.

56  28 × 20

Head of a Crossbowman
Madrid, Prado
A repetition with variants (cross on the beret, crossbow rest) of the head of the soldier pounding the crown of thorns into Christ's head in the Antwerp copy of the *Crowning* (55). The Prado catalogue (1963) lists it among the authentic works.

57 73 × 59 1508-09

The Crowning with Thorns
London, National Gallery
This was in the Hollingwood Collection at Colworth and in the Magniac sale in London (1892), and was then in Italy until 1934. Its authenticity is unanimously acknowledged

(except for doubts expressed by Conway [1921]); it was dated to the mature period (Tolnay, 1937 and 1965; Combe, 1946 and 1957), after the Madrid *Ascent of Calvary* (41); or to the transition from maturity to old age (Baldass, 1943 and 1959) on the basis of an affinity to *The Epiphany* of the Prado (62); according to Davies (Catalogue, 1955²), this is a youthful work. It is one of the first Passions with large busts grouped at the back (according to Baldass, Tolnay and Combe, it was preceded by the lost original of the Antwerp *Crowning* [55]). The calm nobleness (which Combe related to the lost original of the Cologne *Adoration* [54]), the breadth of the modelling, the physiognomical types, reverse a fully mature work of art. Concerning the iconography, Baldass (1947) referred to paintings of the Passion by the German Frueauf (the staff, the armour); whereas Combe drew attention to the enigmatic nature of such elements as the arrow through the hat, a motif typical of Bosch, the crescent, the collar bristling with nails. It has been suggested that the four heads surrounding Christ represent the four temperaments: sanguine and choleric (below), phlegmatic and melancholy (above). The state of preservation is not perfect; some parts were repainted and infra-red rays revealed variants and 'second thoughts' (Davies).

58 165 × 195 1510*

The Crowning with Thorns
Escorial, Monastery of San Lorenzo

58

Usually – though wrongly – identified as one of the paintings sent to the Escorial by Philip II in 1574 (Justi, 1889); this is, in effect, the painting accurately described in the dispatch to the monastery of San Lorenzo carried out on 8 July 1593 (Zarco Cuevas, 1930). Its authenticity is unquestioned; it was erroneously dated to the youthful period by Lafond (1914), Demonts (1919) and Escherich (ZK, 1940), the latter claiming it to be a satire against Austrian rule over Brabant, after the

59 Pl. LIII

death of Charles II the Bold (1477). The rest of the critics consider it a rather late work in view of the accomplished technique, the penetrating study of physiognomies and the plasticity of the rendering. According to Combe (1946 and 1957), it is not far removed from *The Delights* (30); according to Baldass (1917), it is Bosch's last work, where Rogier van der Weyden's influence reached its apex (1943), and is, at any rate, the last version of the theme (1959); according to Tolnay (1937 and 1965), it is not later than 1511, in view of his claim that Christ's face is imitated from Matsys' *Deposition* in Antwerp (1511). It is considered as the remnant of a polyptych (Justi; Friedländer, 1927; Baldass) because of the gold used for the ground and by the comparision with the complex in the Valencia Museum (ascribed by

Dollmayr (1898) to Master M'); the latter work bears at the centre the signed copy of the present *Crowning* and, at the sides, within ovals, the Seizing of Christ and the Flagellation. The symbolism of the tondo as the world is accentuated by the grisaille ground illustrating the Battle and Fall of the Rebel Angels (Tolnay; Combe). The pose of the soldier resting his foot on the parapet was borrowed from the lost original of the paintings in Berne and Philadelphia (55); the soldier's brooch, with the Austrian two-

60

headed eagle, and the glass globe depicting Moses receiving the tables of the Law – held by the figure on the left (according to Tolnay Pilate; to Escherich, Louis XI; to Baldass, a Hebrew official) – are said to symbolise the contrast between temporal and spiritual power (Baldass). The figure with the curly hair is said to be a portrait (of Galeazzo Maria Sforza or the Chancellor Simonetta, according to Escherich; a self-portrait, according to Mosmans [1947]) the hired ruffians have animal-like features: Tolnay mentioned – without, however, inferring from this any direct connection – Leonardo's studies of human heads resembling animals. In addition to the one in Valencia, other copies and variants are at the Rijksmuseum in Amsterdam, at the Lázaro Galdiano Museum in Madrid, at the Museo Provincial in Segovia, and one was on the London art market in 1911 (Friedländer).

59  70 × 51 1510*

The Temptation of St Anthony
Madrid, Prado
Although it came from the Escorial, this work is not identified in the old inventories (nonetheless, Puyvelde [1952] held it to be one of the *Temptations* sent to the royal palace in 1574 [see Outline Biography]). It bears at the top the marks of a semicircular frame, perhaps not the original one (Tolnay maintained that the corners reveal Bosch's hand; Baldass that they were repainted). The authenticity is unquestioned (Cohen, 1910; etc., up to Baldass, 1959, and Tolnay, 1965). The dating, set by Friedländer at 1490, was referred by all the other scholars to the final period (according to Combe, this was the artist's last work, in view of the analogies with *The Epiphany* of the Prado (62), first noted by Baldass 1917 who also mentioned affinities with Geertgen tot sin Jans). The saint, wrapped in purest contemplation, untroubled by the rather harmless deviltries that surround him, recalls Ruysbroeck's mystical writings, such as *The Mirror of Eternal*

Salvation ('The light of God holds wide open the eye that it has rendered simple; thus it remains forever, nor can we ever close it') and the *Book of the Supreme Truth* (his eye sees 'the things that are beyond all knowledge'). Among the iconographic models proposed are, (Combe) the woodcuts of the *Exercitium super Pater Noster*, relating to the circle of the Brethren of the Common Life (see Outline Biography **1486-7**); in the 1445–50 reprint, the first plate of the volume represents a brother meditating in the open air, with a similar stream, hut and chapel (the hut illustrating the hermitage of Groenandel, where Ruysbroeck lived). In the painting being examined the entrance and the saint's habit bear the Anthonin symbol of the letter T. The shelter in the shape of a hollow tree with a stubble roofing recalls the 'natural' huts on the exterior of the shutters in the Anderlecht Triptych (63) (Baldass); near the saint is a pig, his attribute with the little bell in its ear which enabled these animals, the property of the convent, to wander freely also in the town (Combe). A debatable hypothesis was advanced by Fraenger (1957 and 1958) about Bosch's anticipation of Jung's doctrine on the internal dialogue between the ego and its internal mirror, the 'Self'. This picture echoes *St John the Baptist in the Wilderness* (34) in the calm, delightful landscape, (the Devil's activities seem unimportant) and the harmony between it and the saint.

60 40 × 26.5

The Temptation of St Anthony
Berlin-Dahlem, Staatliche Museen
Donated to the museum in 1904 from a British collection. Believed to be an original by Friedländer (1927) and the work of an imitator by Baldass and Tolnay (1965) who drew attention to the inspiration from the *St Anthony* of the Prado (59). Deviltries and 'grylli' belong to Bosch's usual repertory but relative emptiness of the space and the precious execution of the figures seem foreign to Bosch's style.

III

61 ⊞ ⊗ 71×70.6 1510* 🔲 ⋮

'The Prodigal Son'
Rotterdam, Boymans-van
Beuningen Museum

A panel cut down to an
octagonal shape, perhaps in the
seventeenth century; according
to Baldass (1943 and 1959), it is
the surviving exterior wing of a
lost triptych. Formerly in the
Schiff and, later, Figdor
Collections, in Vienna; it came to
its present location with the
Van der Schilden bequest in
1931. After Glück's attribution
(1904) its authenticity was
unquestioned and so was the
late dating: Hannema
(Boymans Museum, 1931),
followed by Tolnay dated it to
about 1510, by analogy with
The Epiphany of the Prado (62).
It used to be thought that it
represented the Prodigal Son;
Hannema claimed that it was a
self-portrait. Baldass (1926,
etc.) and Sudeck (*Bettler-
darstellungen*, Strasburg, 1931)
suggested instead the moralising theme of the wanderer (an
old pedlar), similar to that on
the outside of the wings of *The
Triptych of the Hay Wain*
(21 A); Pigler (B M 1950) held
the figure to represent one of
'Saturn's children' and called
attention to a Florentine
engraving of 1460 representing
a wanderer, a pig and a scaffold;
his suggestion was taken up
and elaborated by L. Brand-
Philip (1958) as part of her
conjectured series on the four
planets, elements and temperaments (1 and 6); this was
denied by Bax (NKJ, 1962) and
by Tolnay (1965). The painting
does not obviously depict the
story of the Prodigal Son, as
told in Luke xv; 11–32, where
the son is still a young man at
the time of his return. Such
features as the ramshackle
public-house and its inmates do
not belong to the biblical story:
Tolnay tries to account for these
motifs by saying that the man is
not simply the Prodigal, he is
Everyman, and thus Bosch can
give himself scope in his
motifs. Mrs Brand-Philip offers
a carefully worked-out
explanation which at least has

the merit of being a thorough
and sympathetic analysis of the
painting. She interprets the
peddler (as she considers his
profession to be) as the type of
the Melancholic humour (thin,
pale, poor, cheerless); the cow
is linked with *terra*, the Element
corresponding to the Melancholy humour; Saturn is closely
associated with Melancholy,
and the Peddler is represented
as one of his 'children' (the
author refers to Pigler's
Florentine woodcuts). She also
points out that Saturn is often
given a limp, and the peddler
seems to be lame (one foot in a
boot, the other in a shoe, not to
mention the staff, sometimes
also held by Saturn). Finally she
identifies the background
figures with signs of the Zodiac.
Her theory is linked to her
interpretation of *The Conjuror*
(6) and *The Cure of Folly* (1),
which, with a putative lost work
she would associate together as
a quartet of the four humours
(etc.) in their worst aspects –
the peddler, like the charlatans,
is a dishonest person: the scene

of his business is the seedy
house in the background. His
end will be the gallows, to be
seen beyond the gate he is
about to pass.

62 A   Pls. LVI–LVII A

62 B   Pls. LVI–LVII B & LVIII

62 C   Pls. LVI–LVII C & LIX–LXI

62 D   Pls. LVI–LVII D

The Triptych of the Epiphany
Madrid

This is the last of the great
triptychs known to us (Madrid,
Prado); it represents the
Adoration of the Magi at the
centre and two kneeling donors
with their patron saints at the
sides; closed, the triptych shows
the Mass of St Gregory. An
attempt has been made to
identify it as the painting which
decorated the chapel of the
Sweet Mother of 'sHertogenbosch in the cathedral (not to
be mistaken for the chapel of the
Brotherhood of Our Lady): but
Gramaye mentioned it as being
still in its original location in
1610 (see 106) whereas the
present painting was confis-
cated in 1568 by the Duke of
Alba from its owner, Jean de
Casembroot, near Brussels
(Pinchart, 1860) and presented
to Philip II who sent it to the
Escorial in 1574 (Justi, 1889);
it went to the Prado in 1839. It
is probably the Epiphany
'without any eccentricities'
mentioned also by Brother José
de Sigüenza (1605). Signed in
the central panel; its authenticity is unquestioned. The date,
put at one point in period of
early maturity (Baldass [1917],
about 1490, on the basis of the
costumes; Demonts [1919];
Friedländer [1927], about
1495), was correctly moved to
about 1510 by Tolnay (1937)
(later followed by Baldass,
1959, and by others), precisely
in relation to the costumes,
and to the reassertion of a new

monumentality derived, it is
claimed, from the Master of
Flémalle and Van Eyck. According to Tolnay (1937 and 1965),
followed by Combe (1946) and
by Delevoy (1960), the triptych
is an allegory of the sacrifice of
the Mass (see also 8), attended
by the donors. L. Brand-Philip
(1953) held it instead to
symbolise the contrast
between Christ and Antichrist,
between the ancient and the
new Law, wherein the Magi,
kings of this world and
worshippers of the divine,
occupy an ambiguous position.

62 ⊞ ⊗ 138×66 1510* 🔲 ⋮

**A. The Mass of St
Gregory**
Exterior of the wings, forming a
single composition, painted in
grisaille. Pope Gregory is
portrayed celebrating mass
before an altar surmounted with
the sarcophagus of Christ. The
emergent figure of the Saviour
and the episodes of the Passion,
represented as carvings on the
frame of the altarpiece, come to
life through the saint's im-
passioned prayer (Tolnay).
Alternating from left to right and
from bottom to top, the scenes
illustrated are: the Prayer on the
Mount of Olives, the Seizing of
Christ, Christ before Pilate, the
Flagellation, the Crowning with
Thorns, the Ascent of Calvary
with St Veronica unfolding the
veil, the Crucifixion; this last
is animated by secondary
scenes, such as the Devil making
away with the cross of the bad
thief, and the burgher taking his
child to see Judas hanged. The
style recalls, though with
greater vigour, the grisailles of
St John on Patmos and of *The
Lisbon Triptych* (Combe)
(33, 43). L. Brand-Philip
interpreted the stations of the
Cross as depicting the seven
sins, in preparation for the
contrast with the subject
depicted inside: in their order,
Sloth, Wrath, Pride, Lust and
Gluttony (the figures surrounding the Flagellation and the

Crowning with Thorns), Envy
(the bad thief), Avarice
(struggle for Christ's tunic).
According to Tolnay, Gregory's
mass prefigures the Epiphany-
Mass on the central panel; of the
two kneeling laymen, the one on
the left is said to portray the
deceased father of the donor;
the small figure on the right, the
Roman woman who doubted
the miracle of transubstantiation
(Fraenger, DJV, 1957).

62 ⊞ ⊗ 138×33 1510* 🔲 ⋮

**B. St Peter and the
Donor**
Interior of the left wing,
portraying the kneeling donor,
Peter Bronckhorst, recognisable
by the patron saint, St Peter,
and by the family coat-of-arms
(identified by Lafond, 1914),
surmounted with the inscription
Een voer al (one for all). In the
middle distance, against the
ruins of a pagan structure
(according to L. Brand-Philip,
the remains of Solomon's or
David's palace), St Joseph is
drying the Child's swaddling
clothes over a fire. Subtle
manifestations of the evil
present in the world are illustrated by the toad balanced on
the key-stone of the Gothic
gate, the demons springing out
of the bases of the archway
the peasant dance to the sound
of the bagpipe.

62 ⊞ ⊗ 138×72 1510* 🔲 ⋮

**C. The Adoration of the
Magi**
Central panel, signed
'Jheronimus bosch' at lower
left. Under the projecting roof
of a crumbling hut recalling, as
does the whole composition,
The Adoration of the Shepherds
by the Master of Flémalle in
the Dijon Museum (Schubert-
Soldern, *Von Van Eyck bis
Bosch*, 1903; Tolnay), the
Virgin solemnly holds the child
upright on her knees. Tolnay
thought her inspired by Van
Eyck's *Madonna of Chancellor
Rolin*, in the Louvre. The

sculpted gold group represent-
ting the Sacrifice of Isaac, an
offering to the child, recalls the
sacrifice of Christ: the precious
object crushes the toads of
heresy under its weight. The
embroidery on Melchior's
cloak, depicting the Queen of
Sheba's visit to Solomon,
prefigures the Magi's journey to
Bethlehem according to the
Biblia pauperum (Tolnay;
Combe): it stands above
another scene illustrating the
Sacrifice of Manoah and the
Annunciation to the sterile
couple of the birth of the Baptist,
Christ's precursor (Fraenger).
The bowl of myrrh held by
Caspar bears a relief representing the three heroes asking
David for water (a foreshadow-
ing of the Epiphany) and is
surmounted with a pelican
(Christ). Although the bird
seems to be in its traditional
attitude – pecking its own
breast in order that its young
can drink its blood – this
appearance is misleading. It is

Messiah (Isaiah, LIII: 3–4), a
prefiguration of the Passion of
Christ; Combe thought he was
spying on the believers;
Fraenger that he was Adam, a
witness of the miracle of
Epiphany (and behind him,
Abraham). L. Brand-Philip put
forward a detailed interpretation
of the picture based on this
figure. The golden chain and the
leprous sore she traces to old
Jewish accounts of Antichrist.
The crown of thorns is a
mockery of Christ's own crown
of thorns, for Antichrist will
imitate Christ's Passion. She
suggests that Bosch's source for
Jewish lore would have been
Jacob van Almaengien (the real
existence of whom is the basis
for Fraenger's 'Adamite'
theory of Bosch's work). This
Jew was for a time a member of
the Brotherhood of Our Lady at
'sHertogenbosch. She points
out that Antichrist will over-
come the three kings of the
world; in the picture he holds
the hat of one of them, and

Interior of the right wing,
portraying Agnes Bosshuyse,
recognisable by her patron saint
and her family coat-of-arms
(identified by Lafond). Behind
them is the lamb, symbol of St
Agnes, near the staff of the
Good Shepherd who protects
mankind from evil, symbolised
in its turn by the bear and the
wolf attacking the wayfarers in
the background.

The Triptych
of the Epiphany
Anderlecht

Bequeathed in 1844 by Father
E. H. Moens to the church of SS

Peter and Guyon in Anderlecht
(Brussels) – where it is at
present. Believed at one time an
authentic work of 1500 or
later (Hulin de Loo [*Catalogue*]
1902; Lafond, 1914; up to
Friedländer, 1927); judged at
present to be the work of an
imitator, inspired by *The
Epiphany* of the Prado (62)
(Tolnay, 1937 and 1965
[dating it to about 1520–5 on
the basis of the Italianate
building in the left wing]), or a
copy (Combe, 1947); Puyvelde
(1956 and 1962) considered it a
copy of the central panel in the
Prado. According to L.
Ninane (*Le siècle de Bruegel*,
1963) the wings are superior in
quality to the central panel and,
in view of the originality of the
subjects, she did not feel they
could be copies; the unity of the
composition on the exterior of
the shutters is in the style of
Bosch. The state of preservation
is not good; the faces were
repainted in the second half of
the sixteenth century (Tolnay).

Exterior of the left wing,
portraying St Peter in prayer
inside a cave-hut; as concerns
the setting on the exterior of the
two wings (see also 63 B).
Baldass (1959) pointed out a
resemblance to St Giles in *The
Altarpiece of the Hermits* (40 C).
A preliminary drawing of the
figure of St Peter is reported to
be in the N. Beets Collection in
Amsterdam (catalogue
*Middeleeuwse Kunst der
Noordelijke Nederlanden*,
Amsterdam 1958).

Exterior of the right wing,
portraying Mary Magdalen
doing penance in a setting
similar to that of the left wing.

63 A   63 B   63 C   63 D   63 E

in fact pecking at a strawberry,
symbol of wantoness, as we
have seen in *The Garden of
Delights* (30). This detail adds
to the ambiguity of the figure
of Caspar (the theory of the
'anti-pelican' [43 C] may be
recalled). The edge of Caspar's
cloak displays further
birds, some with human heads,
pecking at fruit, and the erotic
theme is continued in the swan
on the helmet lying on the
ground to the right. Combe
attributed to this black king an
ambiguous significance:
either the conversion of the
infidels or the persistence of
evil. The strange half-naked
figure that appears on the
threshold of the hut – with a
scarlet mantle and a prisoner's
chain made of gold, a wound on
his leg, a turban encircled with
a crown of thorns and surmounted with a miraculously
verdant twig – represents,
according to Tolnay, the Judaic

because of the equivocal
symbols they carry (in addition
to their sacred gifts) she sees
them as half under his sway
already. This ambiguous note
is echoed in the rest of the
picture. In the background,
despite the apparent calm and
beauty of the landscape are to
be seen indications of the perils
and evils of the world into
which Christ is born. A couple
walk toward an inn, of the ill-
famed sign of the swan (see 47
and 60); on the right, people are
attacked by wolves, and
soldiers are in evidence – the
sinister shepherds on the roof of
the hut (the old Dispensation)
are those mentioned in John
x:1 who climb like robbers into
the sheepfold, not through the
Door (Christ), the only way to
Salvation. Many copies of this
central panel survive
(Friedländer, 1927) in Philadelphia, Amsterdam, Bonn,
Avignon, etc.

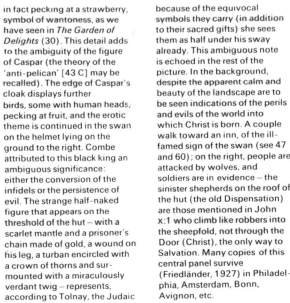

64

65 A

65 C

63 ⊞ ⊕ 80,5×26,5 目 ⦂

C. St Joseph
Interior of the left wing, representing St Joseph drawing water; in the background, an Italianate building; an angel washing the swaddling clothes.

63 ⊞ ⊕ 78×62 目 ⦂

D. The Adoration of the Magi
Central panel of the triptych, inspired by that of the Prado (62), but displaying a reversed composition. The peculiar figures on the threshold of the hut are replaced by two men in secular dress; the shepherd on the roof turns to look, as in the Prado version.

63 ⊞ ⊕ 80,5×26,6 目 ⦂

E. The Retinue of the Magi
Interior of the right wing. In the Adorations of unquestionable authenticity, the theme of the retinue is usually omitted.

64 ⊞ ⊕ ——— 目 ⦂

The Adoration of the Magi
London, Bearsted Collection
Tolnay (1965) drew attention to this triptych, the central panel is a copy of the Prado *Epiphany* (62 C) except for the absence of the shepherds on the roof. The interior of the left wing represents St Joseph drawing

water, against the background of an Italianate building; the right wing depicts the mounted retinue of the Magi (see 63 C and E). The exterior of the shutters, forming a single composition, bears a tondo with a representation of the *Ecce Homo*, recalling Bosch's mature, half-length compositions. In our opinion, this is a composition made up of various Bosch-like elements.

The Kleinberger-Johnson Adoration

Triptych reconstructed at the 1939 exhibition at the Worcester Museum, with two wing fragments from the Johnson Collection in the Philadelphia Museum — judged authentic by Friedländer (1927) — and an

with a dog before a porticoed building. Tolnay (1965) thought that the detail of the dog revealed Bosch's hand. Combe (1946 and 1957) judged it a copy of a lost youthful work.

65 ⊞ ⊕ 70×22 目 ⦂

B. The Adoration of the Magi New York, Kleinberger Gallery
Central panel of the triptych, bought by Kleinberger in 1929; its height is less than that of the wings, as shown by the Vught copy. The perspective architectural setting, in a sixteenth-century Italianate and Dürer-like style, seems foreign to Bosch's style, while the figures echo motifs from the Epiphanies at the Prado, in Anderlecht and also from the youthful work in Philadelphia (62, 63, 8).

Copy of 65 A–C (Vught, W. A. Moonen Collection)

Ideal integration of 65 A–C carried out with the help of the copy in the Moonen Collection at Vught

65 ⊞ ⊕ 33×21,6 目 ⦂

C. The Retinue of the Magi Philadelphia, Museum of Art (Johnson Collection)
Fragment of the right wing, displaying some affinity with the right wing of the Bearsted *Adoration* (64). The style might suggest a relatively early dating, close to the Vienna *Ascent of Calvary* (19), but it also contains figures from the *Calvary* in Madrid (44). Thought by Combe (1946 and 1957) to be the copy of a lost youthful work.

66 ⊞ ⊕ 182,8×142,2 目 ⦂

The Adoration of the Magi New York, Metropolitan Museum
Painted in tempera and oils. Formerly in the Lippmann Collection in Berlin; it came to its present location in 1912 with the Kennedy Fund. Friedländer (1927) believed it to be a youthful work spoiled by restorations; its authenticity was rightly refuted by Wilenski (1960) and Tolnay (1965); the latter proposed as a term *post quem* the architectural setting of Dürer's *Epiphany* in a woodcut of the Life of Mary, of

Adoration of the Magi from the Kleinberger Gallery in New York as the central panel. A complete copy of the work is in the Moonen Collection at Vught (formerly in that of the Marquis Casa Torres in Madrid). The general layout and the Italianate architectural details closely recall, more than the Anderlecht altarpiece (63), that of the Bearsted Collection in London (64). The Worcester catalogue proposes a dating prior to 1500; in our opinion, this is a workshop product, subsequent to the above-mentioned triptychs.

65 B

65 ⊞ ⊕ 33×21,6 目 ⦂

A. The Adoration of the Shepherds
Philadelphia, Museum of Art (Johnson Collection)
Fragment of the left wing, representing two shepherds

66

67 A   67 B

about 1502–05. Among the Bosch-like elements in the figures of the Magi, of the St Joseph and of the landscape, is inserted a small Virgin in a Primitive Flemish taste, which perhaps reflects the archaicism of Bosch's late period, ingenuously interpreted in the workshop. An almost identical panel, though of lower quality, has been in the Boymans-van Beuningen Museum of Rotterdam 70 × 56.7 cm. since 1958; Puyvelde (Paris Exhibition, 1947) maintained it to be a youthful work by Bosch, whereas the museum's catalogue lists it among the workshop products.

67 ⊞ ⊗ 247,5×84 ‖ ⦙
1513

A. Madonna and Child
'sHertogenbosch, Cathedral

68

Together with 67 B, this originally formed one of the two shutters on the left of a large clock, signed 'I S B' and dated 1513. On the reverse is an inscription in Gothic letters: *Bosch delineavit et p(in)xit* (Bosch drew and painted it). The two panels were made known by Mosmans in 1950; the figures are larger than life size. The painting is done in grisaille, with the exception of the heads and hands, and of the red ground. The state of preservation is bad; the two paintings were heavily restored in 1949. According to Tolnay, they were painted in the workshop, perhaps after a model by the master.

67 ⊞ ⊗ 247,5×84 ‖ ⦙
1513

B. St John the Evangelist
'sHertogenbosch, Cathedral
Originally the right shutter of a large clock dated 1513 (see 67 A).

68 ⊞ ⊗ 46,5×36,5 ‖ ⦙

Christ before Pilate
Rotterdam, Boymans-van Beuningen Museum
Formerly in the Kilmansegg (Vienna) and Von Nemes (Munich) Collections, later with Goudstikker of Amsterdam (Friedländer, 1927); it came to the museum with the Van Beuningen Collection (1958). Considered authentic by Friedländer (who titled it 'Christ before the High Priest') and by Puyvelde (*Primitifs flamands* catalogue, Paris 1947), who, in view of the

physiognomical rendering, related it to *Christ Bearing the Cross* in Ghent (70), after having erroneously named it (Antwerp, 1930) 'The Mocking of Christ'. Tolnay and Baldass considered it the excellent copy of a lost original datable to the artist's final period, while the copy itself might be set at about 1520–30. The human types, especially that with a ring through his lip, prefigure those of the analogous subject at the Princeton Museum (69), where the basin and the jug with the big spout also reappear. The latter refer to Pilate washing his hands.

69 ⊞ ⊗ 84,5×108 ‖ ⦙
1513-15

Christ before Pilate
Princeton, Art Museum
Bought in London in 1891 it was bequeathed to the Museum by Allen Marquant. It was considered authentic by most scholars, except for Baldass (1943 and 1959), although in 1917 he had stated it to be authentic and subsequent to *Christ bearing the Cross* in Ghent (70), and Combe (1946 and 1957). According to Tolnay, it preceded the similar subject in Ghent, the last version of the theme, confined to the heads only, while the Princeton composition displays

69

70 Pls. LXII–LXIV
coincidences – which he felt were probably unintentional – with the half-length Italian paintings by Giovanni Bellini and Titian. The half-length conception was at any rate prefigured in Bosch's art by *The Crowning with Thorns* in London and by that in Madrid (57 and 58). The physiognomical emphasis, the reduction of the faces to bestial masks, have caused references to Leonardo's caricatures. In effect, these

scoundrelly types had been gradually elaborated in the course of Bosch's career, from the *Ecce Homo* in Frankfurt (10) to the *Ascent of Calvary* (44) and *The Crowning with Thorns* (58) to *Christ before Pilate* in Rotterdam (68), and it seems to us that analogies should be sought with similar types in German art. A certain metallic hardness and the coarse emphasis on the grotesque types, with a repetition of motifs such as the rings stuck through the flesh of the rascals, suggests some doubt as to its authenticity. The inscription BVS FACIEBAT has been made out on Pilate's sleeve, but Tolnay thought it improbable that it could be a signature. The work was cleaned in 1948.

70 ⊞ ⊗ 76,5×83,5 ‖ ⦙
1515-16

Christ bearing the Cross
Ghent, Musée des Beaux-Arts
This is a most striking work, perhaps Bosch's last. The panel entered the museum in 1902 with the Hulin de Loo purchase. It was slightly cut down at the corners, and restored in 1956–67. Its authenticity is unquestioned and so is its late dating, with the exception of Puyvelde's listing (1962) among the works of the first period. Combe (1946 and 1957) related it to Hell in *The Triptych of the Garden of Delights* (30 D); Baldass (1959) thought it one of the last works. Tolnay (1937 and 1965), the last. It is undoubtedly subsequent to the calm, expanded style of *The Epiphany* and of *St Anthony* at the Prado (62 and 59). Concerning the device of showing only the heads, Baldass (1938 and

71

72

1943) referred to Dürer's *Jesus among the Doctors* (1506) in the Thyssen Collection, Lugano, to which Tolnay also added a Dutch miniature (*ca.* 1470) with six heads above the altar. Bosch imposed onto his crowded picture three moments of formal and spiritual pause: they are the faces of St Veronica, of the Saviour and of the good thief subjected to the ferocious charity of the Dominican friar. It is not by chance that the faces of these three close their eyes to the sight of the degraded humanity around them.

71 ⊞ ⊗ 50,8×80,3 ‖ ⦙

The Kiss of Judas
San Diego, California, Fine Arts Gallery
Published as authentic by Henkel (*Pantheon*, 1931), the work must in fact be considered as the copy of a lost original (Cohen, *ibid.*; Tolnay, 1965). Another version of this work is at the Rijksmuseum in Amsterdam. The composition recalls the oval on the left of the Valencia Triptych (cf. 58): it displays many figures of Bosch's last period, from *The Crowning with Thorns* in London (57) to *Christ before Pilate* in Princeton (69) and *Christ bearing the Cross*, in Ghent (70).

72 ⊞ ⊗ 29×74 ‖ ⦙

Christ before Pilate
São Paulo, Museu de Arte
Originally with Goudstikker in Amsterdam; then (1942) at the Heimann in New York. While some ascribe it to Bosch, it is in all probability the work of an imitator of Bosch's late style, inspired by the Princeton painting (69), but with elements borrowed from Lucas van Leyden and Dürer's woodcuts; it is listed as authentic in the museum's catalogue.

73 ⊞ ⊗ 102×155,5 ‖ ⦙

The Expulsion of the Merchants from the Temple
Copenhagen, Statens Museum for Kunst
Tempera and oils. Tolnay (1965) considered it a pastiche of various elements borrowed from Bosch and Breugel. Of the two versions of this painting mentioned by Friedländer (1927), one was in the Brunner sale in Paris in 1910 (111 × 172 cm.) and the other, formerly in the Claude Phillips Collection in London (75 × 59 cm.), was displayed at the Bruges Exhibition 1902.

73

Other works mentioned in the early sources

In addition to the work which it was possible to insert in the chronological sequence of the Catalogue (see **14** *and* **32**), *a list follows of the works which sources ascribe to Bosch and of which there is neither a trace nor the possibility of a chronological classification. They are, therefore, cited on the basis of the location (in alphabetical order) mentioned by extant documents and in accordance with the antiquity of such documents.*

FLANDERS
ANTWERP

74 The Temptation of St Anthony Formerly in Rubens' Collection, as appears from the inventory drawn up after the painter's death (Pinchart, *Messager des sciences de Gand*, 1858).

75 Heads Two paintings of this subject are listed in the inventory mentioned above.

76 Wedding Banquet This also belonged to Rubens, and is described in the above mentioned inventory as a work *à la façon de Jeronimus Bosch* (in the manner of Jeronimus Bosch). For a possible identification with the *Marriage of Cana* in Rotterdam, see 3.

77 Subject unknown Canvas painting mentioned in the 1552 inventory relating to the estate of Michiel van der Heyden (Denucé, *Les galeries d'art à Anvers*, 1932).

78 Figure with Physiognomical Studies Canvas, inventoried like the preceding one.

79 The Seven Deadly Sins Work listed in the 1574 inventory of Margaretha Boge's estate (Denucé, 1932).

80 Subject unknown Canvas mentioned in the 1583 inventory of Jan van Kessel's estate (Denucé, 1932).

81 Man Who Repairs Bellows and Lanterns Panel painting, listed in the inventory (1603) of the estate of Marco Núñex Pérez (. . . *un hombre que concierta fuelles y linternas*) (Denucé, 1932).

82 Temptation (The Temptation of St Anthony [?]) Appears in the 1642 inventory of Herman de Neyt's estate (Denucé, 1932).

83 Pastorale Mentioned, like preceding painting.

84 Hell Mentioned, like the two preceding paintings.

85 A Sovereign (?) Panel painting, listed with the three preceding ones (*Eenen voesterheer . . . op paneel, met binnenlyst*).

86 The Temptation of St Anthony Listed in the 1644 inventory relating to the estate of Sara Schut (Denucé, 1932).

87 The Temptation of St Anthony Listed in the 1652 inventory of Jan van Meurs' estate (Denucé, 1932).

88 Subject unknown Panel, mentioned in the inventory (1657) of Susanna Willemsens' estate (Denucé, 1932).

89 The Last Judgement Triptych, listed (1660) among the property of Jean Petit (Denucé, 1932).

BRUSSELS

90 Subject unknown Large painting (*grand tableau*), formerly in the collections of William of Orange (the Silent) according to its listing in the corresponding inventory of 1568 (Pinchart, 1860).

91 The Cure of Folly Formerly in the palace of Grand Duke Ernest of Austria, as stated in a 1595 inventory (Pinchart, 1860), in which it is said to represent 'physicians and surgeons intent on extracting a stone from the head of a patient'.

92 Sicut Erat in Diebus Noë Like the preceding work, formerly in the palace of Ernest of Austria and is mentioned in the above-mentioned inventory (see also 25).

93 The Crucifixion and the Descent into Limbo Mentioned like the preceding work; stated to have been bought for one hundred and six florins (Hymans, 1884).

GHENT

94 Christ bearing the Cross Formerly in the church of Ste Pharailde, according to an indication by Marc van Vaernewijk in the 1500s (*Troubles en Flandres . . .*, Brussels 1905).

MALINES

95 The Temptation of St Anthony Formerly in the collection of Margaret of Austria, according to its listing in the 1516 inventory of the House of Hapsburg (see Outline Biography) and, particularly, in that of 1524, from which it appears that the saint held in his hands a book and spectacles, and a staff under his arm, against a background of wooded country with strange figures. In spite of this description, Glück (1935) identified the painting as the *Temptation* in Amsterdam (47).

GERMANY
BONN

96 Life of Christ Triptych, formerly in the cathedral, perhaps as the result of a purchase (1518) by Canon Gerard de Haen. The centre depicted the Entry into Jerusalem; the wings, the Nativity and the Resurrection. The work may have been destroyed in the 1590 fire (Brans, 1948).

97 Christ bearing the Cross According to a document in the archives of Bonn University, studied by M. G. Kinkel (Hymans, 1884), a painting of this subject was in the city's cathedral in 1584 and might be the same as that listed under 102. Van Mander's testimony is in contrast with the above.

ITALY
VENICE

98 Jonah Canvas; Michiel saw it in 1521 in Cardinal Grimani's Collection and described it as: *fortuna con el ceto che ingiotte* (tempest at sea with the whale swallowing [Jonah]).

NETHERLANDS

The worst destruction of works of art occurred during the 1566 reaction against Philip II of Spain and in 1629, when the Protestants occupied sHertogenbosch. The principal sources, as concerns Bosch's native town, are Gramaye (*Taxandria*, 1610) (who copied almost literally a chronicle drawn up for him in 1608 by Everswijn, Loeff and Van Balen, the authors of a history of the city up to 1565) and J. van Oudenhoven (*Beschryvinge der Stadt ende meyereye van 'sHertogenbosche*, 1649); for the rest of the country, see C. van Mander (1604).

Location unknown

99 The Flight into Egypt A privately owned work seen by Van Mander (1604), who mentioned some of its details: St Joseph asking a peasant the way, and a bear dancing in the background.

100 The Descent into Limbo Privately owned painting

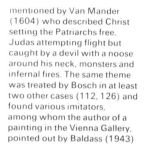

Engraved by an unknown author (Iheronimus Bos invètor) published by Cock, with St Martin and the horse in a boat (see 129)

mentioned by Van Mander (1604) who described Christ setting the Patriarchs free, Judas attempting flight but caught by a devil with a noose around his neck, monsters and infernal fires. The same theme was treated by Bosch in at least two other cases (112, 126) and found various imitators, among whom the author of a painting in the Vienna Gallery, pointed out by Baldass (1943)

101 A Prodigy Privately owned work mentioned by Van Mander (1604) who described a king and other figures falling to the ground in terror (perhaps of divine intervention).

AMSTERDAM

102 Christ bearing the Cross Seen by Van Mander (1604) in a private collection, and stated by him to be infused with an unusual solemnity of style (see 44). Hymans (1884) mentioned a document in the archives of Bonn University, from which it appears that in 1584 the work was in the cathedral of that city; and there it may have been destroyed in the 1590 fire (but see *Bonn*, 97).

HAARLEM

103 The Proof of Heresy Van Mander (1604) mentioned it as being in Jan Dietring's Collection and described its

theme: a monk commits heretical books to the flames together with his own, and only the latter are spared.

104 Various unknown subjects Mentioned by Van Mander as being in the Dietring Collection.

'sHERTOGENBOSCH

105 The Creation of the World The theme, recalling the exterior of *The Triptych of the Garden of Delights* (30 A), unfolded on the exterior of the shutters of a carved and gilded wooden altarpiece (with scenes illustrating infernal punishments), placed on the high altar of the cathedral. The interior of the shutters represented monsters and antediluvian animals painted in light colours (perhaps a grisaille ?). The work was mentioned by Gramaye (1610) who described it together with the shutters of the altarpiece belonging to the Brotherhood of Our Lady (14). The paintings in question were sold in 1617 to the municipality of 'sHertogenbosch, and they may have been destroyed in the fire which ravaged the building in 1669 (Mosmans, 1931 and 1947; reports by H. J. H. Bossink and H. Hens, 1966).

106 The Epiphany This was in the chapel of the 'Sweet Mother of 'sHertogenbosch' (*Altari D. Virginis Inferioris*) in the cathedral, not to be mistaken for the altar of the Brotherhood of Our Lady (*Divae Virginis Superioris*) where 14 stood. The painting was mentioned by Gramaye (1610) and by Van Oudenhoven (1649). In 1566 it had been transferred to the Municipal Building to preserve it from the rage of the iconoclasts (Mosmans, Bossink and Hens, as for 105), but subsequently it was probably returned to the chapel: there is no documentary basis (report by P. Gerlach, 1966) for its identification, attempted by some, as the painting at the Prado (62).

107 Scenes from the Lives of Judith and Esther Gramaye (1610) and Van

The Descent into Limbo, *by an imitator of Bosch. Vienna, Kunsthistorisches Museum (see 100)*

Oudenhoven (1649) mention this altarpiece on the altar of St Michael in the cathedral; Gramaye listed its themes: Siege of Bethulia, Beheading of Holofernes, Flight of the Assyrians, Triumph of the Hebrews, Mordechai and Esther. Judith and Holofernes also appear in the *Altarpiece of the Hermits* (40B).

PORTUGAL
ALENQUER

108 The Crowning with Thorns Panel, donated to the church of Sta Maria da Várzea, after 1526, by the Humanist Damiao de Góis, the agent of Manuel I and Juan III. Listed in a 1571 document (Vieira Santos, B M N A, 1958).

LISBON

109 The Patience of Job Formerly in the collections of Juan III, for whose account it was probably purchased by De Góis (1523–4) at two hundred *cruzados* (see Outline Biography).

SPAIN

Spanish inventories of the seventeenth and eighteenth centuries (Justi, 1889) mentioned numerous paintings by Bosch; but they are often works by others, especially Bruegel and Cranach or

Location unknown

110 St Mary Magdalen A painting of this theme apparently belonged to Queen Isabella the Catholic, according to unpublished documents in the Simancas archives summarised by Pedro Madrazo (*Viaje artistico . . . por las colecctiones de los reyes de Espana*, 1844). Isabella, mother-in-law of Philip the Fair, maintained close relations with the Flemish court; the inventory of her estate, drawn up (1505) the year after her death, mentions a painting by a 'Jheronymus' identifiable as Bosch.

ESCORIAL

111 The Seizing of Christ Canvas ($4\frac{1}{2} \times 5$ *pies*) sent (1574) by Philip II to the monastery of San Lorenzo (Escorial) (Justi, 1889 [see Outline Biography]), where it was still stated to be in the late eighteenth century by Ponz (1777) and Ceán Bermúdez (1800). (For its alleged identification as *The Crowning with Thorns* of the Prado, see 58).

112 The Descent into Limbo Panel (2×3 *pies*) sent to San Lorenzo with the preceding work (see also 100 and 126).

A. de Hameel, The Besieged Elephant, engraving with the inscription 'bosche', possibly related to 130

imitators of theirs, which, when ascertained as such, were excluded from the present catalogue. However, even of the forty or so works mentioned here below many may be copies or workshop products; among the works most plausibly ascribed to Bosch are those that belonged to De Guevara, and those sent by Philip II to the Escorial in 1574 and 1593. The greater part of these paintings was destroyed or ruined in the fires of the Pardo (1608), of the Escorial (1671) of the Royal Palace (1734), and during the French occupation of the Escorial, in 1809–10. The dimensions are quoted in *varas* (that is to say *braccia* [yards], equivalent to 83 cm.) and *pies* (feet, 27.8 cm.): from the comparison with the extent originals, they appear for the most part to be in excess, suggesting that the frames may occasionally have been included in the measurement.

113 The Temptation of St Anthony Triptych on panel ($4 \times 3\frac{1}{2}$ *pies*; the wings were painted on both sides), sent to San Lorenzo with the preceding works. Possibly a copy of the *Lisbon Triptych* (43), the interior of its wings is at the Prado (Brans, 1948).

114 The Temptation of St Anthony Panel ($3 \times 4\frac{1}{2}$ *pies*) sent to the Escorial by Philip II together with the preceding works.

115 The Temptation of St Anthony Panel (3×2 *pies*) sent to the Escorial by Philip II together with the preceding works.

116 The Seven Sacraments Mentioned by Brother José de Sigüenza together with the panel of the *Sins* (2).

117 The Last Judgement Oil on panel ($1\frac{1}{4} \times 1\frac{1}{6}$ *varas*), sent to the Escorial in 1593

after Philip II had acquired it in the sale of the property of the Prior don Fernando, the illegitimate son of the Duke of Alba (Zarco Cuevas, 1930). The same sale included *The Triptych of the Garden of Delights* (30).

118 The Temptation of St Anthony Small triptych in oil ($1\frac{1}{6} \times 1$ *varas*) which Philip II acquired through the sale mentioned above and sent to the Escorial in 1593.

119 Deviltries Panel painted in oils ($\frac{3}{4} \times 1\frac{1}{4}$ *varas*), purchased by Philip II and sent to the Escorial like the two preceding works. It may have

J. Cock (engraver and publisher in Paris, 1601; HIERONIMVS BOS INVE), The Besieged Elephant (see engraving at left)

illustrated the temptation of St Anthony (Brans, 1948); Brother de Sigüenza saw five such subjects at the Escorial.

MADRID

120 Three Blind Figures Canvas ($1\frac{1}{3} \times 3$ *varas*) purchased in 1570 by Philip II from the De Guevara heirs (Justi, 1889; Viñaza, 1889 [see Outline Biography]). It represented a blind man leading another and, behind them, a blind woman. It also appears in the inventory of the Royal Palace, drawn up in 1607. Later on, it was perhaps transferred to the Pardo, where a canvas in tempera with blind figures is listed in the inventories subsequent to the 1608 fire (Justi) (see 144).

121 Flemish Dance Canvas (1×2 *varas*) which Philip II acquired like the preceding work. It also appears in the inventory of the Royal Palace drawn up after the king's death (1598), with the indication *tempera*. At the end of the eighteenth century it was at the Buen Retiro (Ponz, 1777), where Ceán Bermúdez (1800) also saw *una borrachera con figuras ridiculas* (a drunken feast with ludicrous figures).

122 Blind Men Boar-Hunting Canvas ($1\frac{1}{3} \times 1\frac{2}{3}$ *varas*), purchased by Philip II like the preceding works. Mentioned in the inventory of the Royal Palace drawn up after the king's death (1598).

123 A Witch Canvas ($1 \times 1\frac{1}{3}$ *varas*), purchased by Philip II like the preceding works and listed in the same 1598 inventory (but see 137).

124 The Cure of Folly Tempera on canvas ($1\frac{1}{3} \times 1\frac{1}{3}$ *varas*), purchased with the preceding works and mentioned in the 1598 inventory. (With reference to its possible identity with the painting now in the Prado, see 1.)

125 The Crucifixion Oil on canvas ($1\frac{1}{4} \times 1\frac{1}{3}$ *varas*), mentioned in the 1598 inventory of the Royal Palace.

126 The Descent into Limbo Oil, on panel ($\frac{1}{2} \times \frac{1}{2}$ ca.

varas), with the figures enclosed within a tondo against a black ground; mentioned, like the preceding work (Justi, 1889). Its very dimensions confirm that it is not the analogous subject cited at the Escorial (112). It is also mentioned in the Royal Palace inventory compiled in 1747 and in those of 1772 and 1794 pertaining to the Buen Retiro, where it was seen by Ceán Bermúdez (1800). (Concerning the imitations, see 100.)

127 The Temptation of St Anthony Oil, on panel ($\frac{1}{2} \times \frac{3}{4}$ *varas*), mentioned like the two preceding works; immediately after 1598 it was sold to the heirs of Pedro Álvárez (Brans, 1948).

128 St Martin Tempera on canvas ($2\frac{1}{2} \times 3$ *varas*), where the saint was represented 'with many poor'. Mentioned, like the three preceding works. Along with the painting, the 1598 inventory also lists a 'sketch' of it ($2\frac{1}{8} \times 2\frac{2}{3}$ *varas*), about which it is not clear whether it was the cartoon for the painting or a large painted outline.

129 St Martin Grisaille ($2\frac{1}{8} \times 3\frac{1}{4}$ *varas*), representing the saint on one boat and his horse on another. The work is mentioned, like the four preceding ones. Justi (1889) referred to an engraving by H. Cock with a similar subject (reproduced here). A second print was made by J. Galle after

a drawing by Bosch, and bears at the top the inscription: *La vie joyeyse et sans souci des estropiés* (the merry and careless life of the crippled) followed by two verses: *Contemple ung peu tous ces boiteux // au beau milieu de leur misère // rire et danser, estre joyeux // sans se soucier de la guerre* (Do look upon all these lame people // right in the midst of their misery // laughing and dancing, making merry // with not a care about the war); at the bottom, another inscription in Dutch with the French translation: *Saint Martin, pensant faire aux pauvres charité, causa par son manteau la guerre aux estropiés* (St Martin, wishing to extend his charity to the poor, caused a war amongst the cripples because of his cloak) [Castelli, 1952].

130 The Elephant Oil (outline at a highly advanced stage) on canvas ($2\frac{5}{8} \times 2\frac{5}{8}$ *varas*); mentioned like the five preceding works. There is no certainty as to its connection with the engraving by De Hameel and with that published by Cock, both reproduced here, and based, at any rate, on a drawing by Bosch (Lehrs, 1930 and Bosch Cat. 1967, n. 92 and 95). The theme of the elephant with the tower appeared in playing cards about the year 1455 (Tolnay, 1937 and 1965); Hennema (Rotterdam Exhibition, 1936) referred it to Eleazar's fight against an elephant of the pagan army, led by a Moor (Maccabees VI. 28–47), pointing out, moreover, that in 1484 an elephant was displayed for the first time, so it seems, in the cities of the Low Countries. Combe (1946) thought Bosch's lost original to have been coeval with the Vienna *Judgement* (50)

131 The Disputation with the Doctors Painting mentioned in the 1607 inventory of the Royal Palace (Brans, 1948).

132 St Christopher Oil, on panel, mentioned in the 1636 inventory of the Royal Palace (Justi, 1889). The saint was depicted while fording the river, and strange figures completed the scene, against two fires, which recalls 38.

133 St Christopher and St Anthony Work mentioned, like the preceding one. The former saint wore a yellow robe under a red cloak; the latter, further back, was represented with a staff, a rosary and a lantern; in the background, a castle in flames.

134 The Temptation of St Anthony Work mentioned, like the two preceding ones, in conjunction with which it may have constituted the remains of a large polyptych (Justi, 1889). The episode was represented as a night scene, in the light of a lamp inside a hollow tree.

135 An Old Woman on Her Threshold Listed, like the preceding works. At the top of the tiled roof the head of an animal could be seen.

136 A Sorcerer Tempera, mentioned, like the preceding works.

PARDO

137 The Monster Argote (*Discurso sobre el libro de la Monteria*, 1583) described this work as displayed in the hunting pavilion of the Pardo: 'a strange child born in Germany, who at the age of three days appeared to be seven years old . . . whom his mother is wrapping in swaddling clothes'. It reappears in the Pardo inventories subsequent to the 1608 fire. Justi (1889) conjectured its identity with the *Witch* formerly in the Royal Palace (see 123), but this is in contrast with the dates of the corresponding documents.

138 The Temptation of St Anthony Argote (1583) stated that the Pardo housed, including the preceding work, seven paintings by Bosch on this subject. It is likely that many of them were destroyed in the 1608 fire.

139 St Anthony The work represented the saint kneeling, with the Child next to him. It is mentioned in a Pardo inventory subsequent to the 1608 fire (Justi, 1889).

140 St Anthony Fresco (this designation is somewhat perplexing), mentioned like the preceding work. The saint appeared with the usual small bell.

141 Lent and Carnival Mentioned in Pardo inventories subsequent to the 1608 fire (Justi, 1889). The work may have come from the Royal Palace, the 1607 inventory of which records a *Mardi Gras* ('Martes de carnaval') (Brans, 1948). Painting 23 might be a copy.

142 The Sbirri Oil, on canvas, listed at the Royal Palace in 1607 (*Las Justicias*); presumably identifiable as a large painting which was later in the Pardo, after the 1608 fire, and representing 'the *sbirri* (constables, police) leading a prisoner, with the executioner's wife riding a horse'. Francisco Granello painted a copy which is also lost.

143 The Marriage Agreement This is described as a fresco in the inventory of the Pardo drawn up after the 1608 fire. Its likely provenance was the Royal Palace, where a wedding subject is listed in the 1607 inventory. It may be the painting of the same theme (treated in an ironical manner) seen by Ponz (1777) and Ceán Bermúdez (1800) at the Buen Retiro.

144 The Blind Tempera on canvas, mentioned in the Pardo inventory like the preceding work. Justi (1889) attempted to identify it with 120.

145 Assistant Organist Mentioned at the Pardo like the

118

preceding work; the man portrayed was represented while working the organ-bellows.

146 Man on the Ice Mentioned in the Pardo inventory like the preceding work; the figure had a horse's skull on his head.

The illustrations on these two pages show some of the more common symbols from Bosch's works, and those at the bottom of this page are from the Tarot pack.

Hollow tree

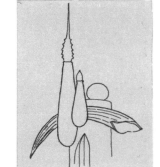

Horn

Indexes

Index of Titles

Abigail and David 14
Adoration of the Child (Cologne) 54
Adoration of the Child (Kleinberger-Johnson) 65 A–C
Adoration of the Child (New York) 66
Adoration of the Child (Madrid) see Epiphany
Adoration of the Child (Anderlecht) see Epiphany
Adoration of the Child (Philadelphia) see Epiphany
Allegory of Pleasures 17
Ascent of Calvary 19 A, 20, 44
Ascent into the Empyrean 26 D

Battle between Carnival and Lent 23

Carrying of the Cross 70
Child at Play 19 B
Christ and the Adulteress 4
Christ before Pilate 68, 69, 72
City in Flames 24 A
Concert in the Egg 7
Conjuror 6
Creation of the World 30 A
Crowning with Thorns 51 A, 55, 57, 58
Crucifixion 9
Cure of Folly 1

Deadly Sins, the Seven 2
Death of the Just Man 13 A
Death of the Miser 15
Death of the Reprobate 13 B
Delights, see Garden
Devil in the Country 25 C
Devil in the House 25 B

Ecce Homo 10, 11, 27, 28
Epiphany 8, 62, 63, 64
Expulsion from the Temple 73

Fall of the Damned 26 A

Garden of Delights, Triptych of 30
Garden of Eden 21 B, 22 B, 26 C, 30 B, 31, 50 C

Harbour 24 C
Hay Wain, Triptych of 21
Head of a Crossbowman 56
Head of a Woman 18
Heaven 52 C
Hell 2 (detail), 21 D, 26 B, 30 D, 48, 50 D & E, 51 D & E
Hermits, Altarpiece of 40

Jesus among the Doctors 12
Job, Tribulations of 42 B

Kiss of Judas 71

Last Judgement 2 (detail), 48, 50 D, 51 D, 52
Lost Soul 25 C

Madonna and Child 67 A
Marriage at Cana 3
Mass of St Gregory 62 A

Passion of Christ 33 B
'Prodigal Son' 61

Retinue of the Magi 63 E, 64 E, 65 C

St Agnes (and donor) 62 D
St Anthony, Temptation of, 29 B, 35, 40 A, 41, 42 A, 43 C–E (Lisbon Triptych),

45, 46, 47, 49, 59, 60
St Bavon 50 B
St Christopher 36, 37, 38
St Giles 40 C
St James 50 A
St James and Hermogenes 29 A
St Jerome 39, 40 B, 42 C
St John the Evangelist 67 B
St John the Baptist in the Wilderness 34
St John the Evangelist on Patmos 33 A
St Joseph 63 C
St Julia 24 B
St Liberata, Altarpiece of 24 A–C
St Mary Magdalen 63 B
St Peter (and donor) 62 B
St Peter in prayer 63 A
Saved Soul 25 F
Seizing of Christ 43 A
Ship of Fools 16

Temptation, see St Anthony
Tondalus, Vision of 53
Two Priestly Heads 5

Wanderer 21, 22
World after the Flood 25 D
World before the Flood 25 A

Bagatto

Chariot

Hermit

Fool

Topographical Index

AMSTERDAM
Rijksmuseum
Temptation of Saint Anthony 47

ANDERLECHT
Church of the SS Peter and Guyon
Triptych of the Epiphany 63 A–E

ANTWERP
Musée Royal des Beaux-Arts
Crowning with Thorns 55

BAYTOWN (USA)
Princess Kadjar Collection
Last Judgement 52

BERLIN-DAHLEM
Staatliche Museen
St John on Patmos 33 A
The Passion 33 B
Temptation of St Anthony 60

BERNE
Kunstmuseum
Crowning with Thorns 55

BOSTON
Museum of Fine Arts
Ecce Homo 11

BRUGES
Musée Groeninge
Triptych of the Patience of Job 42 A–C
Triptych of the Judgement 51 A–D

BRUSSELS
Musées Royaux des Beaux-Arts
Crucifixion 9

Van Buuren Collection (formerly)
Temptation of St Anthony 45

CHICAGO
Art Institute
Garden of Eden 31

COLOGNE
Wallraf-Richartz Museum
Adoration of the Child 54

COPENHAGEN
Statens Museum for Kunst
Expulsion of the Merchants from the Temple 73

ESCORIAL
Monastery of San Lorenzo
Crowning with Thorns 58
Triptych of the Hay Wain 22

FRANKFURT
Staedelesches Kunstinstitut
Ecce Homo 10

GHENT
Musée des Beaux-Arts
St Jerome in prayer 39
Christ bearing the Cross 70

THE HAGUE
Cramer Gallery
Battle between Carnival and Lent 23

KANSAS CITY
Gallery of Art
Temptation of St Anthony 41

LILLE
Musée Wicar
Concert in the Egg 7

LISBON
Museu Nacional de Arte Antiga
Triptych of the Temptation of St Anthony 43 A–E

LONDON
Arnot Gallery (formerly)
Ascent of Calvary 20

Bearsted Collection
Adoration of the Magi 64

National Gallery
Crowning with Thorns 57

MADRID
Private collection
Small St Christopher 37

Lázaro Galdiano Museum
St John the Baptist in the Wilderness 34.
Vision of Tondalus 53

Royal Palace
Ascent of Calvary 44

Prado
Cure of Folly 1
Seven Deadly Sins 2

Gourd

Thistle flower

Gryllos

Triptych of the Hay Wain 21 A–D
Triptych of the Garden of Delights 30 A–D
Temptation of St Anthony 45
Temptation of St Anthony 47
Head of a Crossbowman 56
Temptation of St Anthony 59
Triptych of the Epiphany 62 A–D

MUNICH
Alte Pinakothek
Last Judgement 48

NASHVILLE, CANADA
Private Collection
Temptation of St Anthony 46

NEW HAVEN (Conn.)
Yale University Art Gallery
Allegory of Pleasures 17

NEW YORK
Chrysler Collection
Temptation of St Anthony 35

Wildenstein Gallery
Triptych of the Judgement (fragmentary) 13 A–B

Kleinberger Galleries
Adoration of the Magi 65 B

Metropolitan Museum
Adoration of the Magi 66

PARIS
Roland Barny d'Avricourt Collection
Concert in the Egg 7

Louvre
Jesus among the Doctors 12
Ship of Fools 16

PHILADELPHIA
Museum of Art
Christ and the Adulteress 4
Epiphany 8
Jesus among the Doctors 12
Ecce Homo 27
Crowning with Thorns 55
Adoration of the Shepherds 65 A
Retinue of the Magi 65 C

PRINCETON
Art Museum
Christ before Pilate 69

ROTTERDAM
Boymans-van Beuningen Museum
Marriage at Cana 3
Two Priestly Heads 5
Head of a Woman 18
Triptych of the Flood 25 A–F
St Christopher 36
'Prodigal Son' 61
Christ before Pilate 68

SAINT-GERMAIN-EN LAYE
Musée Municipal
Conjurer 6

SAN DIEGO (California)
Fine Arts Gallery
Kiss of Judas 71

SÃO PAULO
Museu de Arte
Christ before Pilate 72

SETTIGNANO
Weinzheimer Collection
Jesus among the Doctors 12

'sHERTOGENBOSCH
Cathedral
Madonna and Child 67 A
St John the Evangelist 67 B

Cathedral (formerly)
Abigail and David, Solomon and Bathsheba 14 (copy now in private collection, Switzerland)

Fr. van Lanschot Collection
Temptation of St Anthony 49

. . . (Switzerland)
Private collection
Ecce Homo 28

VALENCIENNES
Musée des Beaux-Arts
St James of Compostela and the Sorcerer 29 A
Temptation of St Anthony 29 B

VENICE
Palazzo Ducale
Altarpiece of St Liberata (Altarpiece of St Julia) 24 A–C
Scene from the Last Judgement 26 A–D
Altarpiece of the Hermits 40 A–C

VIENNA
Akademie der bildenden Künste
Triptych of the Last Judgement 50 A–E

Kunsthistorisches Museum
Ascent of Calvary 19 A
Child at Play 19 B

WASHINGTON
National Gallery of Art (Kress Collection)
Death of the Miser 15

WINTERTHUR
Reinhart Collection
St Christopher 38

YALE
University Art Gallery
Allegory of Pleasures 17